THE WORLD IN PLAY

THE WORLD IN PLAY
Portraits of a Victorian Concept

Matthew Kaiser

STANFORD UNIVERSITY PRESS
STANFORD, CALIFORNIA

Stanford University Press
Stanford, California

© 2012 by the Board of Trustees of the Leland Stanford Junior University. All rights reserved.

This book has been published with the assistance of the Faculty of Arts and Sciences at Harvard University.

No part of this book may be reproduced or transmitted in any form or by any means, electronic or mechanical, including photocopying and recording, or in any information storage or retrieval system without the prior written permission of Stanford University Press.

Printed in the United States of America on acid-free, archival-quality paper

Library of Congress Cataloging-in-Publication Data

Kaiser, Matthew, author.
  The world in play : portraits of a Victorian concept / Matthew Kaiser.
    pages cm
  Includes bibliographical references and index.
    ISBN 978-0-8047-7608-0 (cloth : alk. paper)
  1. English literature—19th century—History and criticism. 2. Play in literature. I. Title.
PR468.P55K35 2012
820.9'3579—dc22
                                                              2011005797

For Ken Urban

Contents

Acknowledgments ix

Introduction: A Modern Sensation 1

PART I *The World in Play*

1 Mapping the World in Play 13

PART II *Portraits*

2 Fair Play in an Ugly World:
  The Politics of Nautical Melodrama 51
3 Toying with the Future in *Wuthering Heights* 85
4 A Joy on the Precipice of Death:
  Muir and Stevenson in California 117
5 Wilde's Folly 144

Notes 173
Index 199

Acknowledgments

This book elbowed its way into the world several years ago in Victoria, British Columbia, where I was presenting a chapter from another project, a book on the neurobiology of historical consciousness in Victorian literature. As luck would have it, Herbert "Chip" Tucker, one of the most brilliant, stylish, and generous writers I know, was in the audience, and on learning that play was one of my research interests, he graciously invited me to contribute an essay to a special issue, devoted to play, of *New Literary History*. Chip turned out to be one tough editor, mercilessly pushing and prodding my original paradigm (timid creature that it was!) and encouraging me to go back to the drawing board, to question everything I knew about play that I might discover it anew. Thanks to Herbert Tucker, I discovered a world in play. What began as a short article insisted on becoming a book, and at every stage it has benefited from Chip's wisdom and rigor.

I am also indebted to George Levine, one of the great Victorianists of his generation. Luckily for me, he was one of the first readers of this book. His encouragement, advice, and faith in this project have meant the world to me. I thank Carolyn Williams too for her friendship, support, and mentorship over the years. She will always be part of my internal audience (the best sentences in this book were written for her). My big-hearted, no-nonsense editor, Emily-Jane Cohen, piloted this vessel expertly into port. I am in awe of her editorial skills and delighted that Emily Brontë is her namesake. I offer heartfelt thanks to my agent, David Patterson, to Tim Roberts at Stanford University Press, to Annette Fern at the Houghton Library at Harvard University, to Georgianna Ziegler at the Folger Shakespeare Library, to Gayle Barkley and Donna Stromberg at the

Huntington Library, and to Harvard deans Diana Sorensen and Heather Lantz for funding this project. Portions of the Introduction and Chapter One are Copyright © 2009 *New Literary History*, The University of Virginia. They first appeared as an article in *New Literary History*, volume 40, no. 1 (2009): 105–29. I thank managing editor Mollie Washburne, the University of Virginia, and Johns Hopkins University Press for permission to reprint them here. For their support and advice, I am indebted to my colleagues at Harvard University, in particular Daniel Donoghue, James Engell, Marge Garber, Elaine Scarry, and James Simpson.

The following individuals also contributed to *The World in Play*. Some provided me with public venues in which to test my ideas; others read early drafts and offered helpful suggestions; others opened doors for me, inspired me, or extended a hand in friendship. Still others challenged me, roughed up my ideas, asked incisive questions to which I had no immediate answer. Months later, their words still in my head, an answer would suddenly come to me, and a new dimension to my book would emerge. I also thank Tanya Agathocleous, Stephen Arata, Derek Attridge, Homi Bhabha, Lawrence Buell, James Buzard, Ed Cohen, Leo Damrosch, Carol Dell'Amico, Christine DeVine, Richard Dury, Stephen Greenblatt, Molly Clark Hillard, Anne Janowitz, John Jordan, Gerhard Joseph, Sally Ledger, Teresa Mangum, Ankhi Mukherjee, Elisa New, Leah Price, Catherine Robson, Werner Sollors, Richard Stein, Maria Tatar, Robyn Warhol, and Roderick Watson. I am lucky to have been accompanied on this journey by Susan Hoffman, Robert Fiddaman, and Sybil Kaiser. To Ken Urban, playwright and musician, I dedicate *The World in Play* with love and gratitude. For the past fifteen years he has used his tremendous theatrical talent to feign interest in all things Victorian.

Introduction

A MODERN SENSATION

> They cry fie now upon men engaged in play; but I should like to know how much more honourable their modes of livelihood are than ours. The broker of the Exchange who bulls and bears, and buys and sells, and dabbles with lying loans, and trades on state secrets, what is he but a gamester? The merchant who deals in teas and tallow, is he any better? His bales of dirty indigo are his dice, his cards come up every year instead of every ten minutes, and the sea is his green table.
> —William Makepeace Thackeray, *Barry Lyndon*[1]

What did modernity feel like to the Victorians? What trusted metaphors did they employ to describe the sensation of modern life? Some felt modernity in their guts: the jolt of a railroad carriage, the lurching landscape, the rattling window. Modernity filled the ears of others: a deafening doubt roused by the ocean, its endless surface, its mockery of heaven. For some, modernity meant an exhilarating leap into darkness, or a mechanized march into light, or the tread of ghost feet beside one's bed. This book explores one modern sensation in particular: a trope invoked frequently by the Victorians to describe a world unhinged from a past. Despite its ubiquity in Victorian literary and cultural texts, despite its centrality to nineteenth-century British self-understanding, few critics today pay it much heed. At first glance, it seems a slight creature, incapable of bearing the cultural and political weight it did.

The modern sensation is *play*, specifically the bewildering experience of a world in play. A world in play is not the same thing, of course, as a world *at* play, which is how the Victorians depicted that apocryphal age known as Merry Old England, a time when the omnipresence of play was still satisfying, its expression enchanting. A world in play means two things. First, it means a world in flux: an inconstant and unsettled condition, a queasy state, as Marx and Engels describe it, in which "all that is solid melts into air."[2] But a world in play also means a world that throws itself headlong *into* play, inside it, where it constructs a parallel universe, a ludic microcosm of itself, which eventually displaces that world. The membranes of play, its elastic fibers, stretch to the point where they encircle all of existence. Modern life is subjected simultaneously to a miniaturizing, reductive pressure and to an increasingly erratic, oscillating motion. Recall for a moment *Alice's Adventures in Wonderland* (1865), in which Victorian England, in the shape of a little girl, leaps into a microcosm of itself, a world of toylike objects and childish creatures, a world riven with epistemological undecidability and political strife, where a queen with a penchant for beheadings reigns. Lewis Carroll's rabbit hole captures, in whimsical fashion, the precise psychological state that many Victorians associate with modernity: a narrow space without a floor, constricting but unfixed, finite but unending, a world in play.

Consider, too, the quotation from *Barry Lyndon* (1844) with which I began. Thackeray's notoriously unreliable narrator, the professional gambler and con artist Redmond Barry, regards himself as a vestige of an aristocratic world at play, the last of a dying breed, in a modern middle-class commercial world that is very much in play. Writing from prison, utterly defeated in his various schemes, Barry has come to the startling metahistorical conclusion not that he is being punished for his outmoded playfulness but that modernity has expertly outplayed *him*, the commercial ethic that governs modern life proving more ruthlessly ludic, more winning, than his own more modest con artistry. Formerly confined to the casino, the game has expanded exponentially, shrunk the sea to the size of a gaming table, and turned bales of merchandise into dice, the very calendar into a turn at the table. A man at play feels, for the first time, the overwhelming reality of a world in play, grasps the extent to which modern play has no outside, no floor. Like Alice, who shrinks to the size of a rodent, a diminished Barry has been baptized into modernity and awakens in a labyrinth of play. As J. Jeffrey Franklin has so superbly documented in the context of the nineteenth-century realist novel, "play functioned as a linch-pin concept within the discursive infrastructure by which Victorian society represented itself to itself."[3] Franklin is one of the few critics who recognizes the extent to which the logic of play shapes nineteenth-century British culture and identity. We can gaze at the railroad, the factory chimney, the clunky nineteenth-century camera on its tripod. The Victorians themselves, however, in considerable numbers, located modernity—felt its presence most powerfully—in the interstices of play, in its jumbled folds and myriad overlappings. It is down this rabbit hole we now plunge.

For we postmodern subjects are all too familiar with the world in play, with the uncanny sensation—a decidedly nineteenth-century one—that the boundaries have blurred between signifier and referent, not temporarily but irrevocably. We alternately frighten and titillate ourselves with thoughts that modern consciousness has become permanently mired in a ludic representation of itself. From virtual reality to artificial intelligence, from the game theory of WTO economists to the war games of NATO commanders, from *The Matrix* (1999) to *The Truman Show* (1998), from online "communities" and flash mobs to so-called reality television and the pornographization of sex, from the ever-expanding "infotainment" industry to people "tweeting" their own suicides, from our phantom hordes of Facebook "friends" to the South Korean couple arrested in 2010 for raising a virtual child online in an Internet café, while their flesh-and-blood baby starved to death in an empty apartment—the evidence increasingly suggests that we live in a world of lotus-eaters, weaned on a digital perfume more consequential, more compelling, than the reality it enhances and supplants.

Skeptics will wonder what all the fuss is about. "All the world's a stage," they remind us. "Been there, done that!" The concept of a ludic world order, they insist, is no freak of the modern imagination. Some will trace it to antiquity, to Plato's shadow-flecked cave, or to Heraclitus's capricious Cosmos making and breaking the lives of men. They will claim that Jaques's meditation upon the seven ages of man proves that the world in play predates the Victorian period by at least two and a half centuries, with its stilted, earnest play, so naïve and one-dimensional by early-modern standards, or by ours. Compared to the world at play, however, the concept of the world *in* play is a relatively recent invention. While its protracted birth might be contemporaneous with the gradual coalescence of modernity in the late sixteenth and early seventeenth centuries, it finds its voice and flexes its young muscles in the eighteenth century. It comes of age and acquires its mature, historically coherent shape in the nineteenth century. Today, we see it in its prime. How long it will persist is unknown.

It appears to be fairly hearty. Although Shakespeare's metaphor of the world as a stage, we as actors, contains a prescient glimmer of our trope, it differs in a significant way. A stage implies the existence of an audience, an orchestra pit, a mezzanine, balconies, or in other words, an *outside*, a psychological and epistemological vantage from which to observe oneself, one's world, at play. Jaques has perspective, philosophical distance. *The World in Play* makes the case that this epistemic foothold offstage, this solid ground outside the game, dwindles and eventually disappears, in the minds of a growing number of people, by the early nineteenth century, swallowed by the totalizing concept of a world truly in play, by the modern conviction that we are trapped in the infinite regress of ludic representation, in a game that never ends, in the illusion's reflection. To put it bluntly: the Victorians wipe the smirk off Jaques's face.

How does one survive and thrive in a world in play? How does one forge political and ethical agency, experience meaningfulness and the fullness of being, in modernity's funhouse mirror? While this book cannot provide conclusive answers to these questions, it does provide what I hope is a compelling account of how various Victorian misfits, underdogs, and iconoclasts—antiestablishment literary figures with a penchant for questioning the middle-class worldview—grappled with, transformed, or in some cases made reluctant peace with the world in play: not from outside it, for the world in play has no exteriority, but from *below*, from their subaltern positions as oddballs and Others. If you want to learn the truth about a respectable family, don't ask Mama or Papa, ask the chambermaid; she will take you to the family portrait gallery and peel off those masks. While there is no "outside" to the world in play, there is a "below": an opportunity to achieve critical distance from within, to hack into the mainframe of Victorian culture. I toyed with the idea of titling this book *Play and Its Discontents*, but it sounded too fatalistic and clinical. It failed to capture the spirit of rebellion and intellectual dexterity with which certain Victorian writers and thinkers—melodramatists of the 1830s, Emily Brontë, Robert Louis Stevenson, John Muir, and Oscar Wilde, among others—battled the world in play in the name of play, struggled valiantly, like Alice, to find their footing in a seemingly innocuous logic that had swallowed the cosmos whole.

For all its purported fun, play is a notoriously inscrutable philosophical concept. Mihai I. Spariosu and James Hans have documented how Western philosophers and cultural critics, over the last two and a half centuries, have cloaked the concept of play in an airy undecidability, an aesthetic mysticism, making it all the more difficult to grasp even as these same thinkers—Schiller, Kant, Ruskin, Arnold, Nietzsche, Husserl, Gadamer, Derrida, Feyerabend, Deleuze, and Rorty, among others—have asked play to do some heavy lifting, to act as a cornerstone in their respective philosophical systems (or antisystems, as the case may be).[4] In Part I of *The World in Play*, I bring the concept of play back down to earth, while preserving its definitional complexity. Building on the groundbreaking scholarship of play theorist Brian Sutton-Smith, and using Dickens as my primary touchstone, I present an extensive albeit provisional taxonomy of play in nineteenth-century British literature and culture, revealing the surprising extent to which the concept of play infiltrates the infrastructure of everyday life in the Victorian period, indeed, how a network of contradictory and overlapping logics of play constitutes the very architecture of *being*.[5] Part I provides readers with a user-friendly planimeter, an analytical frame, with which to map the various logics of play in hundreds—indeed, in thousands—of nineteenth-century literary and cultural artifacts. Whence did the world in play come? What caused play to proliferate conceptually in the first place, to spread virally through modern consciousness? At the end of Part I, I provide some tentative answers to these difficult questions.

The World in Play encourages readers to rethink their relationship with play not just theoretically or historically, but emotionally as well, to sweep aside the sentimental fluff, thoughts of frolicking toddlers and utopian politics, that has accrued around the concept of play over the years, even in hard-nosed academic circles, obscuring its ugly and sometimes brutal underbelly, its breathtaking ubiquity, the extent of its ideological work. While it would be unwise to claim that play is inherently bad, it would be no wiser to declare it inherently good. Many may find this painful to accept, for the concept of play has come to function in the popular imagination as a readymade philosophical and political antidote to all things unpleasant: unfreedom, regimentation, suffering, somber seriousness, uncomfortable truth, overweening power, repression, stifling conventionality, and joyless work, for example. Let's face it, we love play, or rather, we are in love with play, blinded by affection. Thinking rigorously about play means breaking our own hearts.

In the four chapters that comprise Part II of *The World in Play*, I break hearts. I present each chapter as a portrait of a nineteenth-century writer or group of writers, misfits all, who struggled to make sense of play from within what they perceived as the prison house of play, its infinite regress. Portraits of ludic angst, these four chapters lay bare the paranoia, rage, and melancholy induced by this fixed game called modern life. Portraits too of survival and heroism, however, these chapters tell the story of how these same writers succeeded, sometimes at a high cost to themselves, in gaining an ethical and political perspective on play from within play, turning play against itself, discovering ludic worlds within worlds, pockets of possibility, hope, and love. These writers made the most of the world in play. In the process, they taught their Victorian contemporaries the joyful art of modern life: how to be at play in a world in play. If Part I is a map, then Part II is a record of four literary voyages, each of which sets off in a different direction at a different moment in the nineteenth century, their dotted lines diverging and crisscrossing on our map, each subsequent voyage coming a bit closer to discovering that elusive cove, a treasure trove of peace, in this choppy world in play.

We begin in the 1820s and 1830s with an account in Chapter Two of nautical melodrama, which constitutes, at first glance, a relatively crude phase in nineteenth-century British theatre. Though we can trace the melodramatic tropes that punctuate so much of Victorian literature to these scrappy texts, critics today all but ignore them, for extant copies of scripts are difficult to acquire. Taking as its subject the trials and tribulations of Jolly Jack Tar and of the seafaring life, nautical melodrama, and the unruly working-class theatres that showcased it, delighted plebeian audiences by indicting the world in play, by exposing the alienating and unsettling effects of global capitalism on the lives of industrial workers. Nautical melodrama mourned a bygone world at play, an apocryphal order, pastoral and customary. These wildly popular plays provided audiences with underdog strategies for outwitting predatory authority, for achieving fair play in an increasingly unfair world. If working-class literary skirmishes with the world in play erupted in the intersubjective space of the public sphere, in London's gaudy theatres, then middle-class literary attempts to make sense of the world in play were confined, for the most part, to the private realm of interiority: to that rabbit hole we call bourgeois subjectivity. Hence, in Chapter Three, we turn our attention from raucous representations of sailors to the existential musings of a Yorkshire recluse, to Emily Brontë's *Wuthering Heights* (1847). I read this famously recalcitrant novel as a polemic against the middle-class pedagogization of child play, against the modern impulse to transform play activity in children into an industrious expression of psychic development. Invoking the circular logic of cosmic time, Brontë plucks the ludic child from the stifling telos of domesticity and forges instead a future-destroying model of child play, which refuses to subordinate itself to the demands of socialization. It is a refusal that leads to a sacred death that is more life-affirming, in Brontë's eyes, than life. In Chapter Four, one sees a similar though less brutal, more hopeful dynamic at work in the California travel narratives of Scottish free spirits Robert Louis Stevenson and John Muir, who set out to purge the Victorian cult of leisure, specifically, outdoorsy sportiness, of its proprietary egoism. They reimagine the Golden State, their adopted home, as a sublime Romantic playground where the middle-class male ego disintegrates in the face of destructive nature, and where competitive men are reborn as little cosmic boys. Stevenson and Muir's literary efforts to rebrand California as a postapocalyptic, neo-Caledonian playground, as a land of death and play, helped shape the fledgling state's image of itself as an otherworldly and exceptional place. Modern California is a product, in part, of the Victorian world in play.

If these three literary attempts to outplay modernity, to outmaneuver the world in play, seem nostalgic, to varying degrees, for an outside that does not exist, that is because, as I demonstrate in my concluding chapter on Oscar Wilde's anti-athleticism, it is nearly impossible psychologically to confront the viral logic of the world in play, in all its nihilistic fury, head on, without emotional recourse to an outside, a fantasy of primitivism or premodernity, howsoever illusory that outside may be. Wilde, however, achieved the seemingly impossible. Though many critics still cling to the popular image of Wilde as ludic martyr in a tragically unplayful age, his relationship with Victorian culture was more complicated than that. What made Wilde so controversial was his refusal to take play seriously or show it the proper respect by competing with his fellow Victorians in the mandatory sport of modern life. Wilde considered earnestness a form of moral athleticism, the apotheosis of the competitive impulse: an ugly desire to win. Wilde was a spoilsport. He refused to catch the ball or score a manly victory, enraging his fellow players and inviting the wrath of the world in play to rain down upon his head. In his courageous willingness to lose a game from which there is no escape, and thus to live forever in *loss*, Wilde discovered the art of love. For this reason, he is the hero of this book.

Early nineteenth-century melodramatists and their working-class audiences experienced a very different world in play than did Wilde or Brontë or Stevenson and Muir. The world in play has a thousand faces, yet there is an underlying structure. Rather than a narrative of chronological development, an account, for example, of the minute changes that rugby or dollhouse construction underwent between 1856 and 1879, this book focuses mostly on capturing that elusive and, in some academic circles, dubious creature known as historical constancy. What is constant in the world in play, however, is not some ontological entity or metaphysical category called "play," but the proliferation of ludic multiplicity itself, the definitional dynamism of this fluid concept, the play of play. The world in play is constant much as the ocean is constant, for it expresses itself steadily in endless waves of variability. It is this steadiness I want to capture, the rhythm of change, the pattern of play. Wilde, for instance, defines modern consciousness as the internalization of violent sport. Brontë, on the other hand, defines modern consciousness as the moment one directs one's play impulses toward a socially productive end. What is constant is not a specific logic of play or the meaning of play, but the idea that one always already operates from within play, that one must therefore combat discourses of play with counterdiscourses of play. Wilde presents Christian folly as the antidote to sport. Brontë presents the deadly play of the cosmos as the antidote to rational play. The logic might have changed but the dynamic, the historical rhythm, the form, remains the same. For too long the Victorian world in play has gone uncharted, the breathtaking ubiquity of play ignored. We have been taught to distrust big pictures, and play is *big*, so big we cannot see it, like the curvature of the earth. "The Game is so large," Rudyard Kipling writes, "that one sees but a little at a time."[6] Equipped with the map from Part I and the historical models from

Part II, readers, I hope, will feel emboldened to strike out on their own, to be done with fear, to explore the vast stretches of the world in play that bend beyond the confines of this book.

To readers who have a vested intellectual or psychological interest in the notion that the Victorians were unplayful, or that they were playful in a circumscribed, innocent, or crude way, *The World in Play* will seem like a brazen attempt to overturn decades of conventional wisdom, to turn Victorian studies on its head. I sympathize with these readers. As I discuss in detail in the chapter on Wilde, the world in play is a disturbing idea; it disturbs *me*. For years I resisted it, sought to discover some phenomenon, some flicker of an idea or cultural force that could not be co-opted by play or subsumed in it, some phenomenon that is *intrinsically* antithetical to play and escapes its totalizing grasp. Such a phenomenon does not exist. This does not mean that everything, therefore, must be understood as play. A world in play is not the same thing as a world in which everything is straightforwardly ludic. Rather, it is a world in which nothing is immune to the infectious logic of play, in which everything—death, war, earnestness—has the capacity in theory to be exposed to play, overwritten by it, infiltrated by it, represented by it. An unsettling ludic potentiality lurks within the logic of modernity. Like Vesuvius, play threatens to erupt at any moment. The very ground beneath our feet—our convictions, rootedness, truth—is haunted by an epistemologically catastrophic illusoriness, by a nagging modern sensation that, to quote Marx and Engels, "all that is solid melts into air." With this book, I do not seek to impose a totalizing concept on history. My intention is merely to write the history of a totalizing concept, a concept that the Victorians themselves imposed on history.

PART I

The World in Play

CHAPTER I

Mapping the World in Play

But while every single player differed markedly from every other, there was a certain uniform negativeness of expression which had the effect of a mask—as if they had all eaten of some root that for the time compelled the brains of each to the same narrow monotony of action.
—George Eliot, *Daniel Deronda*[1]

In politics you are used as the counters of a game, each side plays with you: not for you, mind. You get nothing, whichever side is in: you are the pawns.... And if I might advise, it would be that we give that game over and play one by ourselves in which there really is something to be got.
—Walter Besant, *All Sorts and Conditions of Men*[2]

At dinner she is hostess, I am host.
Went the feast ever cheerfuller? She keeps
The Topic over intellectual deeps
In buoyancy afloat. They see no ghost.
With sparkling surface-eyes we ply the ball:
HIDING THE SKELETON shall be its name.
Such play as this the devils might appal!
—George Meredith, *Modern Love*[3]

The Totality of Play

The list of nineteenth-century British writers and thinkers who take it upon themselves to voice official anxiety about play—frustration with idle children, roughhousing workers, playboy bachelors—is long. Let us not mistake anxiety about play, however, for hostility toward it. Because so many Victorians perceive modern life as structured by play, and because play is a perennial object of contemplation and worry, even the smallest or most quotidian play phenomenon becomes magnified, distorted and transformed into an opportunity for self-reflection. A mirror in which the Victorians admire themselves or shudder, play is not a problem to be eliminated or alleviated. Rather, the Victorians seek, in contradictory ways, sometimes inelegantly or heavy-handedly, to improve play. They set out to reform and manage it, mapping its varied terrain, getting to the bottom of it, coming to terms with its daunting range. They wrap metaphors of play around all aspects of their lives. Charles Darwin transforms biology into an endless act of competition, a life-and-death sport, and transforms sexual reproduction into a first-place trophy. John Ruskin conceives of Gothic architecture, and the life-affirming model of sociality it communicates, as a ludic enterprise. Flying buttresses become stony maypoles. Thomas Hughes and other reformers transform football into a vehicle for the political indoctrination of the working classes. The Victorians christen a new recreational institution "the weekend." They build hundreds of parks and playgrounds in a democratizing (and normalizing) effort to cultivate play. Leisure becomes big business. At times they attack play, yes, rail against it, but they do so from within play, from a world perceived as in play.

What prevents us from seeing clearly the degree to which Victorian representations of modernity—indeed, Victorian senses of self—are interoperable with tropes of play? Why are we such spoilsports when it comes to the Victorians? The problem is only partially attributable to our mistaking Victorian anxiety about play for hostility, or our facile conflation of play with notions of fun. Fundamental flaws exist at the methodological, ideological, and historical levels in the ways we think about play. We think about play almost exclusively in quantitative rather than qualitative terms. How playful were the Victorians? This unanswerable question implies that play is quantifiable, that a historical epoch is either rich in play or impoverished. Rather than measure the Victorians against ourselves in a quixotic effort to determine who possesses the most play, or enough play (which is very Victorian of us, actually), we might ask the "how" question differently: In what ways were the Victorians "playful"? What logics of play shaped Victorian self-understanding? Why is it sometimes so difficult to detect play in the act of invading or absorbing various nonplay concepts? How do divergent logics of play vie for supremacy, clash, overlap, merge, and produce hybrid logics, only to subdivide once again, confronted by upstarts? Conversely, which logics of play harmonize with or hide behind one another, downplaying their presence? Answering these questions will give us a better sense of the double meaning of *in play*, of the play of play, the simultaneity of play as "ludic activity" and play as "constant flux." On the one hand, the Victorians recognize and embrace the multiplicity of play, the taxonomic proliferation of various play logics (sport, recreation, mischief, and so on), which they project onto the world in order to give it structure; on the other hand, there is an accompanying sense of the inherent instability of these same logics, their reversibility, the tendency of play's conceptual boundaries to blur and thereby to unsettle the very world to which play gives structure. At the same time that play makes the world cohere, it betrays the illusoriness of that coherence. The Victorian desire to control play is as anxious as it is confident. Even the most straightforward Victorian expressions of play are haunted by a potential for definitional fluctuation. Festivity, for instance, can in an instant metamorphose into mischief, and a leisurely pastime can metamorphose into a competitive sport. The state of being at play can never completely shake the sensation of being in play.

We insist, too, upon measuring play against its supposed antitheses: work, seriousness, suffering, truth. But what if nothing was intrinsically external to the concept of play, a concept that many Victorians describe, as we have seen, in startlingly totalizing terms? As Gerhard Joseph and Herbert Tucker have documented, the Victorians could view even death itself as a "prize," a moral reward for a race well run, a life well lived.[4] The point is not that those famously elegiac Victorians, with their crepe, black bunting, and funeral etiquette, experienced the passing of a loved one as fun, but merely that the concept of death has no conceptual immunity to the logic of play, which wears an appropriately somber (a theatrically somber) aspect for the occasion. Dickens in particular takes macabre delight, in *Oliver Twist* (1837) and *Martin Chuzzlewit* (1843–44), in exposing the ludic underpinnings of the Victorian funeral industry. Play does not die; it shifts shape. As philosopher Eugen Fink explains, when backed into a corner by its definitional opponents, "[p]lay, so to speak, confronts them all—it absorbs them by representing them."[5] As play theorist Edward Gross notes, "work can *become* play in a genuine sense ... when forms bec[o]me ends in themselves," when "hunting for food evolved into The Fox Hunt," or more generally when "play becomes the life-work of the players."[6] The relentlessly porcine logic of play can absorb, without causing much of a stir, the most horrific and depressing Victorian phenomena: wars of imperial expansion, or the dehumanizing conditions of crime- and disease-infested slums. Readers barely bat their eyelashes. In *Kim* (1901), for example, Kipling metaphorizes the British conquest and occupation of India, including the impending Second Afghan War, as a game played by—literally facilitated by, at the level of plot—a mischievous boy spy, who is motivated, in the end, by "sheer excitement and the sense of power."[7] Here, the invocation of play, child play in particular, masks ideology while downplaying geopolitical violence and imperial espionage. An Indian matron marvels at how the British "dance and they play like children when they are grandfathers," playing tricks on a disoriented India and running circles around it.[8] But the wily and shamelessly transideological logic of play proves equally adept at exposing ideology and at inspiring radical change when necessary, for play wears the mercenary, reversible colors of relativistic modernity. Thus, Victorian social reformers alert the public to the deplorable conditions of urban slums by depicting the brutal sport to which the lives of the poor have been reduced. In *How the Poor Live* (1883), George R. Sims provides his middle-class readers with a sketch of a typical woman of the slum, a young mother with "the fist of a prizefighter."[9] In *The Nether World* (1889), George Gissing repeatedly metaphorizes *want*—the slum dweller's instinct to cheat and steal in the struggle for scarce resources—as a "game."[10]

One of our worst intellectual habits, however, when it comes to theorizing play, is to divide ludic phenomena into *games*, on the one hand, which have "a certain formal *logic*," Nancy Morrow suggests, rule-boundness, and structure, and so-called *pure play*, on the other hand, which is "not so much about reaching a particular goal," as it is about "open-endedness," imaginative freedom, and "infinite substitutions."[11] Proponents of the games-are-bad-and-play-is-good school of thought, as well as of its less countrified cousin, games-have-structure-and-play-does-not, remind me of those employees in maternity wards who used to tape blue bows to the bald heads of male infants, pink bows to the bald heads of female infants, in order to create a heartwarming illusion of the inevitability of one of our most heavy-handed, culturally imposed binary oppositions. If "game" and "play" are as antithetical as many sophisticated people persist in believing, then the sentence "She's playing a game" would sound, at least, in certain contexts, paradoxical. But it never does. "No, no, I don't mean 'play' in *that* sense of the word," a proponent will explain, smiling at my simplicity. But already, you see, the binary has collapsed. The baby has lost its bow. Do you really propose that we now use *duct* tape? For that is what it would take to preserve this tired opposition. The Victorians had no difficulty whatsoever (and neither do we) characterizing chaos as a game or believing that unstructured play has the capacity to induce a sense of psychic constriction in a player. Such radical abuses of language confused no one. The Victorians had no qualms about obliterating the distinction between "game" and "play" altogether, fusing these terms into one seamless megaconcept; nor did they have qualms about fracturing each half of this dubious binary into myriad irreconcilable concepts: a cacophonous litter of mewing mini-ideas. In the eyes of the language police, Victorian society no doubt made a mess of these concepts. While I recognize the necessity of pinning down our terms, mapping the topography of play, there is a more efficacious and nuanced way to go about it than by erecting an artificial semantic barrier between "game" and "play," a barrier that has trouble withstanding even the most pedestrian expressions of quotidian speech.

When Victorian writers and thinkers praise or disparage play, they do so from within constellations of play logics; the praise or disparagement comes, implicitly or explicitly, at the expense of or on behalf of multiple logics of play, between which boundaries often prove quite porous. Consider the following statement by Dickens in *Hard Times* (1854): "I entertain a weak idea that the English people are as hard-worked as any people upon whom the sun shines. . . . I acknowledge to this ridiculous idiosyncrasy," he adds, "as a reason why I would give them a little more play."[12] Yes, Dickens uses quantitative logic here to suggest that the working classes deserve an increase in play, reminding us obliquely that they deserve an increase in *pay*. But the real tension exists not between play and work but within the contending senses of the word. Dickens uses "play" as a relatively benign synonym of "freedom," the power to maneuver—economically, politically, and socially. He also uses it as a synonym of "recreation."

In associating freedom with increased recreational opportunities for the working classes, and with rational, civic-minded amusements, of which he was a passionate advocate, Dickens attempts to sever the connection in the middle-class imagination between working-class political agency and another kind of play: mischief, tomfoolery, and ludic incivility. Rather than a blistering attack upon his own supposedly unplayful epoch or upon a society that distributes its ludic resources unequally, Dickens tacitly pits one play logic against another. He attempts to rescue play (freedom) from play (mischief) in the name of play (recreation).

No text has done more to reinforce the historically myopic view that Dickens waged a lonely battle on behalf of play than *A Christmas Carol* (1843). It is tempting to view Ebenezer Scrooge as the ultimate Victorian party pooper, the personification of an individualistic, middle-class hostility toward communitarian fun. It is tempting to view Tiny Tim as the embodiment of an increasingly obsolete ethic of festivity, indulged once a year at Christmas. Yet Dickens has a more nuanced, less evangelical understanding of the role of play in modern life. For Scrooge's miserliness is just as pervasively marked by play as Tiny Tim's mirth. Scrooge embodies competition: the agonistic impulse to win, to outplay one's opponent. He greets people not as fellow revelers at a party but as potential competitors in a contest. "[E]dg[ing] his way," Dickens writes, "along the crowded paths of life," Scrooge even competes with the "wintry weather" itself for the title of most cold: "No wind that blew was bitterer than he, no falling snow was more intent upon its purpose, no pelting rain less open to entreaty." "Foul weather," Dickens adds, invoking the image of a hapless wrestler, "didn't know where to have him."[13]

A Christmas Carol provides a vivid account of the civil war raging within the concept of play during the Victorian period. "Bah, Humbug!" and "God bless Us, Every One!" are sides of the same coin. Our experience of reality is shaped, Dickens suggests, by the clash of these divergent logics, which, for all their incommensurability, uncannily and symbiotically interconnect. The fact that Christmas cheer, a moral corrective to competition, soundly defeats Scrooge—that it *wins*, by forcing him to wrestle with his conscience—raises questions about the intractability of the logic of contest, about the moral hollowness of triumphing over the urge to triumph. Beneath the text's communitarian bonding, blighting its merriment, lurks an urge to vanquish Otherness, to crush resistance to fun. Dickens made play central to so many of his writings not because he viewed it as a panacea, but because he understood in his bones the extent to which the world as we know it, our experience of modernity, is in play. Rather than blindly embrace it, Dickens gingerly navigates play, searches for a foothold, a place to call home, in a slippery and expansive and multifarious concept from which no exit appears.

A Cartographic Approach to Play

What follows is a map, a necessarily provisional and modifiable map, of play in the Victorian period, with its moving parts and its labyrinthine contours. My cartographical endeavor is inspired, as I noted in the Introduction, by play theorist Brian Sutton-Smith, who recently brought a bit of cohesion to the fractious field of play studies—which attracts anthropologists, literary critics, philosophers, folklorists, psychologists, among others, all of whom approach the topic with markedly different priorities and assumptions—by identifying seven primary rhetorics of play that currently operate, often at cross-purposes, within this interdisciplinary field. It is my contention that all seven of Sutton-Smith's academic rhetorics of play have popular precursors in the correspondent logics that delineate and structure nineteenth-century quotidian life, from the ethic of competition that pervades the middle-class worldview, through the therapeutic faith in recreation, to the political efficacy of holidays in the promotion of national identity. The rhetorical dissonance that marks play studies today is a rarefied echo, in my view, of the popular debates that reached a boiling point in the nineteenth century about the meaning and value of play as a central component of human experience. What follows, then, is an effort not merely to "Victorianize" Sutton-Smith's seven logics of play, some of which I have taken the liberty of renaming, but to scrutinize each in isolation, through the lens of Victorian modernity, in order to appreciate how each triggered in its nineteenth-century proponents a distinct act of metahistorical self-definition. Rather than types of play, the logics that follow—which I present, on properly aleatory grounds, in no particular order—should be understood as constellations of cultural and ideological assumptions about the function and value of play.[14]

Every map, of course, distorts. Greenland looms larger than South America in my desktop atlas. Spatial distortions inevitably result when we flatten three-dimensional phenomena such as spheres into two-dimensional representations on a mere piece of paper. This is the price we pay for knowledge of our world. Stoics that we are, we do not pronounce Earth nonexistent, or proclaim cartography fantastical, simply because an oversized Antarctica startles us. In order to avoid confusion, then, I would like to take the opportunity here to explain how best to read the map that follows, before proceeding with our efforts to situate Victorian literary and cultural texts within the rolling landscape of play in Great Britain between 1820 and 1900. Readers will rightly point out that the entirety of play—assuming, of course, that the Victorian concept of play is as totalizing as this book claims—cannot possibly be reduced to seven principalities, time zones, or zip codes. The seven logics of play outlined below, and I invite readers to contribute as many additional logics to my list as they desire, should not be viewed as compartments or containers. They are not *places*. They function as openings, doorways, vectors. As I mention in the Introduction, the world in play unfurls infinitely, stretching beyond the confines of this little book.

How should we imagine these seven play logics, if we are not to think of them as discrete territories comprising the totality of play? A placeless map, after all, is a useless map. In his *Philosophical Investigations*, Ludwig Wittgenstein provides an answer. Wittgenstein observes that certain complex signifiers—common words, such as "heart," as opposed to specialty words, such as "aorta"—have so many multiple meanings and senses that one cannot possibly gather them together under one unifying definition, for even though twenty threads of commonality might run through the lot of them, loosely binding them, no single thread runs through them all: "[T]hese phenomena have no one thing in common which makes us use the same word for all," he explains, for "similarities crop up and disappear," "but they are related to one another in many different ways."[15] In order to understand how the various senses of a complex concept like "heart" relate to each other, Wittgenstein recommends drawing a map of "family resemblances," a portrait gallery of sorts, across which one can trace the generational "overlap and criss-cross" of "build, features, colour of eyes, gait, temperament, etc. etc." Members of the Kennedy clan, for instance, share many facial features—toothy grin, big shock of hair, strong brow and jaw, large heads, eyelids heavy in the outer corner—which mark them as "Kennedy-esque," even though no single feature is intrinsic to *all* Kennedys. Some Kennedys do not even look alike. Gathered together, however, for a family portrait at Hyannisport, sailboats conspicuous in the distance, a sunny lawn stretching toward the past, even the outlier cousins begin to make sense, for subtle threads of resemblance weave from face to face, a gossamer map of relatedness spreading in our brains. We do not experience a unitary Kennedy signifier, so much as a "complicated network" of sibling logics: the simultaneity of related and sometimes contradictory features spread out in a nonlinear fashion across four generations. A granddaughter might look more like a younger version of her grandmother's sister than like a younger version of her own mother. Certain features skip generations. We might detect three species of Kennedy nose. In family portraits we experience diachronic history, change across time, synchronically as present variation or patterns of resemblance, which both express time and transcend it, causing time to circle back uncannily on itself. Maps of family resemblances are necessarily open-ended: the number of possible resemblances is arbitrary. Do Kennedy-esque crow's-feet or earlobes exist? Perhaps. Do we need to get mired in that level of detail in order to ascertain whether someone is a Kennedy? Probably not.

Think of the pages that follow, then, as a panoramic family portrait of Victorian play, in which I attempt to capture three generations of Victorian culture simultaneously and synchronically in a map of ludic resemblances, early, mid-, and late Victorian society standing shoulder to shoulder: grandfathers, fathers, and sons. In deference to Sutton-Smith, and for the sake of convenience, I have opted to focus on seven logics of play. At first glance, some might seem incommensurable or unrelated. Taken together, however, they form a family, a map of ludic resemblances, and a portrait of modernity. Seven is not so large a number as to test the patience of readers, I hope, but it is certainly large enough to give a sense of play's conceptual variation. In the end, however, number is unimportant. My "family portrait" approach to Victorian play differs markedly from a traditional diachronic approach to play, which would place the emphasis upon the subtle changes that any given logic of play undergoes over six or seven decades. It would be the equivalent of historicizing the Kennedy grin, determining whether community water fluoridation rates in Massachusetts from the late 1940s to the present correlate to perceived toothiness levels in Kennedy smiles over that same period of time. While I respect this latter method of historical analysis, performing a version of it myself, in fact, on a smaller scale in Part II, it does have its drawbacks, as even its most ardent adherents will admit, for it emphasizes difference over similarity, change over constancy, the evolving content of history over history's more steady form. Producing a map of family resemblances means giving ourselves permission to step outside our diachronic comfort zone, and loosening ourselves a bit from the supple arms of historical change. In our case, it means taking a step back, so that we might listen for the familiar rhythms, the familial patterns, which underlie the protean concept of play, the play of play. A final note on Wittgenstein before we begin: it seems a happy coincidence, one might even say propitious, that Wittgenstein presents as *his* example of a complex signifier, as his fans already know, not the word "heart," which is my attempt at an example, but the word "game."

Seven Logics of Play

Play as Competition

No logic of play inspired more enthusiasm or more outrage in Victorian society. To play means *to contest*. Life is perceived as a rule-bound game in which contestants compete meritocratically for rewards, prestige, and authority. Rather than cooperative or autotelic, the will to play is seen by proponents of this logic, especially from the politically ascendant middle class, as an impulse to be the best, to gain power: over oneself, over others, over one's environment. Here is a logic that puts the "victor" in "Victorian." Heroes and tyrants, selfless saints and soulless materialists, all epitomize in their way this ethic of competition, this struggle to crush the weakness against which one defines oneself. The will to compete becomes for many Victorians synonymous with civilization itself, with its most and its least reassuring aspects, whether these be economic, in the form of the capitalist marketplace; geopolitical, in the form of Britain's ever-expanding empire; or intellectual, in the form of the scientific method, whereby the most meritorious theory prevails.

To the proponents of this view of life, history looks something like this: in the nineteenth century, competition finally displaces its age-old nemesis, custom, as the ethic credited with maintaining social order. Thus, any socialist or "paternal" attempt by the state to temper "antagonism or competition" would be, to quote Herbert Spencer, "fatal to the species."[16] The middle-class athlete, his muscles hardened by sport rather than by labor, becomes a synecdoche for national greatness. A cult of boy-sports sweeps the nation, making minor deities of cricket, football, and rugby heroes. Samuel Smiles trumpets the Duke of Wellington's apocryphal statement that on "the play-ground at Eton" "the battle of Waterloo was won."[17] Oxford, too, is Hellenized, infused by Benjamin Jowett with the sporty ethic of the Greeks, making men of milksops and inflecting with Olympian glory A.E. Housman's furtive glances at Shropshire athletes. Charles Kingsley sends Jesus to the gym, makes Christianity muscular, purging male virtue of its passivity and softness. As Donald Hall has argued, the athleticizing Victorian impulse to infuse modern life with pugilistic limberness is motivated as much by "insecurity and turmoil" as by confidence; by an urge to refashion subjectivity for a changing world, for a life that seems perpetually to outpace those who live it.[18]

We often associate twentieth-century thinkers, such as Johan Huizinga or José Ortega y Gasset, with the quasi-anthropological theory that civilization is rooted in the logic of contest. In "The Sportive Origin of the State," for instance, Ortega argues that human society begins with the rowdy athleticism of young men, whose institutions of physical bonding, fraternal ascesis, act as a political counter to matriarchal power.[19] To credit sports with igniting history: it is such a nineteenth-century impulse! Nietzsche, for instance, argues in "Homer's Contest" that civilization begins only when the Greeks sublimate the desire to kill their enemies into the urge to compete with them.[20] British Victorians, too, award the Greeks the honor of having sparked the competitive essence of culture; for at its height, Walter Pater writes, Greek civilization defines itself not in "battle against a foreign foe" but in the "peaceful combat" of athletic and artistic contests.[21] The Greeks awarded prizes, Pater gushes, for everything under the sun, from fleetest foot to most "beautiful eyebrows," even for "the deftest kiss."[22] One part self-congratulation, one part paranoia, the ethic of contest wends its way through all aspects of Victorian lives: economic behavior, child-rearing practices, views of love and marriage, racial ideology. Indeed, the word "race" has a double meaning for the Victorians: a category of ethnic difference, race is at the same time a contest to outdistance others, a competition between anatomical teams, with biological winners and losers. In *The Races of Men* (1850), for instance, anatomist Robert Knox presents himself as scientific referee, measuring racial groups against each other and concluding that the winner is his own Saxon race, whom he praises for their respect for order, their "matchless" power to accumulate "wealth," their "love of fair play," as well as their talent for "sparring matches," "rowing," "horse racing," and "gymnastics."[23] The will to compete courses, apparently, through English veins.

In the wake of Charles Lyell, Alfred Russel Wallace, and Darwin, nature itself is radically transformed in the Victorian imagination into a contest between species for territory and food, and within species for the privilege of mating. The first-place prize is the female of one's species. Last place means extinction. Darwin peppers his descriptions of natural selection with sportive metaphors and analogies: "Just as man can improve the breed of his game-cocks," he muses, "by the selection of those birds which are victorious in the cockpit, so it appears that the strongest and most vigorous males, or those provided with the best weapons, have prevailed under nature."[24] Here natural selection is literalized as sport. Although Darwin occasionally frames his analysis of animal behavior using other logics of play, as when he credits birds with having a sophisticated "taste for the beautiful," in the end, the logic of contest subsumes all other logics of play, just as all bird songs, no matter how beautifully or pleasurably chirped, are sung for the ultimate purpose of fertilizing that prize egg.[25] While Stephen Jay Gould, George Levine, and Alfie Kohn, among others, have explored, quite compellingly, various noncompetitive dimensions to Darwinian evolutionary theory, the fact of the matter is that, to many of Darwin's contemporaries, it is precisely its logic of contest that makes his narrative of nature so disturbing and so convincing.[26]

The Victorian ethic of competition has plenty of detractors, of course. In *The Bertrams* (1859), for instance, published the same year as *The Origin of Species*, Anthony Trollope confesses that "[t]here is something very painful in these races which we English are always running"; it is something that tears at the fabric of society and dilutes the common good.²⁷ *The Bertrams* is a novel about the high social price that one pays for coming in second and the even higher moral price for coming in first. In *Man and Wife* (1870), Wilkie Collins blames the brutality of modern life in part on the Victorian "mania" "for muscular exercises," "which has seized on us of late years," suggesting that this athletic approach to life, for all the charm of a well-honed bicep, is synonymous with "stupidity."²⁸ In his lecture "Traffic" (1864), Ruskin detects in competition the "vice of jealousy," imploring his audience to look to their souls, for "fox-hunting and cricketing will not carry you through the whole of this unendurably long mortal life."²⁹ If the Greek gymnasium is lauded as the cradle of civilization, then graphic depictions of the Roman amphitheatre, by contrast, with its blood lust, warn readers of historical novels like Edward Bulwer-Lytton's *The Last Days of Pompeii* (1834) and Pater's own *Marius the Epicurean* (1885) against the moral danger of competition for its own sake.

Dickens, however, captures best the Victorian ambivalence toward competition. The plot of *Nicholas Nickleby* (1838–39) revolves around a power struggle within the Nickleby family between the "handsome," "well-formed" Nicholas and his "hard-featured" and "cunning" uncle Ralph.³⁰ Both vie for guardianship of Nicholas's recently widowed mother and sister. Nicholas's "comeliness" "gall[s]" the competitive Ralph, causes him to "hate[ ]" to his "heart's core" his charismatic nephew. Like a poison, the spirit of competition creeps through the opening chapters, setting the events of the novel in motion. But Nicholas's heroism, his cocky determination to defeat his tyrannical uncle, is also rooted in competition. With his Greek first name, which in rough translation means "victory of the people," Nicholas embodies fair play: the ethical beauty of contests, the drive to excel, to right wrongs. Competition is the disease from which modern life suffers. Competition is the only cure.

Play as Self-Creation

The proponents of this next logic view play not as a contest with Otherness but as a self-directed activity. It is the loneliest logic of play, a touch bittersweet. For even when people play together, surrounded by company, they play alone, inwardly. More than work or pain or religious devotion, play opens a window onto interiority. Whether one's model of subjectivity is essentialist or performative, play reveals the machinations of self. This view of play is at the root of a variety of Victorian cultural phenomena: the middle-class cult of leisure, the mania for hobbies, the emergence of Saturday as an official day of recreation, and the effort by the Metropolitan Early Closing Association, established in 1842, to encourage shops to close early so that overworked clerks could pursue self-improving pastimes.[31] We see it in the burgeoning Victorian entertainment industry, in the celebritization of actors and actresses, those ultimate ludic subjects. We see it in the vacation and tourism industries that explode in the wake of the railroad, in the reformist efforts to build more public parks, and in the Great Exhibition of 1851, with its message of rational recreation.[32] We see it in the middle-class cult of sexuality that Foucault describes, the association of erotic pleasures, tastes, and practices with the truth of the self. We see it in the rampant consumerism of the Victorian middle class, the metamorphosis of shopping into a form of entertainment and self-expression. We even see it in the late-century institutionalization of the industrial work break or "coffee break." A dollop of play in the midst of work refocuses the worker. With its range of subtle and pungent pleasures, play was seen to optimize the self, tingle the deadened fibers of subjectivity. A defense against mechanization, it is a declaration of uniqueness and a sign of aliveness.

Mr. Wemmick in *Great Expectations* (1860–61) exemplifies this idea perfectly. An unassuming clerk by day, flattened by paperwork, he becomes a true character in our eyes only when we learn of his unlikely hobby: the transformation of his suburban house into a Gothic castle, replete with diminutive drawbridge and moat, over which he and Pip shake hands one evening. Two hands clasped over a toy moat is a convenient metaphor for the touching yet defensive logic of leisure. By erecting a wall around subjectivity, leisure preserves one's humanity, making one, in turn, more inviting. When it comes to play, Dickens is one of the most rhetorically promiscuous of Victorian writers, regularly invoking all seven of our logics, as well as others, and breeding a menagerie of hybrids among them. He has a soft spot, however, for this one. A professional entertainer, he made his living and fanned his fame in the quiet corners of his readers' afternoons. His first work, *Sketches by Boz* (1836), stands as a monument to early Victorian leisure and is a bustling panorama of his countrymen's recreational pursuits. The word "sketch" connotes informality, fleetingness, a drawing done for fun. Just as the paucity of lines in a sketch freights each pen stroke with meaning, so the transitory way Dickens flits from London's minor theatres, to Greenwich Fair, to a boat race on the Thames—providing glimpses of the English winding down, or raising their spirits, or lifting a "heavy sandwich" from a "large wicker" basket—captures in concentrated form the essence of Britishness, the soulfulness of leisure.[33] "These are their only recreations," Dickens writes, "and they require no more." Indeed, "[t]hey have within themselves, the materials of comfort and content."[34]

As Thorstein Veblen argues in *The Theory of the Leisure Class* (1899), and as historians Hugh Cunningham and Peter Bailey have documented, underlying the logic of leisure is a tendency toward social insularity and individualism, a callous disregard for the world beyond the self.[35] The affluent characters with strange hobbies and unnatural pleasures who punctuate nineteenth-century British literature threaten to unravel the frayed fabric of society even further. Embodying the excesses of leisurely self-cultivation, Dorian Gray and Dr. Henry Jekyll remind us that what separates recreation from re-creation is mere emphasis.

Most middle-class Victorians, however, felt not hostility but ambivalence toward the new recreational ethic of the age. They feared appearing dull as much as they feared appearing too interesting. George and Weedon Grossmith's *The Diary of a Nobody* (1892) records the daily thoughts of a flummoxed suburbanite, Charles Pooter, bombarded by the forces of middle-class play: parlor tricks, card games, dinner parties, séances, and a theatrically inclined son embroiled in perpetual self-discovery. Repelled by the ascendant play ethic around him, Pooter nevertheless finds himself drawn to it, desiring the sense of self that it imparts to his friends and family: the sense of being a *somebody*. And then there is Douglas Jerrold's *Mrs. Caudle's Curtain Lectures* (1845), a masterpiece of early Victorian humor, in which a husband—a toy merchant, appropriately enough—records from memory the nagging tirades delivered every night in bed by his late wife. She appears at first a nemesis of play, complaining about his cigar smoking, his trip to Greenwich Fair, his billiards playing, and the party that he throws for his friends when she is at her mother's. As the lectures unfold, however, it becomes increasingly evident that Mrs. Caudle's bitterness bespeaks not antipathy to play but exclusion from it.

Mrs. Caudle's Curtain Lectures reveals the painful truth not just about marriage but about leisure: even when together, we play alone, our recreational impulses passing like pleasure barges in the night.

Play as Subversion

The Victorians who invoke this third logic see play not as a will to compete, nor as an autotelic impulse, but as a desire, essentially, to make mischief. Play here becomes power's Other, a potentially frightening yet decidedly seductive urge to undermine. An ancient logic, this view of play manifests itself in the usual Victorian suspects: a love-hate relationship with all things carnivalesque and all things evocative of the lower bodily strata. It manifests itself in jokes, comedy, profanity, and rowdiness; in a fascination with nonsense and illogicality; and in the Victorian delight in clowns, buffoons, and circuses, which Jacky Bratton and Ann Featherstone have examined.[36] It manifests itself in boisterous city streets and music halls, in thrill-seekers and cads, in naughty and willful children, in bawdy or seductive women, in drunkards and bumpkins, in tricksters, con artists, bullies, and cheats. This logic of play manifests itself in satiric and parodic efforts to deflate high-mindedness and undermine respectability. We see it, for instance, in the hero of Robert Surtees's picaresque *Mr. Facey Romford's Hounds* (1865): a commoner with "little pig eyes," Romford steals the identity of a nobleman of the same name so that he can pursue his life's passion, fox hunting.[37] The eccentric minor characters, especially the itinerant showmen, with which Dickens peppers his novels, embody the Victorian logic of play as subversion; for example, in *The Old Curiosity Shop* (1840–41), Mr. Grinder's stilt-walkers and Mrs. Jarley with her waxworks; in *Nicholas Nickleby*, Mr. Crummles's theatrical troupe; in *Hard Times*, the equine circus of Mr. Sleary. Hovering on the periphery of the normal and on the outskirts of town, these centrifugal figures—governed by their own extralegal code of conduct—remain unassimilated peddlers of discombobulation and critics of convention.

For all its gossamer lightness, this logic of play gives voice to some decidedly ugly Victorian phobias. The criminal, the political radical, the unruly mob, the racial and sexual Other, the working class, all find themselves tangled together in this tacky logic like flies, made discursively inert. The Victorians paint idleness, irrationality, madness, perversion, an-

Mapping the World in Play 29

tiutilitarian behavior of all kinds—indeed, difference itself—in paranoid yet dismissive strokes of play. The mischievous Sally Leadbitter might be "jolly" and "full of fun," Elizabeth Gaskell admits in *Mary Barton* (1848), but only "the devil leaves his children" such "qualities" of "character."[38] For all his affectionate invocation of this particular logic, even Dickens will brandish it threateningly on occasion. When that heavily symbolic cask of wine crashes to the ground in *A Tale of Two Cities* (1859) and the rabble of Paris "suspend[ ]" "their idleness" to slurp up its bloodlike contents, Dickens characterizes the feeding frenzy that foreshadows revolution as a "wine-game," "frolicsome," "sport," "playfulness."[39] Small wonder: Thomas Carlyle delights in reminding us that the French Revolution commenced—when the defenestrated representatives of the people sought shelter on the royal tennis court at Versailles—in a place of "idle teeheeing" and "snapping of balls and rackets."[40] Incapable of manly competition, revolutionary politicians achieve at best, in Carlyle's eyes, a ludic parody of order, a "heroic building of . . . card-castles."[41] Hence Robert Knox, Victorian theorist of race, insists that, just as competition is intrinsic to the Saxon race, "plunder, bloodshed and violence" are to the French: "War," he opines, "is the game for which [they are] made."[42]

Victorian ambivalence toward the unruly ludic inversion of power appears most dramatically in the disturbing yet attractive figure of the trickster, the grifter, and the confidence man (or woman): Becky Sharp, the doll-like Lady Audley, Mrs. Erlynne in *Lady Windermere's Fan* (1892). At once victim and victimizer, hero and villain, self and Other, Victorian tricksters inhabit both the respectable center of modern life and its tawdry margins. Throwbacks to another era, they are harbingers of the world to come. Because they capture the fluctuating essence of modernity, they often bear upon their shoulders metahistorical or geopolitical weight. Think of the ridiculous Bonaparte Blenkins in Olive Schreiner's *The Story of an African Farm* (1883), who counts among his relatives Queen Victoria and Napoleon Bonaparte. Think, too, of those imperial buffoons Daniel Dravot and Peachey Carnehan in Kipling's "The Man Who Would Be King" (1888), who, disguised as sellers of "mud toys," present themselves as gods to the people of Kafiristan, to tragic effect.[43] Or think of adventurer Richard Burton's account of his journey to the holy cities of Al-Madinah and Meccah—a journey marked by "playing" and "seducing."[44] Disguised in an imperial game of "dress-up" as a Muslim physician on Hajj, daredevil Burton infiltrates the inner sanctum of Islam on behalf of British modernity, on behalf of his countrymen's delight in subverting another culture's rigidly sacrosanct order.

Play as Paideia

Victorians adored this logic. With the exception of that self-proclaimed misanthrope Emily Brontë, it is difficult to name a single Victorian writer who aggressively critiques it. Although Dickens and Matthew Arnold poke occasional fun at it, elsewhere even they pledge allegiance. At its core is the sentimental notion, a truism today, that play is intrinsically productive and normative, that children and young animals in particular learn, adapt, and develop through life-enabling play. Nineteenth-century proponents of this logic—educationalists Alexander Francis Chamberlain and Granville Stanley Hall, Kindergarten inventor Friedrich Froebel, animal behaviorist Karl Groos, for example—viewed the impulse to play as an expression of futurity: a preparatory drive to acquire physical, cognitive, and emotional skills that advanced both the organism and the species.[45]

Children and animals are not the only beneficiaries of this infantilizing logic. So too are the working classes, especially working-class men, for whom Thomas Hughes and other reformers founded the Working Men's College in 1854. With its curriculum of sport, the College taught teamwork and self-control. In *All Sorts and Conditions of Men* (1882), Walter Besant extends this logic to women workers, noting that "girls want play as well as work"—"[t]he more innocent play they get, the better for them."[46] He imagines a dressmakers' collective in which members "dance," "romp," and play "lawn tennis" between short productive bursts of labor. Throughout his career, Dickens also lauds the characterologically productive attributes of play, its pedagogical capacity to repair mind, body, and body politic. When the Bishop of London proposed legislation in 1836 to outlaw public amusements on the Sabbath, a young Dickens penned *Sunday Under Three Heads*, a manifesto extolling the virtues of "rational" and "refreshing" working-class play, refuting the charge that play is rooted in excess or idleness, and insisting that those in power should welcome working-class play for its sublimation of seditious impulses into cheerful productivity.[47]

But it is the ludic behavior of children that really commands the attention of proponents of this logic. The ideological tributaries that feed Victorian views of child play are numerous: an Enlightenment model of history as progress; an "Evangelical" "tradition[ ]" that "focused," in the words of Leonore Davidoff and Catherine Hall, "on children's character as the basis for reforming society"; rationalist child-rearing practices that treated children as economic investments; evolutionary models of human behavior; and a Romantic association of childhood not only with cultural authenticity but with the transformative power of nature, as Judith Plotz has documented.[48] We see this logic at work in Hughes's privileging of play over schoolwork in his classic boy's novel *Tom Brown's Schooldays* (1857), where the contrast is stark between boys "hot and ruddy from football" and those "pale and chilly from hard reading"—a sporty echo of the Wordsworthian injunction to quit your books.[49] Hughes even credits sports and games with saving a sick child's life. In his reflections upon the economic devastation that afflicted England in the wake of the Napoleonic Wars, Hughes links the nation's vitality to the quality and quantity of its child play. "The trade," he recalls, "had been half ruined: and then came the old sad story, of masters reducing their establishments, men turned off and wandering about," "children taken from school, and lounging about," "too listless almost to play."[50]

As we shall see in Chapter Three, what makes this particular logic of play so ideologically potent is that it masks its own normalizing violence. Naturalizing socialization, it presents the impetus to conform as its opposite: an autonomous, happy impulse within the child. Dickensian representations of children ooze this logic. On the one hand, we have those productively playful children—Tim Cratchit in *A Christmas Carol*, Sissy Jupe in *Hard Times*, Jemmy in *Mrs. Lirriper's Lodgings* (1863)—who triumph ludically over the modern forces of mechanization, uniformity, and despair. On the other hand, we have those children whose tragic and unnatural inability to play—Jenny Wren in *Our Mutual Friend* (1864–65), Louisa and Tom Gradgrind in *Hard Times*, the inmates of Dotheboys Hall in *Nicholas Nickleby*, the imprisoned boy in *A House to Let* (1858)—is symptomatic of social breakdown at the national level. Louisa's "features," Dickens notes, "were handsome," "but their natural play was so locked up, that it seemed impossible to guess at their genuine expression."[51] Playing on the word *play*, Dickens suggests that the lack of expressiveness in Louisa's countenance is attributable to her stunted ludic growth as a child. In his darkest novel, however, Dickens, to his credit, pulls the rug from under this well-meaning but sentimental logic, debunking the idea that child play is spontaneous and uncoerced future-building. I refer to Miss Havisham's imperious demand in *Great Expectations* that Pip and Estella play—whether they want to or not. The more they play (and they play a lot), the more they become her playthings, their futures deformed by her past.

Play as Imaginary

The logic of play most cherished by those of us who work in literary studies, this one fuels the liberatory claims—the assertions of theoretical or epistemological subversion—that we sometimes make on behalf of the play concept. The Victorians invoke this Romantic logic when they credit play with being the spur of thought, its fluctuating essence. Play is that quality of language—organic, unpredictable, free—that makes it so enchanting. Proponents of this logic envision play, somewhat paradoxically, as an assertion of creative agency, as well as an intuitive surrender to the inexorable motion of the mind. Strategic acquiescence to an unruly force, play is the surfer *and* the wave: a dance atop the collapsing roof of the knowable. Art derives its life-affirming power, we are told, from ludic illusion and flux. The word "illusion," from the Latin *ludere*, means, as Huizinga reminds us, "in play."[52] Hence, Thomas Babington Macaulay's 1825 essay on Milton compares the "illusion" "produce[d]" by "poetry" on the mind to the illusion produced by "a magic lantern" "on the eye," for both are devices that stimulate imagination.[53] At the core of the Enlightenment-Romantic cult of the imagination, fueling its ethic of intellectual and political freedom, play sits, or rather *moves*, for elusive play is never stationary: it slips the confines of system, certainty, and cliché. The logic of play shapes eighteenth- and nineteenth-century understandings of dreams and the unconscious, Wordsworthian eruptions of recollection. As Mihai Spariosu and Mark Johnson have argued, thinkers such as Kant and Nietzsche build their modern philosophies upon a foundation of play.[54] We see this logic in Victorian theories of culture, in Pater's characterization of the Renaissance as the "free play of human intelligence," in Arnold's characterization of Hellenism, in *Culture and Anarchy* (1869), as the "unimpeded play of thought," or in his complaint, in "The Function of Criticism at the Present Time" (1864), that the "practical" "considerations" preoccupying English critics "stifle" the "free play of the mind."[55] In play, the mind becomes a spontaneously burnished surface, pure exteriority: sloshing water, whisking wind, bouncing beams of light.[56]

In 1795, Friedrich Schiller attributed the will to play, or *Spieltrieb*, which he identifies as the source of art, to a physical urge to expend "superabundant" energy.[57] Play, overflowing, militates against fixity and inwardness. In *The Principles of Psychology* (1855), Spencer applies an austere evolutionary patina to Schiller's theory, suggesting that play and art, both of which he considers "useless," are surplus energy left over from a more violent period in man's evolution when humans required more physical strength to survive.[58] Spencer's left-handed compliment to play pays tribute to the power of the logic we are now considering. Although he grumbles about tax increases that pay for "recreation grounds," although he bemoans the proliferation of "idlers" and "loungers," although he insists that the only good kind of play is the competitive play we began by considering, even Spencer, in his cranky way, invokes the idea of play as an imaginative, albeit brutal, organic overflow.[59]

In his chapter on Venice from *Pictures from Italy* (1846), Dickens provides a memorable account not so much of Venice, which recedes into the background, as of the artist's daily, and at times exhausting, surrender to the fluctuating forces of imagination. Suffering from sleep deprivation during this leg of his 1844 and 1845 Italian expedition, Dickens confesses that the border between his conscious and his unconscious has begun to break down. Hence, the city into which he glides one purple night is a "strange Dream upon the water," an oscillating surface of reflections.[60] Around him, from the vantage of his gondola, bleary-eyed, he sees only the undulance of his own mind externalized, like a "dissolv[ing]" "view in a magic-lantern": a "restless flitting to and fro," a "delightful jumble in my brain," the "floating," "rippling," "flowing" sensation of his own thought.[61] The effort of *Martin Chuzzlewit* having exhausted him, Dickens traveled to Italy for a respite from his art. But in Venice he found it anxiously awaiting him in bridges made of sighs and in the incessant lapping at his feet.

The Victorian logic of imaginative play was not always invoked so tenderly. Imagination disorients as much as it enchants. For a portrait of its more ominous aspect, look no further than the opening paragraph of *The Mystery of Edwin Drood* (1870), in which John Jasper's "scattered consciousness," opium-induced, triggers a similar play of thought, his interiority projected onto a reflective urban surface. Cityscape becomes mindscape in a state of collapse. The "ancient English Cathedral town" outside the window, usually the most stable of referents, dissolves, along with the promise of narrative clarity, into a nauseating De Quincey dream, incongruously confected as from *A Thousand and One Nights*. "Ten thousand scimitars flash in the sunlight," as a "spike" intrudes into Jasper's field of vision, "set up by the Sultan's orders for the impaling of a horde of Turkish robbers, one by one."[62] With its play of signifiers, imagination is a double-edged sword: it sends Victorian writers floating in new directions, but it evicts them, too, from the homely truths in which they have taken shelter.

Play as Identity

Here the idea is that humans play in order to connect with other people and experience a primal, intersubjective sense of belonging. "[W]hat religion knits people so closely," Robert Louis Stevenson muses, "as a common sport?"[63] This logic of play underlies the socially cohesive logic of holiday, feast, public spectacle, and all forms of customary revelry. Though shrill at times in the nineteenth century, this antimodern, identitarian logic is usually accompanied by a muted sigh of nostalgia. With the exception of those pillars of the calendar, holidays, this once powerful ethic of play has been purged, so its proponents lament, from Victorian life. They worry that the *spirit* of play—*A Christmas Carol* literalizes this spectral word—has been adulterated by more ascendant play impulses: by the middle-class privatization of pleasure, by a capitalist competitiveness, by a latent anarchy permeating the lower classes. This ghostly logic is the signifier for a referent disappeared, like the old Maypole public house in *Barnaby Rudge* (1841): a structure both "ruinous" and "hale," built upon the festive ground for which it is named.[64] As Eric Hobsbawm has documented, by the end of the nineteenth century partisans from across the British political spectrum had begun to invent tradition, from royal pageantry to May Day celebrations, as a means of legitimizing and inculcating ideology.[65] The Victorian logic of play as identity, which fueled much of this invention, is the most nakedly historical of our logics, as well as the most historically dubious.

We see it at work in the so-called Young England movement of the 1840s, in the welcome accorded by Benjamin Disraeli and John Manners to aristocratic paternalism—the romance of the mirthful peasant—as a remedy for working-class suffering. The feudal lords of Merry England acted not as oppressors but as guardians of customary consciousness, Manners insists in his 1842 *A Plea for National Holy Days*, joining their tenants in the "lawful recreations" decreed by the "Book of Sports."[66] He lauds the "wholesome" nature of early seventeenth-century morris dancing, "archery," and "vaulting," the adjective here denoting not just health but the interworking of parts within a cooperative ethos.[67] Customary play preserves social hierarchy while endowing it with an egalitarian aura. "The lusty apprentice," Manners muses, "shall not fear to outleap his master's son, nor the pauper's child of want to contend with the guardian's brother."[68] The problem is not that Victorian England lacks play, for "whole treatises have been written during the last ten years on every imaginable sport," and "every county in England possesses its pack of foxhounds"; indeed, "reading-rooms" and "gin-shops have sprung up with a mushroom speed of growth."[69] In the eyes of the Young Englanders, what the nation lacks is ludic mutuality, centripetal play. In his sprawling 1801 history *The Sports and Pastimes of the People of England*, Joseph Strutt enumerates the practices of a disintegrating culture like an anthropologist racing against time. He blames the imminent extinction of communitarian sportiveness on "the want of places proper for the purpose," on urbanization, on the enclosure of the commons, and on a landscape "now covered with buildings."[70]

The logic of play as identity functions as the ideological foundation of Ruskin's theory of the Gothic in *The Stones of Venice* (1851–53). It fuels the fetishization by Victorian socialists and by Arts and Crafts enthusiasts of the medieval artisan, who becomes in the nineteenth century a ludic corrective to the alienated modern worker. The "wise play" that is so characteristic, Ruskin insists, of the early Gothic and that stands in such stark contrast to the irreverent and antisocial play of the Renaissance, derives its wisdom from the deindividuating sublimity, the grotesque yet awe-inspiring sense of oneness, that the medieval worker expresses in his crude art, which becomes a conduit for the organic, joyfully connective wealth that is life.[71] Ruskin's theory of the Gothic fuses, then, the logics of play as identity and play as imaginary. It endows imagination with communitarian rusticity, even while redefining intellectual freedom as a willingness "to yield reverence to another," a freedom from self.[72] As E.P. Thompson has documented, thriving pockets of pre-nineteenth-century plebeian revelry such as "wife sales" and "Saint Monday" survived in rural locations well into the Victorian period.[73] Celia Haddon recounts, for instance, how the Cotswold Olimpick Games, which were first played in 1612 and renamed "Dover's Meetings" in the nineteenth century, survived until 1850, though by that date its backsword contests and morris dances had degenerated into cockfighting and an inebriated version of blind man's buff.[74] Unsurprisingly, Victorian middle-class proponents of antimodern communitarian play preferred the revisionist historical fantasy, their own "rustic gatherings," as Jackson Lears describes them, to its nineteenth-century plebeian manifestations, often invoking the logic of play as subversion to dismiss as degraded the latter altogether.[75]

Having convinced themselves that England was dangerously devoid of a vibrant ethic of customary play, middle-class Victorians, assisted by a burgeoning tourism industry and a newfound sense of leisure, proceeded to discover it growing in enviable, frightening, or amusing profusion in every other country under the sun. They journeyed in search of authentic and unadulterated play experience of which their own autotelic recreations seemed a pale imitation. Venice might be a dream, but Dickens experiences the rest of Italy as a nation at raucous play, an endless procession of "festa-days" and celebrations, the deindividuated Italian population "cluster[ing] like bees" in "all the lanes and alleys, and up every little ascent, and on every dwarf wall, and on every flight of steps."[76] In his *Glimpses of Unfamiliar Japan* (1894), Lafcadio Hearn describes in vivid detail the "ancient and merry annual custom of casting out devils," noting with a hint of regret that Japanese of the Westernized "upper classes" "believe" in the "festival just as little as Englishmen to-day believe in the magical virtues of mistletoe or ivy."[77] What England lacks, in Hearn's view, is a ludically credulous and thus charmingly nonthreatening lower class, a people as enchanted by mistletoe as Japanese commoners are by devils. The British fear of communitarian revelry, by contrast, rears its head most often in representations of India. In his descriptions of the deindividuating festival of the Mohorum at Hyderabad in *Confessions of a Thug* (1839), Philip Meadows Taylor recounts in vertigo-inducing detail the "sickening" swaying "to and fro" of "the vast mass of human beings," this "sea of human heads," a rampaging elephant "seiz[ing]," at one point, "an unfortunate" reveler "by the waist with his trunk," "whirling him high in the air," before "dash[ing] him against the ground."[78]

Play as Fate

Rather than something we *do*, play is something that happens *to* us. We are the playthings of the cosmos, the pawns of God, of chance or fortune, of ineffable forces beyond comprehension. Play tugs at our strings. Victorian materialists may call the mysterious force nature, history, or society, rather than God, but they feel the tug nonetheless. Play humbles us. An exhilarating or horrifying sensation, it reminds us just how flimsy, how partial and perspectival, our knowledge and authority are in the grand scheme of things.

The Victorian linkage of play and fate is most pronounced in the love-hate relationship that the middle class had with gambling, which has both profane and sacred dimensions. In his 1898 *The History of Gambling in England*, John Ashton traces the historical and philosophical roots of gambling—a "disease" "most contagious"—to ancient cosmology, to the divine play of Egyptian gods.[79] To gamble is to align one's fate with the cosmic dice throw, with the capricious forces of life. The capitalist impulse is a gambling one, and Ashton (like Thackeray's narrator in *Barry Lyndon*) finds it in commercial speculation, in the "Stock Exchange," in the popularity of "life annuities," even in "insurance," which he deems a "beneficial" "class of gambling."[80] While Victorian critics of capitalism often couch their critique in the logic of play as competition, in the notion that capitalism is an exploitative sport, they also invoke the logic of play as fate. Insofar as the market functions as a game of chance, a "lottery" in Gaskell's words, success is arbitrary and unjust.[81] Whereas competition does violence mainly to the losing player, gaming does moral violence to the winner, too, for it suggests that his or her acquisition of wealth is the result of dumb luck, not merit. "*Alea*," Roger Caillois writes, is "an insolent and sovereign insult to merit."[82] In his early poem "Hap" (1866), Thomas Hardy can bear to think a "vengeful god" is toying with him, "profiting" from his suffering, thwarting him by sadistic design. Unbearable, however, is the idea of mere "dicing Time," an impartial and unfeeling cosmos that "had as readily strown / Blisses about my pilgrimage as pain."[83] Ambivalent about chance, the Victorians unleashed it and suppressed it at the same time. As Elaine Freedgood points out, the growing popularity of risky forms of entertainment, like ballooning and mountaineering, offered the Victorians the chance to hover dangerously on the vertiginous cusp of chance before ultimately mastering it.[84] By the end of the nineteenth century, as Ian Hacking has argued, the very concept of chance had been conceptually tamed, purged in large part of its determinism and fatefulness, and transformed with the rise of statistical reasoning and other methods into a new form of knowledge, a modern epistemology in its own right.[85]

Not everyone, however, was interested in taming chance. The logic of play as fate has some decidedly quirky Victorian proponents who invoke it in defiance of the disenchanting march of reason. We see it in Bulwer-Lytton's fascination with occult wizardry and magic, and most extensively in his novel *Zanoni* (1842). We see it, too, in the Victorian love of ghost stories and all things supernatural. We see it in the popularity of spiritualism, and again in the growing popularity of astrology among the urban middle classes after 1830, culminating in the rise of Alan Leo, astrology's self-declared modernizer and pioneer in the mid-1890s of the daily horoscope.[86]

The logic of play as fate emerges on a more cerebral level in the flurry of interest in Heraclitus among nineteenth-century classicists and philologists, who embraced the notion of ludic flux that makes of time "a game" of creation and destruction "played beautifully by children."[87] While many Victorians marveled at the awesome regularity of the motions of the universe, its astral plan, others detected a childlike whimsy: the power of the cosmos to sweep us away, to discard us like a broken toy. In *Edwin Drood*, a text punctuated by death, Dickens suggests that the very dust of cathedral Cloisterham is comprised of the microscopic "vestiges" of "abbots and abbesses." Thus, "Cloisterham children," Dickens infers, "make dirt-pies of nuns and friars."[88] On occasion, Stevenson too equates child play with cosmic caprice, with the fleetingness of life. In *An Inland Voyage* (1878), he watches children who live with their families on canal boats play together in an "impromptu hamlet," a rustic flotilla, hours before the "four winds" scatter the boats, and the playfellows, "into all parts of France."[89]

The radical assertion attributed to aesthetic philosophers, such as Nietzsche and Pater, that the subjectivist illusion of reality is a state of pure play both diminishes and expands the power of the human intellect. On the one hand, we are constitutionally incapable of arriving at objective truth, yet on the other hand, the world as we know it is an illusory projection of our own minds. While Victorian aestheticism is rooted primarily in the logic of play as imaginary, it is also informed by logics of fate and self-creation. In *The Rubáiyát of Omar Khayyám* (1859), for instance, Edward FitzGerald expresses most eloquently and memorably the Heraclitean notion that we are mere playthings of the unknowable, and that permanence is but a trick of the eye:

> 'Tis all a Chequer-board of Nights and Days
> Where Destiny with Men for Pieces plays:
>   Hither and thither moves, and mates, and slays,
>   And one by one back in the Closet lays.[90]

By adding a veneer of Oriental fatalism to a homegrown Victorian logic, FitzGerald effectively "Others" what is most ethically and philosophically disturbing about it, rendering the aesthetic idea of life-in-play more palatable for domestic consumption. *The Rubáiyát* reconciles at least three ludic subjectivities: the hedonistic self, the fated self, and the poetic or imaginative self. We see the logic of play as fate invoked likewise in Dante Gabriel Rossetti's "The Card Dealer" (1870), which compares life to a card game, an obligatory femme fatale serving as dealer:

> Thou seest the card that falls,—she knows
>   The card that followeth:
> Her game in thy tongue is called Life,
>   As ebbs thy daily breath:
> When she shall speak, thou'lt learn her tongue
> And know she calls it Death.[91]

The Mirrored Chamber

Seven logics of play: seven floor-to-ceiling mirrors—some cracked, some cloudy, some framed in gold—in a heptagonal room of Victorian design. At the center of this play space, claustrophobic yet infinite, modernity stands transfixed, its glimpses catching glimpses of glimpses. This is the world that the Victorians discover in play, from which they sometimes recoil, but at which they cannot help gazing. If you prefer a number other than seven, then add another wall, or three, or twenty. The structure is modular; the effect is the same. The mirrors blur and multiply. The chamber contains infinite space. The important thing—the thing to feel in one's gut, to know in one's dizziness—is that play triggers in the Victorians existential and metahistorical anxiety, endless unsettling reflections upon the condition of modern life. While the Victorians were not the first ludic subjects or the first to perceive the world as structured by play, they were the first to leap through the looking glass hand in hand with history, with the historicist knowledge that the structure is haunted by flux. The Victorians identified in the frictional and reflective space within play a world severed from the past.[92] The Victorians, modernizing play, put modernity in play.

Place a Victorian text inside this mirrored chamber. Which logics of play does it invoke, activate, or contain? In which logics does the modern world recognize itself? In *Culture and Anarchy*, for instance, Arnold presents his "sweetness and light" ethic of the "unimpeded play of thought," rooted in the logic of play as imaginary, as a moral and intellectual corrective to what he deems three dubious logics of play.[93] Arnold associates each with one of the three socioeconomic classes that together threaten to tear modern Britain apart: first, the competitive middle class, with its cult of "games and sports," to which "the passing generation of boys and young men" "is sacrificed"; second, the "rowdyism" of the working class, "our playful giant"; and third, the narcissistic recreations of the nobility, with their "field-sports" and love of leisurely self-cultivation.[94] Arnold diagnoses play as the modern disease: the body politic turned cancerously against itself. He prescribes, however, as its most efficacious cure, the key to political health, nothing more or less than play.

Others are less optimistic. In *Idylls of the King* (1859–85), Tennyson proleptically contemplates the doomed state of Victorian modernity with his portrait of a Camelot teetering on the brink of collapse, its power to cohere gradually undermined by the centrifugal forces of moral dissolution and political dissent. Whereas Tennyson associates civic cohesion with a homosocial ethic of sport, with male bonding and tournaments that temporarily forestall the Round Table's fracturing, anarchy takes the form of a highly sexualized ludic subversion and trickery: the seduction of heroes by loose women, whose actions do not correspond to their words, and whose pleasures are largely self-centered. Tennyson pits his masculine logics of play as competition and play as identity against feminine logics of play as subversion, play as self-creation, and play as imaginary.

He places his sad portrait of the fallenness of modern life in a metahistorical frame of play. Born of play and strengthened by it, civilization will likewise die by its hand. Caught in the darkling plain between life and death, between culture and anarchy, modernity watches impotently as two armies—one sportive, one seductive—bear down in "that last weird battle in the west."[95] At its side, modern poetry, too, stands transfixed, caught between two ludic and gendered aesthetic impulses: the rule-boundness of form and the thrilling undecidability of language. In nineteenth-century Britain, play did not wage war against *unplay*, a foreign foe. Like Tennyson's Balin and Balan, brothers and neighbors took up arms against each other. Logics clashed with fellow logics. The tension in so many Victorian literary and cultural texts lies *within* play, in the civil clash of its disparate logics.

In Part II, we will trace the ludic tensions in specific nineteenth-century British literary and cultural artifacts, and explore the extent to which these Victorian meditations upon the modern condition are meditations, ultimately, upon play. That all of the writers featured in Part II are underdogs, rebels, or outsiders is partly attributable, I confess, to my antiestablishment preferences as a critic, but it is also due to the fact that marginalized, disempowered, or unconventional people tend to bear the brunt of modernity, and are thus exposed in a very personal way to the dark side of play, like no one else. I choose them for my guides. All of the writers discussed in Part II intuit, in their own idiosyncratic ways, that the fault lines of modernity are in play. Melodramatists of the 1830s, for instance, define modern life as a battle between the plebeian forces of fair play and the middle-class forces of foul play: in other words, between the confederate logics, on the one hand, of play as identity (customary revelry) and play as subversion (a trickster ethos) and the marketplace logics, on the other hand, of play as competition (capitalism as a contest) and play as fate (capitalism as a toss of the dice). Emily Brontë, by contrast, sees modern subjectivity as inextricably linked to the middle-class pedagogization of child play. In freeing the ludic child from the demands of productivity, in realigning child play with cosmic destruction, Brontë attempts to displace the ascendant logic of play as *paideia* with a heady mix of two logics: play as fate and play as subversion. Scotsmen Robert Louis Stevenson and John Muir are less offended by the logic of play as *paideia* than by the modern Anglo-American cult of the "weekend warrior," a toxic byproduct of the logics of play as self-creation and play as competition. In reimagining post-Gold Rush California, with its natural wonders and cosmic boyishness, as an ethical corrective to egotistical masculinity, they attempt to loosen competition's violent grip on leisure, aligning the latter instead with the more life-affirming logics (in their eyes) of play as imaginary, play as *paideia*, and play as fate. Oscar Wilde, too, sees competition, the middle-class athleticization of life, as the primary culprit. Morally and philosophically, Victorian athleticism manifests itself as "earnestness," which devours modern subjectivity in one tedious bite. For Wilde, Christian folly, the logic of play as subversion, is the only viable means of undermining competition from within. In refusing to win, in mischievously losing in the sport of life, Wilde hopes to inspire a new culture of love. It should be noted that all of the texts that follow contain additional logics of play, indeed, myriad ludic tensions; in my analysis, I have chosen to highlight those tensions that are most expressive of a given text's sense of the modern, its metahistorical anxiety. Before turning our attention to these writers, however, and to their divergent but equally ludic visions of modernity, I would like to offer some final thoughts on the origins of the world in play, my own theory of how and why modern life has become so closely aligned, increasingly so over the last four centuries, with the concept of play.

The Cosmology of Modernity

One brisk morning in January 1952, anthropologist Gregory Bateson paid a visit to the city zoo in San Francisco, where two young monkeys frolicked in the sun. The monkeys ambushed each another from behind logs and concrete blocks, rolled on the ground in a furry embrace, nipping each other in mock combat, before scurrying off, only to begin their game again. Though the monkeys did not know it, they inspired what would become a classic theory of play. About their nips Bateson would later write, "[n]ot only do the playing animals not quite mean what they are saying but, also, they are . . . communicating about something which does not exist."[96] Or, as Anna Nardo more succinctly puts it, the monkeys are declaring: "This bite does not signify what a bite signifies."[97] "In play," Bateson writes, reality and appearance, frame and context, "are both equated and discriminated."[98] Thus, human infants become mesmerized by their own reflections in mirrors, by the endless slippage between "that is me" and "that is not me," and by the sensation of subjectivity in play. Stephen Nachmanovitch explains that the monkeys are "dynamically rolling together" two worlds—the reality of the bite and the fictional world of the not-bite—in a paradoxical metamessage or metacommunication that undermines the violence of certainty and the stability of knowing in the same way that Epimenides the Cretan inspires in us a meta-epistemological stance toward moralism when he declares that "All Cretans are liars."[99] Because Epimenides is Cretan, by his own definition, he must be lying about being a liar, in which case he is telling the truth, which, in turn, means he is a liar, which starts the ball rolling again. He draws us into the funhouse of infinite regress, depriving us for a moment of a stable vantage point from which to subject him to judgment. This pleasurable blurring of true and false, reality and appearance, bite and not-bite, is the source, some play theorists claim, of the purportedly ethical nature of play, for play constitutes, in the eyes of some, a psychological alchemy in which a bite comes to signify its opposite, having become ironically detached from itself. Nardo explains: "[B]ecause play conflates the defining frame with what is inside the frame, a single play action takes place simultaneously on two levels of reality: the player both participates in his action and stands apart framing the action, thereby gaining distance and perspective on himself."[100] This detachment from the moment, from the heat of *hic et nunc*, is why Nachmanovitch sees in play the logic of "peace."[101]

Critics who are ideologically or emotionally invested in play as an ethical and political corrective to the ills of life—to the world of all-too-real bites—tend to stop here. It is a happy place to stop. We like the idea that a nip is an antidote to a bite. Bateson's celebration of the harmonious dimension to play—indeed, his very theory of play—is based, however, on the assumption that the player clearly recognizes within the paradox of play the boundary between play and not-play. According to anthropologists Don Handelman and David Shulman, Bateson's theory works like this: first, "the invocation of play creates a boundary between not-play and play; second, . . . this boundary is paradoxical; third, . . . this same invocation of play also overcomes the paradox it creates, enabling passage into the reality of play"—the realization, that is to say, that play is play.[102] According to Bateson, at any rate, this is how play *should* work. For some people, however, play does not work so smoothly. Individuals suffering from schizophrenia have lost the ability, Bateson points out, "to recognize the metaphoric nature of [their] fantasies" and "to set metacommunicative frames."[103] If you nip a schizophrenic monkey, it will bite you. Bateson pathologizes the inability or refusal to recognize the passage between play and nonplay; he defines as "schizophrenic" the total collapse of the frame, the sensation of the world in play, of the complete blurring of inside and out. Funhouse becomes madhouse. Mirror devours world. In a sense, the schizophrenic is incapable of experiencing a world *at* play; he can only experience the unsettling sensation of a world *in* play; thus, the "pseudolove and pseudohate" that structure the therapist-patient relationship become indistinguishable in his mind from love and hate.[104] The psychotherapist's challenge is to draw the schizophrenic patient out of the world in play, to rescue him from the cosmos-swallowing abyss of fantasy, and to create a stable sense of an outside, a frame that draws a clear and reassuring line between combat and pseudocombat. Underlying Bateson's theory of play, then, is the seemingly innocuous cosmological assumption that "the ludic" is "formulated," in the words of Handelman and Shulman, "in opposition to, or as a negation of, the order of things."

What happens, however, Handelman and Shulman wonder, when "the invocation of the ludic is embedded in cosmos at a high level of abstraction and generality," when "its fluid, transformational qualities are manifest at all levels of cosmos"?[105] What happens, in other words, when play *is* the order of things, when the frame is the universe itself, and when the world is envisioned as always already in play? According to Handelman and Shulman, such is the case in Hindu-Indic cosmology, in which the world is perceived as the result of a perpetual game of dice between the Hindu god Śiva and his wife Parvati. The dice match, which Śiva invariably loses, constitutes "both a condensed expression" of the "process" of the cosmos "and a mode of activating and generating that process," life itself triggered by the self-alienation of a psychically fragmenting god.[106] Existence, therefore, is literally *in* play. Forget monkey bites or mock bites. Here, reality bites. The mirror in which the infant plays with her reflection expands exponentially, infinitely, its frame corresponding to the rippling, star-bursting contours of the Big Bang. Existence passes through the looking glass, the cosmos turning inside out. A Western psychotherapist might be tempted to diagnose Hindu cosmology as schizophrenic. A better question might be: Is Hindu-Indic cosmology—and Heraclitean cosmology, for that matter, in which time is perceived as a game of destruction and creation played by children—proof, rather, of just how imaginatively meager and epistemologically myopic the Western medical concept of "schizophrenia" truly is? Perhaps the people we label "schizophrenics" are simply individuals with a bit more cosmic perception than the general population.

That said, unlike Gilles Deleuze and Félix Guattari in *Anti-Oedipus: Capitalism and Schizophrenia*, I have no desire to revalue or appropriate schizophrenia, or to view the schizophrenic as the modern subject best equipped to navigate the vicissitudes of capitalist modernity. It is not my intention to attribute untapped political and aesthetic potential to this supposed pathology. Nor do I seek to rescue schizophrenics—whom "Freud doesn't like" and whom he "treat[s]" "more or less as animals," or worse, as "philosophers," "cut off from reality," as people who "mistake words for things"—from the "analytic imperialism of the Oedipus complex."[107] Schizophrenics, Deleuze and Guattari eagerly claim, are "incapable of achieving transference," of setting Oedipal metacommunicative frames, of distinguishing between reality and fantasy. Not one to view the world through a psychotherapeutic lens, I do not really care whether Emily Brontë, for instance, who mentally retreated for hours every day into the imaginary world of Gondal, would today be classified as a borderline schizophrenic.

What intrigues me instead about Deleuze and Guattari's schizoanalysis—indeed, where I see a kinship between their philosophical attack upon Oedipus and my own more modest and historically localized rereading of the Victorian world—is in their characterization of capitalist modernity as a decodifying or frame-collapsing sensation of a world in play. Deleuze and Guattari's modernity is an ominous capitalist-cosmological echo of Śiva's self-alienating dice game, at least as Handelman and Shulman describe it, in which dematerialized, fantastical, and hence phantasmatic money—its circulation, management, and accumulation in the deadly serious game of middle-class capitalism—devours the world and saturates consciousness. In capitalism we maniacally mistake words, or signifiers, for things. The order of things collapses into, and is subsumed in, the fantastical order of its monetary representation. Value in our relentlessly material world becomes synonymous with the radical dematerialization of that very world, its capitalization. Life-and-death economics, the matter of whether our fellow human beings are housed or homeless, fed or hungry, employed or unemployed, seems less immediate to us, less compelling, than the circulation of referentless signifiers: numbers cycling through banks and stock exchanges, endowing us along the way with a sense of self. The mirror swallows the baby. The signifier swallows the referent. The frame between the nip and the bite disintegrates. The outside disappears. Call this modern sensation "schizophrenia" if you like. I prefer to call it the world in play. It is the very sensation that Marx and Engels describe when they characterize the nineteenth century as a world in which "all that is solid melts into air." It is the very sensation that Kipling describes in *Kim*, in which a mischievous Irish boy, disguised as a Hindu, plays his "Great Game" of imperial conquest: his up-to-date dice match for the world's future.[108] Thus does a modern capitalist cosmology impersonate and supplant an ancient Hindu one. It is the very sensation, too, that Thackeray's Redmond Barry describes, when he complains that, under the new regime of global capitalism, the logic of the casino swallows the planet whole, with the very sea—the biggest mirror on earth—serving as the "green table" on which capitalists toss their windward dice. When the last gambler has sailed home, and when the stars bob silently on the sea, vast though it is, it is still a world in play. One cannot escape it, anymore than one can escape the universe. Indeed, the world in play might best be described as the cosmology of modernity.

Capitalism is not the only modern phenomenon that induces cognitive dissonance, the schizophrenic sensation that the ludic order of signifiers has become more real than the order of things. From Copernicus to Galileo, from Isaac Newton to Darwin, from Albert Einstein to Francis Crick, modern science has unsettled the opposition between reality and appearance, noumenon and phenomenon, reminding us, to our terror and delight, that much of what we perceive is a perspectival trick of the eye. Let us begin with a very basic, nonschizophrenic example. We call the orange-pink glow in the distance a "sunset." It feels to us as if the sun has fallen below the horizon. Modern subjects (and high school graduates) that we are, however, we know that the term "horizon rise" describes more accurately than does "sunset" the Earth's rotation away from the sun. For the past four and a half centuries, humans have *played at* watching "sunsets." We have epistemic mastery of the optical illusion. To feel the illusoriness of an optical illusion, to sense simultaneously reality (the Earth's rotation) and illusion (the setting sun) is to be *at play*, to have ludic coordination, self-command, like Shakespeare's Jaques, or like Bateson's nipping monkeys, within the paradox.

Most illusions, however, are not so easy to detect. Modernity triggers an endless avalanche of illusions, many of which we struggle to experience *as* illusions. We tumble like Alice into their depths. Epistemic mastery proves difficult. Modernity does not disillusion us, or disabuse us of our illusions, as some may think, so much as it traps us in illusions that feel more real to us than reality. Our false perceptions of the world have more meaning to us than our scientifically informed awareness of their falsity. Sunsets aside, modern consciousness is, for the most part, *in play*, for that is what "illusion" means. We believe our own lies, even as we confess to ourselves that we are liars. Consider the phenomenon of color. Thanks to modern science, to optical investigations begun by Johannes Kepler and Newton, culminating in the work of Victorian theoretical physicist James Clerk Maxwell, we know that color does not exist outside of our visual cortex. The universe is colorless. The apple we eat is not red. It has no "redness," no color whatsoever, just as grass has no "greenness," the sky no "blueness." The Victorians killed rainbows. What we call "color" is the brain's electrochemical response—patterns of electrical membrane potentials in the neuronal meat of the central nervous system—to different wavelengths of electromagnetic radiation, photons, reflected from molecules on the surfaces of objects to three types of differently sized photoreceptor cells in our retina, which have evolved over millions of years to be selectively responsive to a very narrow range (wavelengths between 370 and 730 nanometers) of all of the electromagnetic radiation bombarding our bodies and ricocheting through the cosmos.[109] This is what we call "color." On occasion, we are reminded of the fact that electromagnetic radiation has no color, only varying wavelengths—when we read a book, for instance, about the neurophysiology of color. Even the most rigorous cognitive neuroscientist, however, forgets on an emotional level that color is inherently neural and succumbs to the joyful illusion that the apple is red and that lemons have an ontological property called "yellowness." "The world," we tell ourselves and our bodies tell us, "*has* color." Or rather, the world seems to have color, the appearance of color, which amounts to the same thing. To equate "reality" and appearance, indeed, to prefer appearance so shamelessly (and schizophrenically) to "reality," even after all that we know, after Kepler and Newton and Maxwell, is to be *in* play. Modernity screams from our bedside that we live in a world of dreams. Modernity shakes us from our slumber. At the same time, however, it slips us another sleeping pill and whispers in our ear, "Dream on, dream on." If the world at play is a daydream, then the world in play is a nightmare from which we attempt—and fail, attempt again, and fail—to wake.

PART II

Portraits

CHAPTER 2

Fair Play in an Ugly World

THE POLITICS OF NAUTICAL MELODRAMA

I am often told by people who never go to the theatre that they like melodramas, because they are so funny. Those who do go know better than that.
—George Bernard Shaw[1]

The Mirrored Curtain

It was not large enough to swallow the world. At five tons, however, it was heavy enough to imperil the roof of the Royal Coburg Theatre in London (The Old Vic today). In December 1821, the managers of the Coburg installed between the auditorium and stage an enormous looking-glass curtain comprised of sixty-three mirrored panels in a gilt frame. It was smudged, Isobel Armstrong notes, with countless fingerprints: the oily residue of the workmen responsible for its installation and maintenance.[2] This wall of metatheatrical reflection greeted spectators at the start of performances, turning—if not all the world—the bustling world inside the auditorium into a stage, and "dissolv[ing] the boundary," Jane Moody writes, "between the consumer and the object of consumption," reminding many theatregoers of a gigantic shop window.[3] Spectators waved at themselves or at each other. They scrutinized cleavage. They chased gazes across panels, dodged whorls of cigar smoke, and caressed the shy plaits of fans. Audiences flocked to the Coburg to behold, and to be held in the greasy palm of, its giant mirror, a moving portrait of modernity: "the most *NOVAL, splendid, & Interesting Object* ever displayed in a British Theatre," or so the playbill proclaimed on the evening of December 26, 1821.

Democratic, the Coburg's looking-glass curtain reduced the socio-economically diverse world of the audience to a single, dynamic representation, and turned everyone into everyone else's object of self-conscious contemplation. Simultaneously hierarchical, however, the mirror preserves for the "highly stratified" audience, Armstrong contends, "a reassuring ideal image of itself"; it captures in a tidy gold frame the working class in its rambunctious pit and middle-class shopkeepers in their balconies and boxes.[4] Delightful to some, unsettling to others, the Coburg's mirror teased its audience with the following question: What would happen to the order of things if a mirror were constructed as boundless as the world it reflected, if the illusion's *inside* rivaled in size its *outside*; if fantasy refused to subordinate itself to reality? The looking-glass curtain is more than a convenient metaphor for capitalist modernity, for the infinite regress of a consumer consumed by consumption. In its celebration of, and gimmicky appeal to, the masses, it is historical proof that the idea of a world in play is no freak of the philosophical or literary imagination. The Coburg's proprietors knew that the uncanny sensation of a cosmos swallowed by its ludic representation was something all Britons would instinctively understand. Everyone felt it, was capable of feeling it. After engineers expressed concern that the Coburg's rafters might snap under its weight, the famed mirror, grown sticky with smoke from "the frying of sausages, stewed eel and trotter," was begrudgingly dismantled, its panels used well into the 1930s, however, in the dressing rooms at the Old Vic.[5]

The Coburg, or the "Blood Tub" as it was commonly known, presented its mirror as a partisan statement of minor-theatre pride in its battle with the big patent houses. The mirror became a symbol of the cultural ascendancy of melodrama, for melodrama is what greeted audiences once the shimmering curtain was raised. Accusing the "giant houses" on "t'other side [of] the water"—Covent Garden and Drury Lane, which had exclusive rights to perform traditional drama—of "giv[ing] to our humility no quarter," of "[s]ay[ing]" that "nought but nonsense lives within our portals," and of "call[ing] our heroes monsters, and not mortals," George McFarren, writing on behalf of the down-market Coburg, brags that the mirror, and thus the melodramatic spectacle it frames, provides the only authentic account of plebeian life: "Our portraits must be true, for you'll behold yourselves!"[6] The proponents of so-called legitimate drama, which had been ceding market share and cultural influence to melodrama for decades, often dismissed the musical spectacles performed at the transpontine Coburg and other minor theatres as vulgar distortions of life. McFarren's celebration of the gaudy mirror of melodrama, his declaration of the obsolescence of traditional language-based drama, and his alignment of the ocular pleasures of melodrama with plebeian "truth," suggest that melodrama, by the early 1820s, was actively reshaping the way the British public saw the world. This chapter examines how melodrama functioned in its heyday as a therapeutic means of making sense of ludic modernity, how it helped working-class audiences find their bearings in an unsettling new world in play.

Just as the Coburg's mirror implicates its audience, resituates them onstage, and reduces the entire world to a melodramatic spectacle, so the "melodramatic mode," as Elaine Hadley terms it, overflows the proscenium, breaks loose from its theatrical frame, and takes to the street, infiltrating modern consciousness, becoming a political tactic and a politics in its own right, manifesting itself in myriad nontheatrical contexts throughout the nineteenth century—in political speeches, in street protests, in countless conversations, as well as in "nonlinguistic forms of representation": "physical gestures, political actions, and visual cues."[7] Emergent in the early nineteenth century, the melodramatic mode—what Hadley defines as an insurgent communitarian form of theatricalized protest against the alienating "reorganization" of society—remained "a prevalent behavioral and rhetorical paradigm to the end of the century."[8] The Coburg's mirrored curtain reminds its audience, to the frustration of traditionalists, of the extent to which melodramatic logic has reshaped nineteenth-century British subjectivity and reframed the experience of life. People live melodramatic lives, think melodramatic thoughts. They see the world with melodramatic eyes. It is not that melodrama is more true than traditional drama, it is simply more real, more ethically and politically useful in navigating the challenges of modern existence. Melodrama has swallowed the world. To its fans, it has no outside. It has become, McFarren proclaims, the new order of things. If global capitalism puts the world in play, then early nineteenth-century melodrama takes its audience by the hand and teaches them to survive the looking glass.

It is no coincidence that the melodramatic subgenre that dominated the British stage between the early 1820s and the mid 1840s, when Parliament dissolved the official distinction between the patent houses and the minor "illegitimate" theatres, was nautical melodrama: highly formulaic and unabashedly jingoistic plays about the Royal Navy, the heroic feats of Jolly Jack Tar, and the tribulations of the seafaring life. More nautical melodrama was performed during this period than any other melodramatic subgenre. A large segment of the audience at London's minor theatres, the most combustible and rowdy, were the sailors, dockworkers, and Thames watermen who lived in the working-class neighborhoods around the theatres, and who fueled the demand for nautical melodrama. This is not the reason, however, that nautical melodrama became so popular; nor does it explain how the long-suffering but good-natured English sailor came to embody modern man in the British popular imagination. A synecdoche for the Navy and hence for British military might, the sailor became in the early nineteenth century the British government's most effective instrument in the expansion of global capitalism, the maintenance of its vast empire, and the policing of its watery trade routes. The sailor stood tall on the fluid surface of modernity, on the biggest mirror on earth. He walked on water. A selfless hero, a victim, too, of the dread press-gang, the sailor of nautical melodrama put a human face on the changes wrought by capitalist bureaucratization, by the worker's alienation from his own labor.

In this unsettling new world, the sailor survived, but barely. He learned to navigate an unfamiliar reality, crossing and recrossing its fluid boundary. In 1804, Sadler's Wells Theatre (the Aquatic Theatre as it was then known) installed an enormous water tank on stage, 100 x 40 x 2 feet, capable of holding over 50,000 gallons of water and fed by the nearby New River. The theatre's repertoire of aqua dramas and reenactments of naval battles, replete with cannon fire and miniature waves, expanded to include nautical melodrama in the early 1820s. Every now and then a curious audience member would leap into the tank during a performance. Of the 1820s and 1830s, stories abound of inebriated sailors at other theatres, leaping from the orchestra pit onto the stage during nautical melodramas or descending from the gallery in order to partake in battle scenes, lending their theatrical counterparts a hand. Audiences loved it. Actors did not. The mirror might have swallowed the world; the signifier might have devoured the referent; existence might be irrevocably in play. These drunken seamen assured their fellow countrymen, however, that the communitarian forces of justice would battle injustice to the bitter end, to the very horizon of the mirror.

How Melodrama Works

According to Peter Brooks, melodrama is a reaction to the desacralized state of the modern world. Structured by an "irreducible manichaeism," by the "bipolar" "clash" of "good and evil," melodrama emerges in the late eighteenth century as a moral-aesthetic response to a century that culminated in the French Revolution: in the "final liquidation of the traditional Sacred and its representative institutions (Church and Monarch)," in "the shattering of the myth of Christendom," and in "the dissolution of an organic and hierarchically cohesive society."[9] In its nostalgic and ritualistic depiction of the triumph of good over evil, in the "fragmentary" "remnants of sacred myth" to which it stubbornly clings, melodrama expresses and cathartically processes the "anxiety brought by a frightening new world in which the traditional patterns of moral order no longer provide the necessary social glue."[10] Hence, the "middle ground and the middle condition are excluded" from melodrama, Brooks insists, for "compromise" is not possible between good and evil.[11] The apocalyptic nature of Brooks's narrative of modernity is due to the fact that he draws his representative texts almost exclusively from a French cultural context, the Revolution functioning in his analysis as the moment the old order spectacularly collapses and modernity rears its fiery head. For obvious reasons, the British narrative of modernity is less overtly cataclysmic than the French. Thus, the British melodramatic critique of the new order of things is rooted, in my view, less in nostalgia for a premodern Sacred than in economic anxiety, alienation, and an uncanny sense of being out of place. Indeed, British melodrama is more a reaction to counterrevolutionary repression than to revolutionary upheaval. Nevertheless, Brooks's classic theory of melodrama can be applied to the British context, insofar as British melodrama constitutes, at its core, as does its French counterpart, a moral response to the psychologically and ethically unsettling experience of modern life.

The good-evil opposition has limited value, however, when it comes to explaining the moral tension at the heart of British melodrama. One can view British melodrama through a lens of moral excess, or as wish-fulfillment or false consciousness, but in doing so one risks reducing melodrama to the unrefined and facile Other to psychological realism and political nuance. While melodrama might be given credit in this scenario for being anthropologically intriguing or historically noteworthy, it is invariably associated with aesthetic and emotional crudity. Melodramatic audiences certainly had a lot of justifiable anxiety about the conditions of modern life, but they were not as naïve as they are often portrayed. In the pages that follow, I outline an alternative theory of melodrama, making the case that melodramatic authors, performers, and audiences were more savvy and pragmatic than they have been given credit for being. I focus primarily on the so-called Golden Age of plebeian melodrama, when nautical melodrama reigned supreme, the period between 1820 and 1840, before this working-class medium was co-opted by middle-class domestic ideology, Queen Victoria becoming in the 1840s melodrama's most famous fan, and before the legal distinction between London's illegitimate minor theatres and its large patentees was dissolved by the Theatre Regulation Act of 1843, which, for the first time, extended the jurisdiction of the Lord Chamberlain's Examiner of Plays to minor houses.

The tension at the heart of early nineteenth-century melodrama is between fairness and unfairness. Modernity is not evil. Life is perceived, rather, as less fair than it once was. The capitalist market has changed the rules of the game, or so it feels, in the middle of the game. Society has become more ruthlessly competitive, less cooperative. The poor and the powerless continue to follow the same customary rules of fair play, but everyone else refuses to recognize these once sacrosanct rules of interaction. The ground shifts beneath the feet of working-class players. Life loses its moral balance. Goal posts move. The playing field contracts and expands arbitrarily. Referees have gone home. What was once out of bounds is now tolerated, or left unpunished. To the lower orders, modernity feels like a rigged game. Rules are absurdly loose one day, ridiculously rigid the next. The rich and powerful rewrite them to suit their needs, to ensure they always have the upper hand. No matter how skillfully or beautifully the working-class player plays, no matter how worthy of advancement or reward she proves herself, the ruling class will make certain, in the end, that she loses the game. The moral tension at the heart of melodrama is between *fair play* and *foul play*: between customary consciousness and capitalist consciousness, between an uncodifiable instinct for justice and the injustice of bending the rules, officially or unofficially, in order to engineer the profitable result one desires. Melodramatic foul play, which sometimes manifests itself as physical violence or even murder, is essentially the killing of a community's organic connectivity. British melodrama is the theatricalized account of working-class victimization, of the befouling of Merry England, of the degradation of a world at play by an unsettling new world in play.

The centrifugal sensation of a world upended, of life disordered, is not limited to the working-class victims of the free-market roulette. In the late eighteenth and early nineteenth centuries, conservative and paternalistic critics of modernity repeatedly invoke the metaphor of *alea*, of the game of dice, to describe what they perceive as the arbitrary and inorganic state of increasingly egalitarian and precedent-shattering modern life. Writing in 1790, Edmund Burke, who, like Brooks, views the French Revolution as a metahistorical cataclysm, complains that the "great object" of France's revolutionary "legislators" "is to metamorphose France from a great kingdom into one great play-table; to turn its inhabitants into a nation of gamesters; to make speculation as extensive as life."[12] Thus, Burke associates modernity's foulness with the "malicious game," with "those who live on chances," who put Time itself in play, on "the destructive table," the revolutions of the roulette tossing tradition to the wind.[13]

An embodiment of fair play, of the increasingly obsolete ethos of an apocryphal Merry England,[14] in which neighbors helped neighbors and justice was intuitive, the sailor-hero of nautical melodrama, invariably a pressed man, finds himself caught between two unjust forces: criminals and villains, on the one hand, who ignore all rules, and the oppressive agents of law and order, on the other hand: naval officers, judges, and bailiffs, with their regulations, floggings, and rigid adherence to rules, no matter how unjust. Simultaneously optimistic and fatalistic, melodrama is not so much a Manichaean battle between good and evil as a protest in the name of fair play—an intuitive, fictive, extralegal expression of justice—against the foul play of the predatory criminal and the coldhearted lawman. Melodramatic morality is triadic, not dyadic. The oppressed are not besieged by an amorphous entity called "evil," they are attacked on two flanks by diametrically opposed forces with seemingly antithetical agendas: crime and law. Crime hurts the poor; law marginalizes them. Caught between those who break society's rules and those who use those rules to disempower the poor, the melodramatic hero enacts, on behalf of his working-class audience, a populist and nostalgic fantasy of fairness, serving as spokesman for a mode of living that is opposed to both law and lawlessness. Melodrama explores the possibility, and the difficulty, of achieving fair play in an ugly world. It longs for moral balance. The transplantation of the sailor-hero from the happy fixity of the English countryside or of homey suburban London, where he tends his crops or plies his trade, to the lurching deck of a storm-battered warship allegorizes Britain's historical and economic shift from a relatively stable agrarian world at play to a capitalist world in play.

Politically, melodrama is neither obedient nor seditious. Its sympathies lie outside crime and law. Radicals distrusted it. So did conservatives. Melodrama reconciles obedience and sedition in an attempt to transcend both, to forge a third way, to escape the foulness of polarity altogether. The melodramatic hero battles criminals on behalf of justice, not law; his profound distrust of law derives not from a criminal nature but from a nature that is all-too-just. The pragmatism of melodrama, and of nautical melodrama in particular, can be traced to its quest for the very middle ground that Brooks claims is foreign to the logic of melodrama. Fair play does not emerge from between good and evil. It emerges from the cultural space between antisocial criminality and ruling-class law: from the fictive, illusory, extralegal, but morally legitimate space of custom.

As E.P. Thompson has documented, "[a]grarian custom was never fact," nor a legally prescribed set of rights. Rather, custom is a concatenation of "sociological norms," "inherited expectations," "neighbourhood pressures," and "rules" that were often invented on the spot.[15] Rooted in the logic of play as identity, custom is more real than true. At times hateful, at times humane, custom acts as counterdiscourse and countertheatre to ruling-class power. The plebeian invocation of custom throughout the eighteenth and early nineteenth centuries functions as a moral and political counterweight to two antisocial types: first, the cretinous working-class individual (or religious or sexual Other) who disrupts the moral economy, the wife-beater, for instance, who is ritualistically humiliated with "rough music" (tied to a pole and "serenade[d]," to quote Frances Power Cobbe, with "cows' horns," "warming-pans, and tea-kettles");[16] and second, the ruling-class tyrant, the greedy landowner, or factory boss, who is targeted with a bread riot or whose workers bring production to a halt every week in honor of "Saint Monday."[17]

Working-class custom exists outside law and crime. It hovers on the periphery of law, is begrudgingly indulged or tolerated by paternalistic landowners and industrial bosses. Custom sometimes crosses the line, however, from inconvenience to crime, in which case the Riot Act is read. Custom is defined by middleness. In the eighteenth and nineteenth centuries, custom functions as a form of compromise. The lower orders invoke custom as a moral and political corrective to both law and crime. In theory, if not always in practice, custom tempers both and quells their violence. It is an island of fairness in a sea of foulness. What is fairness but balance and harmony? Fairness, Elaine Scarry explains, is an "ethical principle" rooted in the aesthetico-moral sensation of "symmetry"; it is essentially "distributive," a "lifesaving reciprocity."[18] Because the foul world that melodrama decries has become so asymmetrical, melodrama channels its moral energy toward the absent middle, toward a cultural and psychological space anterior to foulness, toward a just and peaceful center, which is neither rebellious nor submissive, and which, like custom, provides the working class with a sense of order outside law, justice by other means. This is how melodrama works.

The Ludic Space of the Theatre

Before exploring the politics of ludic compromise or fair play in an assortment of nautical-melodramatic scripts, I would like to focus attention in this section on the ludic dimension to the space inside the early nineteenth-century British theatre, for some readers may not be familiar with the highly interactive manner in which working-class audiences experienced melodrama in the 1820s and 1830s. Carnivalesque, rambunctious, yet highly rule-bound, early nineteenth-century British melodrama looks and feels like a game. Profoundly superficial, its stock characters function as masks without faces, surfaces in a colorful masquerade. Melodrama defaces the human; it flattens, exaggerates, reduces the individual to a type, a set of physical, inflectional, and gestural rules. To deface is not the same as to dehumanize. Melodramatic defacement exteriorizes subjectivity, replaces the person with a game face, transforming characters into agents of play. Melodramatic plot, too, consists of hackneyed convention, a limited universe of options and expectations: "the endless repetition," to quote Michael Booth, "of basic, even archetypal situations and character relationships."[19] Melodrama explores the art of living in a world without options, within the confines of low expectations and narrow perimeters of possibility.

On one level, one experiences melodrama as one might a game of chess, losing oneself in its two-dimensionality, its black-and-white starkness. Even though a rook has no interiority, and pawns feel no ambivalence about being pawns, the game is compelling. Chess pieces embody strategies of survival and tactical maneuvers in a flattened, reduced universe. Nineteenth-century directors often blocked melodramas by moving wooden figurines of various sizes around a board, a tiny replica of the stage. One attends an evening of melodrama as one might a football or basketball game today: more for its ambiance, its atmosphere of play, than for the matchlessness of its plot, or the way it defies expectation. At times one's attention is riveted to the field or court, to the unfolding of a particularly artful play, and at times one focuses on the stands, on one's fellow spectators, on the parallel spectacle of reaction and interaction, the cheering and booing. And sometimes one's hotdog is all that matters. As Tom Gunnel reminds us in Edward Fitzball's *A Sailor's Legacy* (1826), the profound superficiality of plot and character in nautical melodrama, its avoidance of depth, derives in part from its setting: a vast and violent surface on which depth and death are synonymous: "His lovely wife, who had no crime but poverty, foundered with grief. Death had sapped the timbers of her heart, and she struck on the quicksands of distress. Down she went, and there she lays, without a buoy or signal-post to mark the hallowed spot."[20]

On the morning of April 5, 1836, two theatre reviews appeared, one in *The Times*, the other in *The Morning Chronicle*, recounting a raucous evening of nautical melodrama at the Surrey Theatre, where John Thomas Haines's *The Ocean of Life* debuted alongside his crowd-pleaser from the previous season, *My Poll and My Partner Joe*. Although domestic melodrama surpassed nautical melodrama in popularity a few years later, the Navy's centrality to the imperial project ensured that nautical melodrama enjoyed a niche in the theatrical marketplace well into the 1890s, its jingoistic ditties and maudlin ballads implanting themselves in the Victorian cultural imagination. Gilbert and Sullivan's *H.M.S. Pinafore* (1878) and *The Pirates of Penzance* (1880) represent the tip of the iceberg of nostalgic nautical parodies popular from the 1860s to the early twentieth century. The most shamelessly British of melodramatic subgenres, nautical melodrama, usually set during the Revolutionary and Napoleonic wars, takes as its subject the watery frontier that hems the island nation, across which its cultural, military, and economic influence sails, in which it sees its face reflected. The British warship functions as synecdoche for nation; rank and tradition quell mutinous impulses. Beneath it, however, and surrounding it, laps the insatiable sea, keeping it afloat but threatening at any moment to engulf it. Danger lurks not only in the cannons of a foreign navy but below deck, below the hull. According to naval historian G.J. Marcus, in nearly twenty years of war with France, the British Navy lost just ten warships to enemy fire.[21] By contrast, 329 British vessels either foundered or were driven ashore, wrecked on shoals and rocks.

The reviews in the *Times* and the *Chronicle* burst with laughter. So earsplitting is the roar of the Surrey crowd, an audience the *Chronicle* surmises was "one of the most crowded and boisterous," "which perhaps ever congregated," that the already fragile opposition between spectator and spectacle, house and stage, shatters.[22] The deafening laughter displaces the play itself: "To give any account of the plot of the new piece," the *Chronicle* confesses, "would be an impossibility, as such was the constant uproar which prevailed in the house throughout the evening, that not ten consecutive words of the dialogue were heard by the audience, if the term be not a misnomer under such circumstances."[23] *The Times* concurs, admits, "we can speak only [of] the 'action,'" "for hearing was last night wholly out of the question."[24] Despite the fact that the plays cannot be heard or evaluated as *texts*, they receive rave reviews, the *Chronicle* proclaiming the evening an "unqualified success" and noting how "vociferously" the plays were "applauded."[25] Plot and artistry are secondary to audience reaction: *The Ocean of Life* "appeared," the *Chronicle* suggests, "to comprise an abundant stock of the usual materials of melodramatic interest," including, "of course ... a 'female in distress,'" "who is persecuted through three long acts, to the great delight of the hard-hearted spectators." Spectators are not mindless consumers of ideology; they are active participants in melodramatic creation, players familiar with the rules of the game. The crowd delights in the heroine's obligatory travail. Audiences watch melodrama with ironic detachment. As playwright Thomas Morton explained in a statement to the 1832 Parliamentary Committee on Dramatic Literature, audiences have a tendency to "force passages never meant by the author into political meanings": "I think constantly I have observed that; and also we all know that a theatre is a place of peculiar excitement."[26]

London theatres in the 1820s and 1830s, when nautical melodrama reigned supreme, erupted at sunset with sensation and noise, aggression and pleasure. Drunken confrontations and disputes between political factions competed for attention with the play itself.[27] The lights inside early nineteenth-century theatres remained undimmed during performances. Prostitutes plied their trade, providing a more titillating spectacle of female sexuality than the wholesome maidens on stage. Ignoring the world beyond the stage, one might be tempted to interpret these maidens as proof of melodrama's social conservatism. Turn your head, as patrons eagerly did, to the boxes, where lace fans languidly beckon. Theatregoers ate, drank, and smoked in the theatre, engaged in conversation, met friends, and mingled. They hissed or encouraged actors, sang along to songs, shouted their favorite lines, and laughed in all the wrong places. Theatres such as the Surrey, the Coburg, the Adelphi, the Pavilion, and Sadler's Wells, some dingy, some opulent, sold their own brands of vulgarity and danger. The Surrey and the Coburg were downright notorious. Playwrights such as Haines, Fitzball, Douglas Jerrold, George Dibdin Pitt, and William H. Williams wrote specifically for these unruly audiences, not for those inclined to savor every syllable. They wrote with the knowledge that their handiwork would be commandeered and interrupted, used as a vehicle of interaction. It was melodrama's function.

The Wisdom of Nautical Melodrama

Animals and humans instinctively play, zoologist Robert Fagen hypothesizes, not so much to "practice" or "rehears[e]" "motor skills needed in future fighting," as to "develop" their "emotional intelligence," to make themselves "behaviorally and cognitively adaptable, flexible, resilient, and versatile."[28] By ensuring that our intellects are limber, play prepares us "for the unpredictable," for those sticky situations beyond our control.[29] At one point, Fagen suggests that play "makes the world go round."[30] It would be more accurate to say, however, that play enables us to maintain our psychological equilibrium in a world that goes round and round, that shifts unpredictably beneath our feet. Instead of reacting "impulsive[ly]" or "mindlessly" to a novel situation or new environment, we are able "to unhook" "from the here and now," to frame the situation, as Bateson would say, and thus to see it from the outside.[31] Play makes us wise. It gives us the ability to exist on two planes simultaneously, to separate passion and action. Play trains us to outmaneuver our emotions, "keep[ing] emotion" "from being dominating, controlling, exploitative, or selfish."[32] Play makes us just; it balances us ethically in a topsy-turvy world. Some theorists even suggest that play is at the root of love.[33]

While some readers will dismiss Fagen's theory of play as functionalist, it nonetheless provides a compelling explanation of why we so often associate the concept of *fair play* with instinct, with an intuitive sense of justice. To demand fair play is to declare that the conditions of life have become unnatural, asymmetrical, that something basic and life-sustaining has been lost. It means that our ability to be at play, to achieve cosmic balance, has been overwhelmed by a world in play, by an environment that undergoes change more rapidly than our ability to adapt. If early nineteenth-century modernity creates the conditions for such a world, then melodrama, nautical melodrama in particular, provides its discombobulated audience with a fantasy of adaptability and elasticity, a return to the lost world of fair play. "Escapist" is not the right word to describe melodrama's political agenda. Melodrama does not seek to flee modern life. Though inelegant, the word "eludist" comes closer. "Elude" means "to outplay." Melodrama teaches audiences how to slip the ugly grasp of law and crime, how to remain upright in a fallen world. On a formal level, nautical melodramas are rigidly formulaic; on a political level, these plays are remarkably supple, adaptive, and wise. Theirs is a politics of elusion. Melodrama outplays law; it outplays crime. It balances itself wisely between them, between the will to capitulate and the will to lash out.

The political aim of nautical melodrama is to degrade law subtly, not to overthrow it rashly. Like customary consciousness, melodrama bends rules without breaking them. It moves just outside law, in shadows and blind spots: not far enough away to incur its wrath, but not close enough either to be subsumed in it. Custom hovers warily near law's flanks, acquiesces to its demands, obeys its letter—ironically, half-heartedly—but not its repressive spirit. Against the patrician ideal of political economy, nautical melodrama pits a plebeian moral economy: a social order predicated upon an intuitive sense of fairness, illusory rules of social reciprocity that predate the lawgiver. In his depiction of the "crossing the line" ceremony in *Shipwreck of the Medusa* (1820), which theatre reviewer George Daniel considers the earliest nautical melodrama, "a new species of drama," playwright William Thomas Montcrieff equates the seafaring ethos with an extralegal yet nonthreatening customary consciousness.[34] As *The Medusa* crosses the Tropic of Cancer, the crew attire themselves as Neptune, "his fair consort," "and his illustrious court," demanding extra grog from their indulgent captain: "the accustomed tribute due from those / Who, by his kind permission, cross the line."[35] A colonial governor happens to be aboard. The captain finds himself in the awkward position of explaining to his appalled passenger, a representative of officialdom, why ludic custom takes precedence over naval regulation: "We must not attempt to break through customs sanctioned by long usance, and only productive of harmless mirth, Governor; however we may feel inclined to smile at their absurdity or reprobate their inutility."

Melodrama yearns for order without law, a code of conduct without an official apparatus of enforcement. Employing his characteristic nautical metaphor, sailor-hero William says of law in *Black-Ey'd Susan* (1829) that it is "Beelzebub's ship, the Law!": "I'd sooner be sent adrift in the North Sea, in a butter cask, with a 'bacco-box for my store room, than sail in that devil's craft, the Law."[36] When a man claiming to be a lawman attempts to interrogate the cranky seaman Fid, in Fitzball's *The Red Rover* (1829), he is greeted with the following ejaculation: "I am an old fish—d'ye see, and not to be cross-questioned by a land-shark."[37] In melodrama, bailiffs and beadles are invariably corrupt or incompetent. After Goliah Gogmagog, a buffoon beadle in William H. Williams's *The Wreck*, threatens for the umpteenth time to read his neighbors the Riot Act, one mischievous citizen informs him, "The law and you may be lashed together, like a cheating pedlar, and his pack of false merchandise."[38] Williams himself played Gogmagog in the February 1830 production of *The Wreck*. In *Black-Ey'd Susan*, Jerrold reminds us that the bailiff's profession, like the beadle's, is a "trade" in both senses of the word: a profession, as well as merchandise bought and sold.[39] Jerrold sets the play in the coastal town of Deal. When a desperate Susan cannot pay her rent, her corrupt landlord-uncle sends his bailiff henchman to evict her, to enforce the laws of capitalism. The market is more violent, at times, than nature. As Long Luke Layland, the sailor-hero of Haines's *Breakers Ahead!* (1837), succinctly puts it, "we pays no rent at sea."[40]

In melodrama, those who control law inevitably abuse it. To the audience's delight, lawyers are routinely denounced. William blames his impressment on lawyers in *Black-Ey'd Susan*.[41] In Jerrold's *The Mutiny at the Nore* (1830), when Jack Adams, an articulate seaman, is informed by another sailor that he "talk[s] better than any lawyer," he quickly responds, "Ah! that doesn't say much in my recommendation."[42] In Haines's *My Poll and My Partner Joe* (1835), when sailor-hero Harry Hallyard is asked to give an account of himself he sums up his character the following way: "Who am I? I'm the happiest dog on the Thames; got the best craft, and the prettiest sweetheart; will pull a match with any man between bridges; know how to serve a friend, 'specially an old one; always pay my rent; can wash my own shirts; and hate lawyers."[43] Commensurate with Harry's ethos of fair play, his willingness to "pull a match" and "serve a friend," is his instinctive distrust of law and those who profit from its logic. The ubiquity of lawyer-bashing in melodrama in general, and nautical melodrama in particular, can be attributed, at least in part, to the fact that the notoriously unprofitable profession of playwright drew many of its recruits, John Russell Stephens notes, from the ranks of London's disillusioned law students and disgruntled law clerks in the early and mid nineteenth century.[44] Montcrieff "began his working life" "near the bottom," "a humble clerk in a London solicitor's office." So financially fruitless was playwriting, in fact, and so antiquated the copyright laws, that

£60 was all Jerrold was paid for *Black-Ey'd Susan*, the most performed nautical melodrama in history.

Melodrama longs for a world in which those who play by the rules win and those who don't, lose. The criminal is diabolical not because he breaks the law but because he befouls fair play and opens the door to the lawgiver's rigid order. Crime is law's secret accomplice: "[Y]ou must believe passionately in the law," Jean Baudrillard reminds us, "in order to transgress it."[45] In nautical melodrama, distinctions between lawgivers and lawbreakers collapse. Pirates disguise themselves as lawmen. Press-gangs and kidnappers are indistinguishable. Resentful aristocrats send press-gangs after their rivals in love. Magistrates regularly commit fraud and blackmail. Justice is arbitrary. The innocent are arrested for crimes they did not commit. When Long Luke learns that his childhood friend Allan Maydew has been accused of murder in *Breakers Ahead!* he erupts at Maydew's accusers:

> Crime! To old Davy with their accusations, you and crime steer as widely apart, as cowardice and a British tar. Hark ye, you side[-]going land crabs! if you dare accuse an honest lad like him, you are no more fit to live in this merry country, than weevils in a seaman's biscuit; come let us over[haul] your log, or damme part company before I give some [of you] a lurch into port that shall settle you down to the [cold sea] locker.[46]

Raising his grog aloft, Long Luke references the double-headed monster of law and crime, when he toasts: "Here's confusion to the oppressors of the poor."[47]

I agree with Hadley that in melodrama tyrannical lawgivers and corrupt lawmen serve to particularize the "disembodied agents of the bureaucratic state," to embody the "dehumanizing rhetorics" "produced in market culture, such as bureaucratese and statistics."[48] Melodrama's critique of capitalism through its invocation of customary consciousness, through its recourse to what Hadley terms a deferential economy of obligation, is not proof, however, that melodrama is "profoundly reactionary," as she claims, "if not precisely politically reactionary."[49] Admittedly, a culture of conservatism can and does flourish in melodrama, which regularly champions traditional social values and sexual mores. As Thompson has shown, however, neither melodrama, nor the customary consciousness from which it springs, is intrinsically reactionary. Even deference is not inherently reactionary. Deference does not always mean what it says. Sometimes, when a worker doffs his hat to his superior, his doff, to paraphrase Bateson, does not mean what a doff means. Consider Thackeray's *Barry Lyndon*. Upon his dubious ascension to the British aristocracy, Barry notes with dejection that "the farmers on market-days" "touch their hats sulkily, and get out of my way."[50] Plebeians employ deference strategically, not blindly. Acquiescence and complicity often function in melodrama as subtle but effective avenues of critique.

Melodrama is politically pragmatic: it explores the art of eluding power in a world saturated with the marketplace. Conservatives and republicans are united in their desire to wield power. Thus, Dick Dark, the hero of Andrew Campbell's *Bound 'Prentice to a Waterman* (1836), expresses contempt for all politicians: "There's a great many at home in England who, by the power of might alone, talk a great deal to very little purpose; while many others, who have right on their side, jaw a great deal to no purpose at all."[51] Bozzy Bull agrees wholeheartedly with Dick, played by Campbell himself: "I know what you means—I'm wide awake! My mother's brother's uncle's cousin's grandfather's nephew knowed a member of parliament, who said, that in certain place, they generally passed half their time in trying to find out what they'd been talking about the other half."[52] While the melodramatic degradation of law sometimes takes the form of denunciation, when William deems law the "devil's craft" or when Harry Hallyard professes his distaste for lawyers, for example, it usually manifests itself in more subtle ways. Overt critique, after all, has its risks. In an attempt to diffuse the unpatriotic implications of Bozzy's antiparliamentary outburst, Dick issues the following warning: "Avast heaving, mate; you're sailing in an unknown sea! Don't bother yourself about what you don't understand." Nautical melodrama might defer to official order, might obey religiously the letter of the law, but it does not obey, as we shall see, its spirit. Nautical melodrama's wisdom derives from its ludic detachment, its ability to separate action from passion, acquiescence from obedience, the doff from what a doff means.

As Moody has documented, the inception of British melodrama in the mid eighteenth century is marked by ludic detachment. British melodrama emerges, Moody argues, as a response to the draconian Licensing Act of 1737, which not only imposed unprecedented bureaucratic oversight upon London's patent theatres but attempted to deliver a death blow to unlicensed theatres, which proliferated in and around London in the early eighteenth century, fomenting opposition to the ruling class by satirizing political corruption before primarily plebeian audiences. The Act of 1737 essentially forbade stage speech at all unlicensed theatres. The first defiant gasps of melodrama emerged from these same unlicensed theatres. Theatre managers explored an array of strategies for circumventing the law against stage speech, while adhering warily to its letter. Some experimented with puppets and other inanimate "performers." Some resorted to pantomime and dumb show, actors brandishing banners on which complex sentiments were written. The most popular and enduring strategy for circumventing the legal definition of drama, however, was the use of music and song to communicate plot and establish mood. Song is not technically speech. Melodrama gets its name from this defiant *melos*, its ability to obey the letter of the law yet not its repressive spirit. Song was fair play. Melodrama submitted to law's demand that it not speak, but its lack of speech spoke louder than speech itself. In doffing its hat to law, melodrama outplayed law.

Although restrictions on stage speech were eventually relaxed, a popular form of plebeian art had been born. It retained all of its old tricks. Raucous musicality and spectacle displaced patrician textuality; gesticulation eclipsed articulation. So popular had melodrama become, in fact, that, by the dawn of the nineteenth century, Drury Lane and Covent Garden, bastions of cultural legitimacy, showcased it alongside the legitimate drama to which they once enjoyed monopolistic rights. Throughout the Revolutionary and Napoleonic years, government agents, counterrevolutionary spies, and jealous observers from the patent houses descended upon unlicensed theatres, watching for hints of sedition, whispers of republicanism, as well as for evidence that traditional drama was being performed. Because melodrama remained officially illegitimate, considered more spectacle than text, the unlicensed theatres were exempt from the censorship to which licensed houses were subject. Unlicensed theatres, however, enjoyed a highly tenuous foothold in the law: theatre managers were vulnerable to the whims of overzealous magistrates, to prosecution for running "disorderly houses." Early nineteenth-century British melodrama is defined by its uneasy relationship to law, by the threat of government crackdown, neither fully outside law, nor technically within it.

This changed dramatically in 1843 with the Theatre Regulation Act, which superseded the Licensing Act of 1737. As Moody explains, the Act of 1843 abolished the monopolies and privileges of the patentees and granted all theatres the freedom to perform traditional drama, thereby dissolving the official distinction between legitimate and illegitimate theatre, between drama and melodrama. This ostensibly reformist provision in the law changed little, however, for throughout the late 1830s and early 1840s an increasing number of unlicensed theatres were performing traditional drama in flagrant opposition to an antiquated law that the government rarely enforced, for fear of rallying the public on behalf of unlicensed theatres. The true intent of the Theatre Regulation Act, then, was not to liberalize British theatre but to extend government regulation of it, to place illegitimate theatre firmly within the purview of the law. The Theatre Regulation Act of 1843 required all theatres, not just the licensed houses, to submit play texts to the Lord Chamberlain's Examiner of Plays for approval and potential censorship. Law had caught up with melodrama.

It might seem odd that the melodramatic subgenre that dominated the working-class stage during one of the most contentious periods in British history, a period of socioeconomic turbulence and counterrevolutionary repression, was nautical melodrama, an overtly nationalist, unapologetically jingoistic expression of popular culture. Why would plebeian theatre romanticize, indeed, mythologize, of all things, the Royal Navy, which, from a plebeian perspective, epitomized, with its press-gangs and floggings, one of the most repressive institutions in the British arsenal of official order? Why did melodrama become in the 1820s and 1830s so deferential? Jeffrey Cox suggests that melodrama took a reactionary turn in the 1820s, that its centrality in the repertoires of Covent Garden and Drury Lane led to an ideological makeover, a campaign to rebrand itself by replacing its gothic plots of predatory aristocrats with the rallying cry of imperialism.[53] By treating the deference expressed in nautical melodrama as a transparently reactionary phenomenon, however, Cox, like Hadley, ignores the ludic nature of melodramatic acquiescence.

Typically set ten to thirty years in the past, during the Revolutionary and Napoleonic Wars, nautical melodramas do seem, at first glance, to mythologize military order and its concomitant imperial agenda. They idealize the British Tar, present him as the epitome of discipline, or, as one of William's shipmates describes him in *Black-Ey'd Susan*: "The trimmest sailor as ever handled rope; the first on his watch, the last to leave the deck; . . . he has the cleanest top, and the whitest hammock; . . . give me taut Bill afore any able seaman in his Majesty's fleet."[54] The sailor-hero's sense of duty manifests itself in small ways, when he sacrifices his grog to his fellow seaman, or when he "plays upon the fiddle like an angel," as William is said to do. It manifests itself in profound ways as well, when he saves the lives of his fellow sailors and even the lives of superior officers, in the cases of Harry Hallyard in *My Poll and My Partner Joe* and Mat Merriton in *The Ocean of Life*. When an American firing squad prepares to execute Long Tom Coffin's captured commander in Fitzball's *The Pilot* (1825), a grief-stricken Tom throws himself between the marines and his beloved officer:

No, no, you bee'nt in arnest, you can't be in arnest; or, if you be, then let every ball pass through this heart to his; as a youngster I loved him; I taught him to reef the first point, and to hitch the first gasket, he was always so brave, so—[*dashing away tears*]—don't you go to think I'm blubbering—only—what, shoot my commander?[55]

At first glance, nautical melodrama provides an overtly revisionist account of the Navy's contentious relationship during the Revolutionary-Napoleonic period with both the public and its own largely conscript population. In 1812, only 25 percent of a typical British warship's crew consisted of volunteers. Disgruntled and resentful, malnourished, at times seditious, most sailors served the Crown courtesy of the press-gang. Between 1803 and 1805, the Navy suffered approximately five hundred desertions per month. So violent was local opposition to naval conscription that press-gangs could not operate for fear of being murdered in rugged and remote coastal communities. In his memoirs, William Richardson, a naval veteran who served from 1780 to 1819, compares the life of a sailor in the Nelsonian Era to that of a slave: "People may talk of negro slavery and the whip, but let them look nearer home, and see a poor sailor . . . flogged with a cat, much more severe than the negro driver's whip, and if he deserts he is flogged round the fleet nearly to death."[56]

Despite the fact that both William and Harry are "pressed," that

Harry's abduction is enacted within the play (on his wedding day, no less), both recruits thrive in their new milieu, Harry within the space of a scene. So encoded is he by his new profession, so acquiescent is he to naval order, that when his captain asks if he is ungrateful for all that the Navy has done for him, he replies in his newly acquired argot, "May I spring a leak, and go down in the black sea of contempt, if ever I take such a villainous cargo on board!"[57] We can be sure, if the 1836 reviews cited earlier are any indication, that the audience greeted Harry's response with deafening laughter. The comic discrepancy between Harry's angry denunciation of his press-gang captors in the previous scene and his docility in this scene is too stunning to ignore. Harry's obsessive and conventional use of nautical metaphor, too, stands in stark contrast to his relatively jargonless preimpressment speech. In the space of a scene, Harry has become a new person: official sailor-hero of nautical melodrama. Far from obfuscating the State's violence against the working class, the play draws attention to it by highlighting the discrepancy between pre- and postimpressment Harrys. Nautical melodrama's very mythologization of military order, with its excessive jingoism and absurdly pliant sailors, delegitimizes military order. Nautical melodrama couches its critique of officialdom in the conservatively sanctioned discourse of patriotism, providing ideological cover for an amused audience to express its anxieties about the dehumanizing nature of the bureaucratic State. To appreciate nautical melodrama one must first appreciate the ludic politics of *deference as critique*, plebeian fair play, whereby a doff comes to signify what a doff is not. Nautical melodrama is unquestionably patriotic. Most of the men and women who attended nautical melodramas loved their country. No performance was complete without a rousing rendition of "Rule Britannia." But their love was not blind. The "rule" about which nautical melodrama sang was not the rule of law: it was the rule of fair play, the ethos of Merry England.

Three Tactics of Fair Play

We have witnessed some of the overt ways in which nautical melodrama invokes fair play: its privileging of merriment over work discipline; its satirical representations of lawyers, lawmakers, and lawmen; and its intuitive distrust of official order and criminal disorder. As mentioned in the previous chapter, at the heart of fair play is a metahistorical tension between the confederate logics of play as identity and play as subversion and the agonistic and aleatory logics of capitalism. We have also begun to explore how nautical melodrama's acquiescent stance vis-à-vis the law, with its fervent jingoism and customary deference, degrades law, even as it inoculates melodrama against charges of radicalism. Melodrama played a dangerous game with the government, which opted to look the other way most of the time. In this section, we will take a closer look at the melodramatic politics of deference as resistance, focusing on three fair-play tactics that degrade law and deprive it of sanctity, not through open opposition but acquiescence and complicity. Melodrama is one of the first popular expressions in nineteenth-century Britain of the psychic and cosmic suffocation induced in the working classes by the world in play. As politically cautious as these plays might seem from our twenty-first-century vantage, they are a testament to the enterprising spirit and ludic limberness of the men and women on the frontlines of modernity: the workers who bore the brunt of its world-shattering consequences.

Fetishistic Idealization

The first deferential means by which law in nautical melodrama is betrayed as unfair is fetishistic idealization, the literalness with which the naval hierarchy and even the sailor-hero worship the letter of the law, investing procedural and regulatory detail with hyperbolic significance, in effect, at the expense of justice. This phenomenon is evidenced most explicitly in Jerrold's *Black-Ey'd Susan*. After a three-year tour of duty, William returns home, where his wife Susan awaits his discharge from the Navy. That evening, as sailors reunite with their sweethearts, William's intoxicated captain, the lecherous Crosstree, mauls Susan in a shadowy street and is struck by William, who fails to recognize his captain in the dark. The play's action then centers around William's arrest and court-martial for striking a superior officer. Despite the fact that the presiding officers at his trial feel he was justified, despite the endless testimony to his exemplary character, despite Crosstree's acknowledgment that he deserved to be struck, the Court is forced by inflexible naval law, by "the twenty-second Article of War," to sentence the beloved sailor to death, for, "by the rules of the service, William must die."[58] As a pall descends upon the fleet, "true blue" William expresses his respect for the letter of the law, his fidelity to and enthusiasm for naval order, and his willingness to face his fate. He is saved from the yard-arm, however, rescued in the waning moments of the play, when his discharge papers are discovered to be dated prior to the fateful scuffle, revealing that he is not subject to the law he so idealizes.

In *My Poll and My Partner Joe*, Harry Hallyard is also seized by marines. Harry has disobeyed an order, paradoxically, out of his obsessive sense of duty, taking it upon himself to sneak under enemy guns and almost single-handedly capture an enemy vessel. Before Harry's punishment can be meted out, however, a battle ensues between his ship and an approaching slaver. In the mayhem, Harry manages to free himself, invade the slave ship, free the slaves, defeat the slave traders, and, amidst fiery explosions, invade the island fort of their pirate conspirators, where he triumphantly hoists the Union Jack. In *Black-Ey'd Susan* and *My Poll and My Partner Joe*, the sailor-hero's procedural transgression is motivated by valor, duty, and love of nation. Naval officers adhere so unwaveringly to idealized regulation that the regulations become absurdly unjust, heroism itself criminal. At Harry's trial, Captain Oakheart, whose life Harry once saved, faces the dilemma of punishing a sailor for his excessive bravery. He navigates the troublesome discrepancy between ideal sailor and the naval ideal of order:

To preserve the necessary discipline, we are compelled to reprimand a brave man for an act that confers honour on the British flag; yet, while obliged to condemn, we shall applaud and honour in our hearts one of the best seamen that ever trod a plank—one of the most fearless spirits that ever handled a cutlass: his very courage must be restricted with severity, or his example and extraordinary success will banish subordination from the fleet.[59]

So inflated in value are statutory and legalistic minutiae, that law in nautical melodrama is reduced to a fetish, an empty signifier, grounded not in abstract righteousness but in itself. In *Black-Eyed Sukey* (1829), Frederick Cooper's parody of Jerrold's popular play, William is sentenced to be "shoved into the black-hole of this His Majesty's lock-up house" for the murder of a beadle who is not only still alive but who even takes part in the trial.[60] Echoing the admiral who passes judgment on Jerrold's William, the night constable who sentences Cooper's William notes that the "case falls under the three hundred and forty-ninth regulation of the new police."

The metaphysical legitimacy of law derives from its referentiality, from the belief that it is neither epistemologically self-grounded nor politically self-justifying, but grounded in a higher principle—the Good, the primary power from which law derives its own secondary power, and to which it refers. Despite the fact that Kant and other late eighteenth- and early nineteenth-century philosophers had begun to question the metaphysical legitimacy of law, throughout the nineteenth century (and even today) law's legitimacy remained dependant in the popular imagination upon its purported metaphysical referentiality, which functioned to naturalize social hierarchy, mystifying with a veil of inevitability law's tyrannical arbitrariness. According to Marx, fetishism consists essentially of repressing an entity's referentiality; in the case of the commodity, it consists of the devaluation of the labor that produced it and the magical investment of that entity with an autonomous value. The fetish functions as an autonomous signifier, a thing-in-itself. To fetishize law, therefore, that which derives its legitimacy from its metaphysical referentiality, is to endow it with a magical autonomy, a self-groundedness independent of the Good. The more one fetishizes the letter of the law, the more self-referential and thus unjust it becomes. When justice does eventually prevail in nautical melodrama, it is a necessarily arbitrary justice, manifesting itself disconcertingly as luck, chance, or coincidence. Fetishized law is degraded law, the tyranny of rules.

In nautical melodrama, the sailor-hero often interprets naval procedure more fetishistically than do his superior officers. When Metrical Mat, the patriotic coxswain of George Dibdin Pitt's *The Eddystone Elf* (1833), delivers supplies to a remote government lighthouse and discovers that its keeper has been murdered, his first impulse is to proclaim, "Hollo! How's that? He'd no right to die till government gave him orders."[61] Though taken prisoner by the French, whom he "hate[s]" "worse than poison," sailor-hero Martin Roseberry, in Campbell's *Rule Britannia* (1836), so fetishizes naval order and is so disgusted by insubordination that he foils the escape plans of two French deserters, inmates in the same facility, and even saves the life of the French colonel in charge of the prison.[62] Roseberry's blind devotion to authority is transferred to his British superiors only after his ship's crew invades the prison, whereupon he informs the colonel, "I respect but cannot obey you."[63]

Like melodrama itself, which emerges from a defiantly literal interpretation of the 1737 law forbidding stage speech at unlicensed theatres, sailors in nautical melodrama occasionally turn law against itself, adhere to its letter so closely they mischievously thwart its intent, taking advantage of legal loopholes in order to achieve fair play. Though an apprenticed waterman is legally "bound," excluded, in other words, from military service, patriotic Dick Dark, in *Bound 'Prentice to a Waterman*, nevertheless attempts to enlist, exploiting the fact that papers of indenture must be physically present in order to be valid. Having pursued him to the docks, his disapproving parents implore Captain Grant, the impress officer, to disqualify their "bound" son. They are turned away, however, to Dick's delight, when it is discovered they left his papers at home. When Allan Maydew is about to be arrested for wounding a villainous aristocrat in *Breakers Ahead!* his sailor-friend Long Luke bursts onto the scene with a press-gang, announcing, "Hold! I seize him in the king's name, for the royal service!"[64] Luke turns the tyrannical arbitrariness of law against tyranny. Luke's ludic manipulation of law persists throughout the play. When he rescues another friend, a British deserter, from a Chinese prison, and when his captain suggests that prison is precisely where a deserter belongs, Luke points out that the man has not yet been listed *officially* as a deserter: "[S]o you see[,] the law of the case is altered."[65] His amused captain responds, "Luke, you are getting as learned as a Lord Chancellor." The captain's heart is softened by the ludic tactics of Luke, who happens to be a childhood "play fellow" from his "father's estate."[66] Luke's degradation of law through his literal interpretation of regulation, his legalistic exactitude, enables fair play to prevail.

Masochistic Submission

The second acquiescent means by which law in nautical melodrama is degraded is masochistic submission, the sailor-hero's docility in the face of law's violence, his complicity in his own victimization. Despite the fact that Harry Hallyard characterizes naval law as "cruel," acknowledges that he is forced to "defend a country whose laws deprive him of his liberty," he announces to his tearful fiancée as the press-gang closes around him:

"I must submit . . . without one thought of the green hills or the flowing rivers of a country that treats me as a slave!"[67] Despite the fact that William deems law "Beelzebub's ship," which "founders in fair weather," and which is "provisioned with mouldy biscuit and bilge water," he succumbs willingly to the punishment it metes out, embracing with kamikaze enthusiasm its ideal of discipline.[68] He goes so far as to refuse at his court-martial, against the urging of his judges, to reconsider his guilty plea, to equivocate or qualify his actions, claiming that "it is beneath the honesty of a sailor" "to go upon the half tack of a lawyer."[69] His decision results in his death sentence. Placed in irons for insulting his captain in a moment of weakness, Allan Maydew informs his confused commander: "I bless, and kiss these chains—they cool my fevered sense of baseness!"[70] In Fitzball's *The Red Rover*, Fid is derided by his American captors as "passive and unfortunate," when he professes that he would gladly go to the "gallows" for his "commander."[71]

According to Deleuze, masochism constitutes the political strategy of capitulating, surrendering to law so zealously, obeying the letter of the law so literally, that the violent foundations of law, its consequences, are betrayed and its purported nobility debased.[72] The masochist, motivated not by admiration but by contempt for law, does not take pleasure in suffering, so much as endures the greatest pain in order to experience the pleasure of demystifying law, forcing it to reveal itself for what it is: tyranny. Masochism, as Deleuze defines it, exposes the chimerical nature of law's legitimacy, its inherent unfairness and ugliness. With the exception of Christ, history's most famous masochist is Socrates, who delivers his own death sentence with masochistic relish, the knowledge that with each bitter gulp the mask of nobility slips further from law's face. By taking law to its logical extreme, demanding Athens execute him, Socrates forces the law to admit that its only recourse, when its legitimacy is challenged, is the threat of violence.

William, Harry, and the other sailor-heroes of nautical melodrama lack the philosophical acuity and verbal elegance of Socrates. It is the audience itself, however, who experiences the masochistic degradation of law; the sailor serves merely as the submissive body, the docile flesh, upon which the consequences of one's total subjection to law are dramatized. In the Coburg's production of Jerrold's controversial *The Mutiny at the*

Nore (1831), Richard Parker, the lead mutineer and flawed hero, is handed the customary glass of wine before being executed by the Navy for killing his diabolical captain in self-defense. The last line of the play is Parker's farewell toast: "My shipmates, hear the last toast of Richard Parker:—'Here's a health to my king, and God bless him! Confusion to his enemies, and salvation to my soul!'"[73] According to Moody, Parker's masochistic toast was "met with loud hisses from spectators."[74] Had Parker delivered an impassioned denunciation of King and Navy, play and theatre would have been shut down. Parker's patriotic deference nevertheless triggers in the audience the same critical distance as would outright denunciation: disgust at law's injustice, a visceral resistance to its claims of legitimacy. Parker's masochism degrades law, then, while shielding playwright and audience from accusations of sedition.

The sailor-hero's willingness to endure pain and humiliation, his blind devotion to the very powers that crush him, is not irrefutable proof, as some critics have suggested, that nautical melodrama is propagandistic, that it encourages submission. With the passive aggression of a Christian martyr, the sailor shames his oppressor by turning the other cheek, expressing affection and respect for those who inflict pain. When Parker's wife Mary, for instance, denounces the officials who sentence her husband to death as "heartless, savage men," Parker responds, "You judge them harshly, Mary."[75] One can almost hear the working-class audience's mocking groans. In *Black-Ey'd Susan*, William blesses the men who are about to execute him. Recalling his captain, the man who manhandled his wife and whom he is condemned to die for striking, William remembers only the depth and resilience of their homosocial bond: "I loved him—loved him next to my own Susan."[76] When Tobias Pincher in *A Sailor's Legacy* disowns his orphan grandson, a young sailor boy, ordering him to leave his house, the youngster shames the old miser by politely acquiescing, kneeling and asking for his blessing, suggesting, "I'll go to sea—there perhaps I may meet with a watery grave, perhaps a cannon-ball from the enemy may send my soul aloft. No matter which."[77] Penniless, abandoned in a foreign land, his ship having set sail without him, Jack Gallant, the red-blooded Briton in Montcrieff's *Shipwreck of the Medusa*, erupts in anger when invited to join the crew of a French warship:

What! Desert my king and country, you shark?—never! I've fought and bled for old England—I've been wrecked and lost my all, and past [*sic*] my life in her service, and though she neglects and deserts her brave tars just now, damn me if I'll ever desert her: she may one day reflect on our services and reward them; but whether she does or no, when the hour of peril comes and a presumptuous enemy dares to invade her shores, old England will find, as she always has done, her best defences in her wooden walls.[78]

Automatism

The third acquiescent means by which nautical melodrama degrades law is the sailor-hero's verbal and physical automatism, the machinic "inelasticity," as Henri Bergson describes the phenomenon, "of habit that has been contracted and maintained," "something mechanical encrusted on the living."[79] The stylized nature of the sailor's speech and physicality, his rigidity and uniformity, functions ultimately to betray the unnatural, even violent effects of socialization on body and psyche, the transformation of the individual into a machine: a concatenation of verbal and physical gestures, a type. Automatism reduces the person to a thing, a material body, a series of mappable movements and gestures, patterns of speech. "We laugh," Bergson explains, "every time a person gives us the impression of being a thing":

> We begin, then, to become imitable only when we cease to be ourselves. I mean our gestures can only be imitated in their mechanical uniformity, and therefore exactly in what is alien to our living personality. To imitate any one is to bring out the element of automatism he has allowed to creep into his person. And as this is the very essence of the ludicrous, it is no wonder that imitation gives rise to laughter.[80]

When Jemmy Jumble finds himself surrounded by bandits in Haines's *The Ocean of Life* (1836), he resorts to imitating his sailor-friend, Mat Merriton, in an effort to frighten his assailants: "It won't do; so cut your cable, coil up your anchor, get your vessel under weigh, and missle. [*Aside.*] Come, that's nautical!"[81] When Tom Gunnel attempts, in *A Sailor's Legacy*, to convince misanthropic Tobias Pincher to adopt little Charles, his aforementioned grandson, the old man mockingly responds: "Should I meet him in the street and he offered to cling to me, to use your own jargon, I'd throw him off as ocean would a cork."[82] If colorful costume, garish makeup, and the melodramatic mugging of actors—the most legendary being former sailor Thomas Potter Cooke, who immortalized many of the roles discussed in this chapter—were instrumental in solidifying the sailor-hero as a recognizable physical and theatrical type, then his obligatory nautical metaphor reminded audiences that automatism is as intellectual as physical, that rigorous socialization renders mechanical not merely the human body but affect and thought.

The sailor-hero speaks a naval lingo, an obsessive nautical metaphor, that is reminiscent of the impenetrable argot spoken by actual nineteenth-century seamen. In his 1830 memoirs, one theatregoer notes that sailors, when they attend the theatre, use nautical terminology to describe its geography: "the pit they called the hold; the gallery, up aloft, or the maintop landing; the boxes, the cabin; and the stage, the quarterdeck."[83] In nautical melodrama, the sailor-hero's jargon—whereby everything from a woman's curvaceous figure to the sailor's own bodily functions is metaphorized as ship, crew, or nautical paraphernalia—not only reinforces the uniformity and rigidity of naval culture, but is symptomatic of the sailor's total subjection to authority. So hypersocialized is the sailor, his every thought is mediated by the institution to which he is subject. Thus, William in *Black-Ey'd Susan* describes his stifled tears as "standing in either eye like a marine in each gangway," miniature police officers, his repressed emotion a sign, paradoxically, of manly self-control and submission to authority.[84]

Where the sailor's eyes constitute a potential source of leakage, his mouth is the provision-door through which supplies pass, keeping the vessel of his body afloat. In Isaac Pocock's *For England Ho!* (1813), an early precursor to nautical melodrama, a magnanimous Tom Tough informs a famished Frenchman: "I'll line your planks with some English Beef and a can of Grog: that will fetch up your lee-way with a wet-sail, I warrant."[85] In *Shipwreck of the Medusa*, Jack Gallant complains to a lazy barkeep: "Avast heaving, landlord, and bring too [*sic*], you Swab—I've got another shot left still in the locker, so fire us another broadside of your grape aboard, d'ye hear me?"[86] Mouths expel as well as consume. When Martin Roseberry encounters a loquacious interlocutor in *Rule Britannia*, he confesses, "The jaw-tackle of your clipper has been running at such a spanking rate, that the craft of my understanding finds it rather difficult to keep alongside of you."[87] He warns another fellow not to "give me any of your jaw," or "I'll give you a crack over your provision-trap." The sailor views the world through a nautical prism. To a friend in ragged clothing, Mat Merriton remarks, "you've a few seams about your hull want caulking."[88] Receiving some unexpected news, Long Luke exclaims, "Why you've struck my old barky on the rock of surprise!"[89]

The sailor also experiences the metaphysical realm as nautical. One might say of nauticality, as Louis Althusser says of ideology, that it "*has no outside* . . . but at the same time *that it is nothing but outside*": pure exteriority without a "beyond," like the ocean itself, a seemingly endless surface.[90] At his court-martial, William informs his judges, "My actions, your honours, are kept in the log book aloft—if, when that's overhauled I'm not found a trim seaman, why it's only throwing salt to the fishes to patter here."[91] En route to his execution, he tells a superior officer, "you and I, your honour, have laid yard-arm and yard-arm with many a foe—let us hope we shall come gunwhale [*sic*] to gunwhale in another climate."[92] "[T]he vessel of life has her anchor a-trip," he solemnly adds, "and must soon get under way for the ocean of eternity."[93] Echoing William, Tom Gunnel conceives of Judgment Day as the moment "when your log-book is overhauled by the Great Commander aloft."[94] As I stated earlier, *Black-Ey'd Susan* abruptly concludes with the discovery that William had been discharged prior to striking his captain, and that he will not be sailing to "the ocean of eternity" after all. Jerrold does not give him an opportunity to react verbally to news of his salvation. The orchestra erupts; William leaps from the platform; the curtain falls. No longer a sailor, *he has nothing to say*.

Though the sailor's maniacal use of nautical metaphor indicates professional enthusiasm and patriotism, it also makes him appear gesturally stiff, reducing his words to the "immobility of a formula," to quote Bergson, for the comic type "becomes invisible to himself while remaining visible to all the world."[95] Frustrated interlocutors often accuse the sailor-hero of speaking a "horrid jargon" or "sea lingo."[96] "Once our attention is fixed on the material aspect of a metaphor," Bergson notes, "the idea expressed becomes comic."[97] In the sailor's obsessive use of nautical metaphor, the distinction between tenor and vehicle collapses; the sailor's ship and body blur, metaphors for, and extensions of, each other. The sailor-hero is trapped in self-imitation, marked simultaneously by an abundance of personality and by a loss of self. More than a century before Charlie Chaplin's *Modern Times* (1936), melodramatic automatism explores the physical and psychological consequences of working-class self-alienation, the mechanical encrustation of the human body by apparatuses of industrial work-discipline. The sight of a clownish body, of a body blind to its own artifice, inspires in audiences a critical or ironic distance from the power structures that constrain that body. The clown or comic automaton is an emblem of the unnaturalness of socialization. In *Breakers Ahead!* melancholic Barnaby recalls his impressment, his "jollification," as he terms it, his traumatic birth as "Jolly Jack Tar" in a flood of amniotic grog:

> Misfortunes never come alone! I followed up to London—fall in with you—come aboard—have a jollification—get drunk—feel very ill next day—can't get up for three days after, find I'm out at sea, with no *inside* left, and only one kivering for my outside; and here I am among the Chany people, when I ought to be at home. Oh, dear, my innards![98]

The sailor-automaton is the deformed offspring of a violent conception. For Long Tom Coffin, whose very name is infused with death, going ashore is akin to reopening a wound, reliving the trauma of birth, so accustomed is his mechanical body to its lurching warship. Comparing Tom to "a porpoise or a lobster" "born at sea," his impatient commander urges him to "gather your limbs together, and try whether you can walk on terra firma."[99] A frightened Tom responds, "Belay, but this *terror former*, as your Honour nicknames it, tosses and tumbles about like a whale tub afloat among the breakers."

The sailor's profession also deforms his libido. He has one object of desire, his ship. His attraction to women is secondary. When William envisions reuniting with Susan, he conceives of her body as a buoyant ship, imagines how she will "lash and carry, roused up by the whistle of that young boatswain's mate, Cupid, piping in her heart."[100] Even the marriage economy is recast in nautical terms, further abstracting the exchanged bride, literalizing her vehicular function. Introducing himself to his sister's fiancé, Martin Roseberry assures the man, "I am the brother of the little frigate you have taken in tow, and if you promise to convoy her through the voyage of life, you shall have her."[101] In *Breakers Ahead!* Long Luke makes the connection explicit: "Now in my mind, there's no two animals so like each other, as a ship and a woman," for they both require "a good man at the helm"; "they're both fond of flying gear aloft"; and though "man may desert the vessel as she founders," "*she perishes* in his service," "praying for him as she dies!"[102] He makes a distinction, of course, between a wife and a prostitute, a "seaworthy craft" and "a holiday cruise."[103] Needless to say, when a sailor praises his ship or his woman in the presence of a landlubber, a comedy of errors ensues. Overhearing Long Tom Coffin wax romantic about his "sweetheart," an American prisoner makes the mistake of asking her name:

TOM. They call her Ariel.

CAPT. He's a second genuine Caliban, I guess; but this Ariel—

TOM. She's a lovely thing, to be sure; I've seen her in every shape, braced and unbraced, with her stays and without her stays.

CAPT. Mercy on me! Then you've literally seen her undress'd, I calculate.

TOM. Aye, that I have, three times, not a rag flying; and the last time she was so, I tarred her all over myself.

CAPT. The devil, you did! Here's a wretch for you! He'll be tarring me all over, I reckon. And pray, may I venture to inquire what followed the *tarring* exhibition?

TOM. Why then we trimmed her out in prime style, crammed her with grape shot, and sent her off slap to America.[104]

Before his impressment, Harry Hallyard gives his fiancée Mary Maybud the nickname "Polly." To his delight, it happens to be the sobriquet of his new ship, *The Polyphemus*, resulting in a seamless libidinal transference from woman to vessel. If the name "Mary Maybud" connotes virginity, her nickname does not, for "Portsmouth Poll," Marcus points out, was nineteenth-century slang for a prostitute who serviced sailors.[105] No wonder Mary insists, "I don't like your singing about Poll this, and Poll that. My name's Mary."[106]

So encoded is the sailor-hero by the alienating logic of the Navy, he becomes detached from family and old friends. Lobotomized by discipline, emptied of his "insides," he navigates the melodramatic stage in a nautical trance. Encountering an acquaintance from his prenaval days, Harry barely recognizes the man through the distorted lens of his own sailorness, "But—why, there's something about the build of your figure—

head as strikes me—did you ever cross my latitude afore?"[107] "I don't know what you mean by your latitude," his friend replies, "but I've crossed your door-way at Battersea many a time." Reassuring a recent bride that her sailor-husband's long absences from home will not strain her marriage, Metrical Mat, the nautical sage of *The Eddystone Elf*, explains that absence makes the heart grow fonder:

> Why, I was away from my wife last cruise three years and a half, and she was neither sick nor sorry. I found her when I came home again as jolly as a sand-boy, with four young 'uns. I thought she'd only two when I started; but, then, a man can't keep these things in his mind, you know.[108]

To Mat's surprise, the young woman grows more distressed. In *Breakers Ahead!* Long Luke fails to realize that his best friend, Ralph, his "trim tiger," whom he has mentored for six months, is actually his sweetheart Joan, who disguises herself as a boy and enlists in order to be near him.[109] Despite the fact that "Ralph" often professes his affection for Luke, occasionally throwing his arms around him, Luke remains oblivious. When Barnstable's sweetheart Katharine attires herself as a boy in order to pursue him in *The Pilot*, he, too, fails to recognize her, suggesting, with pederastic insinuation, that the "young gentleman," "who hasn't strength enough to carry a beard if he had one," come "aboard with me for the rest of the cruise."[110]

Like Rip Van Winkle, the sailor finds himself out of place, out of time, an animated corpse. T.P. Cooke, the actor and former sailor who made famous many of the roles discussed here—including William, Harry Hallyard, Jack Gallant, Mat Merriton, and Long Tom Coffin—reinforced this impression. Born in 1786, Cooke, who had been an actual participant in the Napoleonic Wars, was forty-three years old when he played William for the first time, forty-nine when he played Harry Hallyard, and fifty when he played Mat Merriton. While some of the sailors Cooke played are middle-aged, even grizzled, including Long Tom Coffin, Metrical Mat, and Fid, the trio of William, Harry, and Merriton are youths, snatched by the Navy in their prime. A press-gang abducts Harry on his wedding day. William and Susan are newlyweds. The sight of a middle-aged man playing a young one is yet another means by which nautical melodrama tacitly degrades the institution it supposedly romanticizes, providing visual proof of just how brutally self-alienating the capitalist reorganization of society is on the minds and bodies of the working class. Cooke performed the role of William until he was seventy.

The Laughter Dies

By 1896, the Coburg's famed mirror had long since been dismantled. Only the oldest of theatregoers would have remembered it. Likewise, the water tank at Sadler's Wells was a distant memory, the decrepit theatre having been transformed into a music hall in the 1880s, after a brief stint as a roller-skating rink. Nautical melodrama was a joke. Middle-class Gilbert and Sullivan poked avuncular fun at it. Others were less indulgent. In his scathing review of Leonard Outram's nautically themed *True Blue*, produced by the Olympic in 1896, George Bernard Shaw insists that the "unspeakable fatuities of the plot" could not possibly have issued "from the same brain" as the "business-like" "dialogue," that Outram must have been assisted by an "unnamed" "idiot."[111] The audience of *True Blue* consists of two classes: those simple-minded enough to be moved by the play's ridiculous plot and those who attend the play in order to laugh in their sleeves at its ridiculousness, or, as Shaw puts it, those "white with . . . pity and terror" and those "red with a voiceless, apoplectic laughter."[112] Raucous early nineteenth-century audiences, who hissed and encouraged actors, or who invaded the stage, or who talked, mingled, and sang during performances, had been replaced at century's end by silent, middle-class spectators who sat in a darkened theatre and trembled with fear or suppressed laughter, alone with their thoughts. The ludic wisdom—the communitarian ethos of fair play—intrinsic to early nineteenth-century nautical melodrama had devolved into yet another form of insularity. In its heyday, however, nautical melodrama was one of the most effective forms of popular protest against the unsettling world in play, against a capitalist, counterrevolutionary reality that seemed frighteningly out of balance. The sailor-hero of melodrama worked miracles. He walked on water and maintained his balance on oceans of global capitalism. He reassured an anxious population that fairness was still possible and had a fighting chance in an increasingly foul world. He made them laugh at those in power. In early nineteenth-century British melodrama, one hears some of the last hurrahs of Merry England. It is a distant laughter from an apocryphal world. By century's end, the world in play had closed its waters over melodrama's head.

CHAPTER 3

Toying with the Future in *Wuthering Heights*

> I could not rescue him—his child
> I found alive and tended well,
> But she was full of anguish wild
> And hated me like we hate hell,
> And weary with her savage woe
> One moonless night I let her go.
> —Emily Brontë[1]

The Bad Teacher

Emily Brontë did not hate children. She hated socializing them. The only Brontë daughter exempt from teaching Sunday school, she succeeded for the most part in avoiding children. Her brief employment at Miss Patchett's school at Law Hill in the fall of 1838 and winter of 1839 ended, as did her other rare ventures from home, in disaster: depression, self-starvation, and return to that boxy brick parsonage at Haworth. Not the most nurturing teacher, she informed her doe-eyed pupils that she preferred the company of the house dog to theirs.[2] The aversion that Brontë felt toward child rearing is as political, however, as it is temperamental. What disturbed her was the discrepancy between the middle-class idealization of child-socialization and its ugly, degrading reality. She recoiled at the notion that children are eager if unconscious partners in their socialization, that they contain within themselves seeds of productivity, their round faces turning instinctively, like sunflowers, to the sun, in cosmic fellowship with the farmer who sowed them. Brontë knew better than that.

The vision of childhood expressed in *Wuthering Heights* (1847) is one of the most brutal in Victorian literature. Brontë's demystification of childhood, and her resistance to cultural pressures to sentimentalize children, extends beyond her memorable depictions of obnoxious and demonic children, or her exposure of the violence underlying the institution of family, or her equation of childhood with psychosexual suffering, or even her frank exploration of the depth of a child's capacity to hate. Brontë shatters the modern cultural fantasy of the child as redemptive agent of futurity. *Wuthering Heights* debunks not just the middle-class cult of the child but what Lee Edelman has termed the "reproductive futurism" at the heart of modernity, the "structuring optimism of politics to which the order of meaning commits us," the idea, that is, that the "[c]hild remains the perpetual horizon of every acknowledged politics, the fantasmatic beneficiary of every political intervention."[3] The figure of the child, Edelman suggests, acts as the motor of history. For the child does not merely embody the future, inspire it, but epistemologically *produces* it by rendering unthinkable the possibility of an asocial, endlessly future-negating present. In nineteenth-century Britain, the hungry child, the exploited child laborer, the criminal child, and Foucault's famous masturbating child function as metahistorical metaphors for the nation's anxiety about its economic and moral trajectory, in the same way that the overweight child, the molested child, and the depressive child function in twenty-first-century America.

If these nonproductive Victorian children, with hunger in their bellies and hands in their pants, embody the possibility of futurelessness, the impending collapse of sociality, then it is the reassuring spectacle of the child at play, the girl with a doll, the boy with a kite, wherein the future once again takes flight. Images of children playing in war zones or in areas ravaged by natural disasters, heartrending though they may be, give us confidence that the future unfailingly self-generates, even as the present collapses. As its title implies, Brontë's turbulent novel precludes the flying of kites. *Wuthering Heights* exposes the ideological underpinnings of functionalist theories of child play. The antisocial ludic activity in which Heathcliff and Cathy engage as children, and in which their destructive intimacy is forged, negates the future by unraveling, at least for a time, the novel's social and economic order.

In the wake of the seventeenth- and eighteenth-century middle-class campaign to pedagogize child play, to transform it into an innately instructional activity, an expression of self-development, psychologists and anthropologists in the nineteenth and twentieth centuries naturalized the socializing potential of play, insisting that child play—indeed, the ludic impulses of all young animals—constituted a biologically productive instinct, a spontaneous form of self-training. Hence, we have the modern ideology of child play, the logic of play as *paideia*: the idea that children at play perform cultural *work*. In light of Terry Eagleton's canonical Marxist reading of *Wuthering Heights* as a text that exposes the very contradictions between "social conformity and personal fulfillment" that Charlotte Brontë's novels, in his view, attempt to reconcile, Emily Brontë's refusal to view child play as the reconciliation of development and enjoyment, as intrinsically entrepreneurial, can be read as a critique of capitalist subjectivity in its embryonic form: the middle-class child at play.[4] Brontë's rejection of bourgeois reproductive futurism, however, does not mean that she replaces it with a revolutionary reproductive futurism. *Wuthering Heights* does not ask us to choose a *better* future, one ethic of futurity, one productivist narrative over another. Rather, Brontë explores in *Wuthering Heights* a future-negating ethic of nonproductivity, which she locates in the play of Heathcliff and Cathy. She opposes this ethic of endless "presentness," of world-shattering immanence, of *presence*, to a morality of futurity, which she aligns with the narrative impulse itself, with teleological causality, with the temporalization and hence obliteration of pure presence. It is no coincidence that narrative, for Brontë, the will to narrate, takes as its primary form an actual nurse, Nelly Dean, who is responsible for rendering comprehensible, for monitoring, the ludic expressions of her mischievous charges. Heathcliff and Cathy succeed for a time in eluding her narrative grasp, running circles around her, causing temporal contortions and gaps: the novel's "stilted and uneven" structure, which Queenie Leavis attributes to Brontë's "inexperience."[5]

It has been over fifty years since the publication of Georges Bataille's *Literature and Evil*, which contains a brief and, by current critical standards, ahistorical reading of *Wuthering Heights*. It is nonetheless a powerfully suggestive essay. Bataille identifies in Brontë's novel an ethic or "hypermorality" of "Evil": an "asocial" renunciation of self-interest, a "disinterested attraction towards death," which he associates with the prerational "kingdom of childhood."[6] Bataille's notion of Evil, which he distinguishes from run-of-the-mill self-interested "evil," anticipates psychoanalytic readings of Brontëan jouissance, as well as the future-negating queerness that Edelman champions in a twenty-first-century context.[7] Unfortunately, Bataille occupies a relatively peripheral place both in Brontë studies and in play studies. After exploring in greater detail the centrality of child play to Brontë's worldview from biographical, formal, and historicist perspectives, I would like to return to Bataille, specifically, to his economic writings, so that we might better appreciate the ethical value of Brontë's stunning capacity for violence: the aspect of the novel that so captivated Bataille.

Wuthering Heights is not a novel for well-socialized people. No matter how painstakingly we elicit from the text and from the mythologized life of Emily Brontë narratives of productivist redemption and rational explanations, countless readers will visit *Wuthering Heights* for what is perceived, fairly or unfairly, as its author's liberating hostility toward the reality principle, her refusal to make peace with the establishment, her stubborn aversion to growing up. From the perspective of play studies, however, the novel is highly productive: further evidence of the degree to which modern consciousness is saturated with play. The tension at the core of modern life is not a Manichaean one between an innately seditious will to play, on the one hand, and the purportedly antiludic forces, on the other hand, of nineteenth-century modernity. No, for Brontë, modern subjectivity is produced, constrained, and normalized by play. As I have claimed throughout this book, the tension is *within* play, in the case of Brontë, between its profane productive tendencies and its sacred future-negating potential. The former produces the reassuring effects of autonomy. The latter leads to madness.

Child Play and the Brontë Myth

The Brontë industry is predicated upon the modern ideology of child play, upon the sentimental-functionalist belief that child play is developmentally productive, preparatory for the work of adulthood. It takes all of the curmudgeonly willpower of the most practiced spoilsport to visit the Brontë Parsonage Museum in Yorkshire and *not* intuit, when gazing at those tiny books constructed from sugar bags and other scraps, the first stirrings of great novels. We are encouraged to trace the novels backward to Emily's early poetry and Charlotte's gothic "juvenilia," then to the elaborate fantasy worlds of Angria and Gondal, assembled from thousands of hours of literary role-play, then to the child game of Glass Town, with its "wild weird writing," as Elizabeth Gaskell termed it, and finally to Branwell's legendary box of wooden toy soldiers: the ludic spark that supposedly set off a literary chain reaction.[8] The Child, to paraphrase Wordsworth, is Mother of the Novelist. In her survey of scholarship on the Brontës' childhood writings, Carol Bock makes the seemingly innocuous observation that "[t]he Brontës began their *apprenticeship* in the profession of literature early": "Escapist as these 'dream' stories may have been, they show remarkable fidelity to the public realm of authorship, reading and publishing in which each of the Brontës later sought to construct a professional identity and earn a living."[9] Even at play, escapist play, those precocious Brontë children busily *work*, laying the groundwork for their literary careers, investing economically in their futures.

The Brontës have come to symbolize the inherent productivity of childhood, the seamlessness between play and work, the naturalness of subordinating present pleasure to future need, the necessarily prophetic and mimetic nature of child play. Polly Teale's 2005 play, *Brontë*, performed at the Lyric Theatre in Hammersmith, London, exemplifies perfectly this conflation of work ethic and child play in biographical representations of the Brontës. In Act One, the adult actors who play Charlotte, Anne, and Branwell metamorphose into their eight- and five- and nine-year-old selves, mounting the kitchen table, where they frolic in painful imitation of child play. According to Teale's stage directions, Charlotte then "writes into a tiny book."[10] That the actor who plays Emily remains an adult throughout this scene, obliviously peeling potatoes at the same table, unperturbed by this analeptic intrusion only inches away, suggests less that she sees through or rejects the modern ideology of child play, as one would hope, and more that she is, in Teale's eyes, merely solitary, famously different. The fact that she performs domestic work reinforces the psychological simultaneity of and symbiotic relationship between children's ludic activity and wholesome social production. We are asked to view her potato-peeling and their play proleptically as preparations for a feast to come. Have we Brontëans become less overtly violent, more brainy versions of the "Little League dad," who projects his professional fantasies and fears onto his child's baseball game, who sees in that homerun a career with the Red Sox, in that missed catch the trickle of part-time jobs? Should we too be ejected from the game?

    At a certain point, the modern ideology of child play interpellates children. They internalize the parental gaze, become accomplices in the pedagogization of their own play, sentimentalizing it even as they experience it. Simultaneously flattered and made self-conscious by this newly perceived weight of futurity, they realize they are actively shaping their future selves. They abandon toys and games that smack of immaturity. They make ludic investments in their futures. Charlotte, in particular, appears, at least according to her biographers, to have conceived of her childhood play as a means to an end, rather than an end in itself, at an early age. In her hagiographical account of Charlotte's life, which is a paean, not surprisingly, to the modern ideology of child play, Gaskell emphasizes the remarkable ease with which Charlotte's childhood pleasure in her "plays and amusements," which were of a necessarily "intellectual nature," translated into full-blown literary and professional ambition.[11] So infused with futurity, so synonymous with job training, is Charlotte's child play, that its status as *play* all but disappears. Her play becomes an ascetic rejection of play, overcoming itself. Gaskell repeatedly underscores how the lives of the Brontë children lacked the pedestrian "sportiveness," the "infantine gaieties," typical of childhood, and how Charlotte read during "play hours" at Roe Head School, excusing herself from a "game at ball," insisting that she "could not play."[12] Charlotte's child writings are ludic, in Gaskell's eyes, insofar as they are natural, uncoerced, and innocent. But, unlike that game at ball, they constitute a future-oriented activity: a practical use, rather than a mere waste, of time. Or rather, Charlotte's play is a more profitable use of time, for activities such as playing ball, experts in child development remind us, teach hand-eye coordination and respect for rules. The legendary sternness of Patrick Brontë, the deaths of Charlotte's mother and older sisters, the family's financial difficulties, appear, in Gaskell's account, as mere contributing factors to Charlotte's workmanlike approach to play, for Gaskell's emphasis upon the "wild weird" nature of the child writings suggests that they emerged organically, uncompelled, almost magically, from a reassuringly autonomous mind. In *The Life of Charlotte Brontë* (1857), child play *is* child labor, but a happy version.

If Emily avoided being interpretively filtered through the modern ideology of child play for nearly a century after her death, it is because her writings and her life story are more difficult to assimilate into a productivist narrative. But assimilated they have been, despite the fact that, until her death, she continued to inhabit—in a compulsive and, some would argue, schizophrenic fashion—her childhood realm of Gondal. She reluctantly agreed to publish her poetry and novel in the face of looming financial crisis and a vigorous lobbying campaign by the more entrepreneurial Charlotte. *Wuthering Heights* protests, however, the very economic imperative, the necessity of rendering one's imagination profitable, that underlies its composition and publication. It militates against the very ideology of child play that so many twentieth-century critics have seized upon as a tool to rehabilitate Brontë's reputation, to rescue her from dismissive (and often sexist) charges of arrested development, to professionalize retrospectively her unusual literary career. Although Brontë was pleased to receive the small payments her publisher sent her, *Wuthering Heights* is a text uneasy about its own existence, about its status as imaginative energy *gainfully reduced*, like Cathy upon her marriage to Edgar Linton, to an object of consumption, a bourgeois plaything. It is a text that writhes uncomfortably against the economic necessity of selling out, of selling oneself, of betraying the profitless domain of childhood.

Some of the novel's first readers sensed this unease on the part of its pseudonymous author, and were concerned that Ellis Bell had not sufficiently relinquished "his" hold on childhood, had not completed his literary training. Writing in the *Palladium* in 1850, and writing under the misapprehension that the novel was penned by the same woman (he suspects) who wrote *Jane Eyre*, Sydney Dobell employs the familiar trope of child play qua protowork to dismiss *Wuthering Heights* as the "immature" "earlier" "fancy" "of a baby god."[13] He contrasts Emily's ludic "hand," which "wanders" clumsily "over the strings of a musical instrument," with Charlotte's light workman's hand: "Whoever has watched a trowel in the hands of a skilful mason has seen an example of a very high excellence in authorship." He believes it is the *same* hand. Only, in the case of *Wuthering Heights*, it has not yet developed its future dexterity, completed its ludic apprenticeship. The notion that Brontë's novel fails to attain the status of *work*, that it is mired in *play*, reaches its critical apogee in 1948, when F.R. Leavis harrumphs at the idea that *Wuthering Heights* is canonical, deeming the text "a kind of sport."[14] The feminist response to Leavis's dismissiveness is exemplified best, perhaps, by Lyn Pykett, who devotes a chapter of her 1989 *Emily Brontë* to refuting Leavis's charge, enumerating the kinds of generic and gender work the novel performs: its painstaking and canonically significant negotiation between gothic and domestic modes.[15] Or take, for example, the first three sentences of Edward Chitham's 1998 *The Birth of Wuthering Heights: Emily Brontë at Work*: "The idea of birth suggests labour. This book will be about that labour. I hope to show how Emily Brontë worked on *Wuthering Heights* to produce the novel we now have."[16] Chitham erases with those ideologically pregnant words, "birth" and "labour," Brontë's childlike reputation, for she is now a metaphorical *mother*, a (re)productive adult. Erased, too, is the self-indulgent or recreational or ludic aura that had for so long accrued around her, for she is now a literary *laborer*, a member of a hardworking *class* of writers. In the span of fifty years, *Wuthering Heights* has been transformed from a childish daydream into one of the hardest working novels in the Victorian library.

Critics have even coated Brontë's excursions into the ludic world of Gondal with a patina of work. Consider Sandra Gilbert and Susan Gubar's reading of a Brontë diary entry from the summer of 1845, written shortly before her twenty-seventh birthday. Recalling how she and Anne metamorphosed into various Gondal characters—"Ronald Mcalgin, Henry Angora, Juliet Angusteena, Rosabella Esmalden, Ella and Julian Egremont, Catharine Navarre, and Cordilia Fitzaphnold"—on a train voyage to York, "escaping from the palaces of instruction [in Gondal] to join the Royalists," Brontë abruptly returns in her diary to her quotidian existence, her "turning and ironing," to the fact that she is "altogether full of business."[17] Rather than view Gondal, where sexually assertive women wage relentless war, as a refuge from and antiproductivist alternative to the demands of domesticity, Gilbert and Gubar breach the scrupulously erected wall between Brontë's discrete worlds, insisting that "play" and "housework" are perfectly compatible varieties of "the same kind of 'business.'"[18] Thus, Gondal is assimilated into the empowering and dignified world of women's labor. The prodigal daughter returns to work. J. Hillis Miller reads the diary differently, viewing the existence of Gondal, and Brontë's tendency to privilege it emotionally over her non-Gondal existence, as the active "*destruction* of the real world by an imaginary one."[19] It is essential that we combat the perennial erasure of women's work from the historical record, indeed, that we militate against the masculinization of labor. It is just as essential, however, that we salvage from the dustbin of history the political and ethical role of play in the lives of women (and men), and, specifically the world-shattering function of child play in the life and writings of Emily Brontë.

Child Play in *Wuthering Heights*

"It was one of their chief amusements," Nelly Dean recounts, "to run away to the moors in the morning and remain there all day, and the after punishment grew a mere thing to laugh at."[20] What exactly do Heathcliff and Cathy *do* on those windswept moors? What form does their "reckless" play take? Brontë refuses to divulge. Their play resists representation. It flees into the proverbial night. We catch only fleeting glimpses of it in the novel's opening chapters. The shadow of a wing, it ripples teasingly across our field of vision, disappears over the narrative horizon.[21] Though we never behold their play directly, its effects, its psychosexual and socioeconomic repercussions, reverberate throughout the text. To come to terms with these effects, to make sense of them, is the diegetic occasion of the text: the stimulus to Lockwood's sensation-hungry imagination, the narrative task with which Nelly Dean is charged. Heathcliff and Cathy's play decenters the narrative, elicits and inspires it, but ultimately resists being fully assimilated into it. Their play is the epistemic void that the narrative circles, attempts to penetrate, but persistently fails to render knowable. Indeed, their play remains stubbornly Other to Nelly's narrative. Does play function, for Brontë, as a kind of narrative unconscious, the repository of unspeakable desire? Is it the limitations of narration, and its spur?

Heathcliff and Cathy's play is certainly *obscene* in the etymological sense of the word: covered in filth and mud, hidden from view beneath dirt. Although D.H. Lawrence famously insists that the English word *obscene* "derive[s] from" the Latin adjective "*obscena*: that which might not be represented on stage," in truth, an obscene person is obscured from view by a coating of grime, not because he is offstage.[22] In *obscenus*, the prefix *ob-s-* ("onto") precedes *caenum* ("mud" or "mire"), not *scaena* ("stage"). That said, Heathcliff and Cathy's filthiness acts, in effect, as a curtain or stage flat, obstructing the audience's view of them. When I ask people what they imagine Heathcliff and Cathy are doing on those moors, what it is that Brontë refuses to represent, they usually respond in one of two ways: either "something sexual" or "something metaphysical." No one says "playing cards" or "jumping rope." This is because its elliptical nature, even before it spawns their illicit adult love, endows their play with an ineffable obscenity, with a sacred irrationality. They are willing to die for their ludic intimacy. Like addicts. Like abject saints. Narrative ellipses, or "refusals," as Robyn Warhol terms them, are reserved, first, for the mundane or obvious, for that which is *beneath* representation; second, for the irrelevant, for that which would be textually or generically extraneous; third, for the improper, for that which *must not* be represented; and fourth, for the inexpressible, for that which *cannot* be represented.[23] The simultaneously sublime and taboo register of Heathcliff and Cathy's play, the fact that Hindley outright forbids it, the fact that they are in danger of "grow[ing] up as rude as savages," belies the idea that its representation would be mundane or irrelevant.[24] Their play smacks of pre-Oedipal eroticism, of mutual masturbation, of reciprocal molestation. There is something profoundly clitoral, in fact, about their child play, and, for that matter, about Heathcliff. He is Cathy's renounced childhood pleasure, that part of her that dissolves her bodily integrity ("Nelly, I *am* Heathcliff"): an extrafamilial, unassimilable member, as Freud would say, of the Earnshaw body politic, threatening to derail her from her reproductive trajectory.[25] That the children are repeatedly characterized as "savage," as mired in "heathenism," that Heathcliff is compared at one point to a "cannibal," suggests, too, that their ludic intimacy has a ritualistic, occultist quality, that it is infused with the power of magic and blood rites.[26]

From the start of the novel, Brontë associates children with pagan precocity, with a mischievous eroticism that representation cannot quite accommodate. In a meta-representational aside, Lockwood "pause[s]" at the "threshold" of the eponymous house "to admire" the "grotesque carving" "over the front," which depicts, among other things, "shameless little boys," presumably naked cherubim or micturating cupids, although we are never informed.[27] At any rate, they are the first children we encounter, and the exact nature of their "shameless" behavior eludes articulation. Heathcliff and Cathy's shamelessness is also heightened by a veil of inexpressibility, by its resistance to depiction. At one point, Cathy ponders "appropriat[ing] the dairy woman's cloak" and having "a scamper on the moors" with Heathcliff "under its shelter."[28] Their ludic intimacy takes place against the cosmic backdrop of the midnight moors and within the surreptitious confines of shared clothing. When disapproving Joseph intrudes upon them earlier that evening, they are playing behind a makeshift "curtain" of their "pinafores," which they had "fastened" "together." We do not see their play. It is offstage, as Lawrence would say, obscured by dirty curtains. Like those "shameless little boys," the act of taking off their clothes renders them invisible.

Its unparticularized and concealed nature, its representational absence, is precisely what makes Heathcliff and Cathy's play, paradoxically, such a powerful textual presence in the novel. It is also how Brontë implicates her reader in their play, makes the reader a ludic accomplice, a colluder. The reader, after all, is invited, indeed, strongly encouraged, to fill the epistemic void left by Brontë's refusal to disclose the nature of their obscene play. It would be a stretch to argue, not to mention impossible to verify, that Brontë triggers in her reader with her ludic ellipsis a return of the repressed, or a fissure in the infantile amnesia that masks from consciousness the autotelic, autoerotic play of early childhood. Can a novel, *any* novel, really do that? Brontë prompts her middle-class readers, however, assuming those readers are playing along and actively reading, to project their own visions of ineffable and taboo child play onto Heathcliff and Cathy's forbidden excursions on the moors. She asks her readers to imagine what she cannot represent. A reader-response critic like Wolfgang Iser will point out that the act of reading is inherently dyadic and interactive, that all texts "prompt acts of ideation on the reader's part," ask their readers to connect events imaginatively, to create logical cohesion, to make narrative "blanks" "disappear."[29] Narrators do not and cannot describe every mundane detail of a room, for instance, the colors of throw pillows and the number of windows, but the reader's mind dutifully and instinctively supplies such details anyway, colors between the lines, connects the dots, and fills all blank spaces, thereby helping to move the narrative along its course. Brontë's ludic ellipses, however, are different in that they resist assimilation and militate against the social harmony, against the productivist mutuality between text and reader that Iser defines as reading. Her blanks refuse to disappear completely. Brontë asks her readers to imagine what cannot be assimilated, what is narratively unimaginable, what must by definition remain bracketed from, in a state of sublime alterity to, the narrative. She makes her reader's imagination obscene. Rather than a tool of assimilation, a vehicle of teleological causality, productively filling in narrative blanks, the reader's imagination is charged with the epistemologically difficult task of defining itself against narrative production, of digging an atemporal hole within the very experience of reading the text, an antitelic and antisocial cavity, a parallel and unrepresentable universe, from which to resist assimilation and militate against narrative incorporation.

Heathcliff and Cathy's child play, therefore, is simultaneously external to and interoperable with the narrative. The narrative pursues their play epistemically, attempts to penetrate the mysterious nature of their bond, only to crash against its elliptical impenetrability: an impenetrability that we are charged, as readers, with maintaining. The novel's profundity is proportional to our powers of imagination. Readers who can imagine only pedestrian roughhousing, or an uninspiring game of tag, will undoubtedly wonder what all the fuss is about. Others, however, who have taken up Brontë's phenomenological challenge to imagine the unspeakable, to erect in opposition to the narrative a supranarrative site of ineffable play, will experience the novel as a dream, as surrounded by a slow-motion shadow world, an extratextual halo. It is a space of impossibility: the narratological equivalent of the space beyond the universe, beyond knowability. Like Heathcliff and Cathy, we can easily lose ourselves in it, succumb to its antiteleological *presence*, its timelessness. Though very little of the action of *Wuthering Heights* takes place on those windblown moors that have come to epitomize the novel, our *experience* of the novel is saturated with their uncontainability. It is the unruly frontier where the text's diegetic empire ends, where its moldering outposts blink into the void.

From the start of the novel, Brontë aligns Heathcliff with an antisocial ludic ellipticality that resists being assimilated into the narrative, socialized, or made coherent. The story of his life is riven by three ludic lacunae, three unsolved mysteries. The *first* is his origin and birth. Who is he? Either a "gift of God," as Mr. Earnshaw terms him, or an envoy, in Nelly's words, "from the devil," Heathcliff leaps preternaturally from the "bundled" heap of Earnshaw's "great coat," a "dirty" "gipsy brat" plucked by Earnshaw from the desperate streets of Liverpool, or so he claims.[30] Full of holes, Earnshaw's story has an apocryphal ring to it. An outraged Mrs. Earnshaw, "ready to fling" the child "out of doors," is forced eventually to "grumble[ ] herself calm." Many readers have hypothesized that Heathcliff is Earnshaw's illegitimate son: the product of a business-trip fling, the fruit of extramarital sport. Whether or not he is connected by blood to the patriarch, his introduction into the family smacks not of Christian charity or paternal responsibility but of recreation, self-indulgence, and whim. He is Earnshaw's plaything, his "favourite," a stray animal to be indulged, "pett[ed]."[31] Heathcliff literally displaces the playthings that Earnshaw had promised to purchase his children in Liverpool: Hindley's fiddle, which Heathcliff "crushed to morsels" in the great coat, and Cathy's whip, which Earnshaw "lost" "in attending on the stranger." A "usurper," he puts in play the contractual obligations between parent and child, the patrilineal transference of power, and thus the future of the family.

The *second*, and least narratively assimilable, ludic ellipsis in Heathcliff's life story is, as I discuss above, his inexpressible play with Cathy. Just as the nature of their play resists representation, so does its inception. Cathy's initial reaction to Heathcliff consists, Nelly remembers, of "grinning and spitting at the stupid little thing." When Nelly leaves Heathcliff "on the landing of the stairs" the night of his arrival, Hindley and Cathy "refus[ing] to have it in bed with them," she is promptly "sent out of the house" by Mr. Earnshaw for her "inhumanity." Upon her return a "few days afterwards," "Miss Cathy and [Heathcliff]," she notes, "were now very thick." The birth of their unlikely friendship, like Heathcliff's own birth, escapes explanation.

The *third* ludic ellipsis in Heathcliff's life is his mysterious three-year absence from Yorkshire, and presumably from England, having fled under the false impression that Cathy renounced for practical purposes the ineffable and paranarrative world of their child play, and aligned herself emotionally with Edgar Linton's gentry value system. Heathcliff returns to Yorkshire a wealthy man, but the question of where he went, and indeed, how he acquired his suspect wealth, is never answered. His "upright carriage," Nelly conjectures, "suggested" "his having been in the army," but this half-hearted explanation withers on the narrative vine.[32] She speculates no further. Heathcliff is destined to remain elliptical. The powers of narrative, in fact, *defer* to his seductive and intimidating ellipticality. It is as if ellipsis has manipulated the very narrative that contains it into pulling its epistemological punches. Heathcliff knows how to play with people. The only expertise he appears to have acquired during his mysteriously lucrative sabbatical is his daunting skill in gambling. His newfound economic power is infused, then, with nonproductivity, and like himself, with ludic illegitimacy. Cards serve as his retributive and aleatory weapon against the game-addicted Hindley. Cards lead to Heathcliff's acquisition of the Heights: an acquisition tainted by ludic means, by his monomaniacal need to "settle [his] score" with Hindley. First as an infant, next as a boy, and finally as a man, Heathcliff emerges "half-civilized" from a playful, antisocial lacuna. A childish space, Brontë's Heathcliffian ellipses resist assimilation or narrative incorporation and refuse to relinquish their demonic incommensurability. At the level of form, Heathcliff's gothic ellipses militate against the future-producing trajectory of Nelly's domestic narrative, the novel's centripetal movement toward social, moral, and logical cohesion. Just as Heathcliff acts as an entropic drag on the Yorkshire community he infiltrates, the three lacunae that punctuate his life story act as pockets of ludic entropy within Nelly's narrative, undermining her ability to explain him coherently to Lockwood, to make him make sense. Heathcliff puts narrative in play and impedes its forward motion toward a logically satisfying resolution.

Wuthering Heights, the novel as well as the house, is haunted by child play, by its unassimilable and uncanny presence, by its hostility to the laws of causality and to temporal and spatial constraints. Enclosed for the night in Cathy's "old-fashioned couch" (a house within a house, a room within a room), and "under the influence of cold and lingering nausea,"

Lockwood pores over her "mildewed books," papers, and diary, "scrawled in an unformed, childish hand."[33] He discovers plans "to rebel," to run away to the moors, to ignore Hindley's order that she and Heathcliff "not play together."[34] Later, tossed by nightmare, he encounters the spectral presence of the little girl, who howls outside his window, clinging with an "ice-cold hand" and a "tenacious gripe [sic]" to his "fingers" through the broken glass.[35] Brontë situates the ludic child outside the socializing and future-producing confines of domestic space, in a state of timeless immanence: "It's twenty years," mourned the voice, "twenty years, I've been a waif for twenty years!"[36] Lockwood views Cathy's attempted entry not as the return of a "lost" child to the hearth but as an invasion by an otherworldly "creature": "I pulled its wrist on to the broken pane, and rubbed it to and fro till the blood ran down and soaked the bed-clothes."[37] Unwelcome visitant from Lockwood's unconscious, gothic demon rather than domestic angel, Brontë's ludic child inhabits an obscene world outside family, time, and logic.

Needless to say, the atavistic child stands in stark contrast to the modern ideology of child play, to the logic of play as *paideia*, wherein ludic activity in children is treated as an expression of psychic and cultural consolidation, not cosmic deliquescence. Despite what some of its early critics might have suspected, however, Brontë's novel should not be interpreted as an orgiastic celebration of obscenity, a self-indulgent advertisement for future-negation. Acutely aware of the nonviable nature of demonic child play, of its "incurable" madness, Brontë knows just how unrelenting a grip the modern ideology of child play has on modern consciousness.[38] A maw that incorporates all Otherness, "ideology," Althusser reminds us, "has no outside."[39] There is no outside to the modern ideology of child play. One cannot escape time. One cannot prevent the future. Brontë knows this. And yet she makes us wonder. She cannot quite bring herself to acquiesce completely, to accept as total the victory of futurity, of middle-class productivity, over timeless presence. She therefore *unsettles* the modern ideology of child play, haunts it, wounds it the best she can, goads it into lowering its defenses. Behind its back, in the wings, lurks a presence, a whisper, causing it to spin around, to betray on its panic-stricken face its underlying violence, its irrepressible insecurity. A haunted Lockwood rips to bloody shreds the arm of that unassimilable, irredeemable ghost-girl.

Beneath the modern ideology of child play, beneath its innocuous veneer, lurks the cultural compulsion to punish nonproductivity in children, to squeeze their lives into a vise of futurity. Brontë lays bare this ugly fact.

"[F]eeble as a kitten" from his ordeal at the Heights, Lockwood surrenders narrative control to Nelly Dean, "a regular gossip," in an effort to make sense of his nonsensical experience.[40] She is the perfect choice. Nelly embodies the modern ideology of child play. The hardest working character in the novel, she is its only (main) character, Pykett reminds us, who "must and does *work*."[41] Even as she narrates, she busily knits.[42] Over the course of her life, by virtue of her class status and gender, Nelly has been employed as nurse, babysitter, or professional nurturer to over half the novel's yeoman and gentry children: Cathy and Heathcliff, Hareton, Cathy's daughter Catherine, and, briefly, Heathcliff and Isabella's son Linton. Although she proves unequal at times to the task, especially when it comes to Heathcliff and Cathy, and occasionally resistant to it, she, more than anyone, is charged with monitoring children, with shepherding their play impulses toward socially productive outlets, instilling in their young lives a *telos* of development. Nelly is also a victim of the modern ideology of child play. Her childhood at the Heights epitomizes the modern conflation of child play and work. In the very first sentence of her narrative, in fact, Nelly grammatically fuses child play and work so naturally, reconciles enjoyment and development so seamlessly, that it is difficult to decide whether she is "patriarchy's paradigmatic housekeeper," as Gilbert and Gubar famously assert, or a subversive Deleuzean masochist, who undermines the purported nobility of power by goading it into unleashing its violence against her.[43] I tend toward the former.

Before I came to live here, she commenced, waiting no further invitation to her story, I was almost always at Wuthering Heights; because, my mother had nursed Mr. Hindley Earnshaw, that was Hareton's father, and I got used to playing with the children—I ran errands too, and helped to make hay, and hung about the farm ready for anything that anybody would set me to.[44]

She views her chores as a natural extension of her play. Having been interpellated by the modern ideology of child play, having internalized the idea that play prepares children for a life of labor, Nelly describes matter-of-factly her metamorphosis from Earnshaw "playmate" to employee.[45]

Whereas Heathcliff and Cathy fail over the course of a novel to reconcile their play impulses with the demands of socialization, working-class Nelly accomplishes it self-effacingly in the span of *one* sentence. The only hint of conceptual suturing, the only ideological scar, is that little dash between "playing with the children" and "I ran errands." Brontë presents the narrative impulse, then, not as the purging of play by work but as their harmonious reconciliation. But there are other textual energies at work in *Wuthering Heights*, paranarrative ludic forces, which prove stubbornly unassimilable. Brontë unfurls Heathcliff and Cathy into the night and projects their apocalyptic ludic intimacy onto the cosmos. Just as Nelly and Lockwood struggle to make sense of Heathcliff and Cathy's impossible friendship, the narrative struggles formally to assimilate its own ludic ellipticality. Nelly and Lockwood outlive Heathcliff and Cathy. Narrative has the last word. Brontë, however, unsettles that word and infuses the novel's domestic resolution with queasy irresoluteness.

The Modern Ideology of Child Play

Before turning our attention to the cosmological features of Brontë's future-negating model of child play, to the tension between the profane logic of play as *paideia* and the sacred logic of play as fate, I would like to take the opportunity here to place Brontë's idiosyncratic views on child play in historical context, to provide an account of the evolution of the modern ideology of child play over the last four centuries. How did the modern ideology of child play come to saturate Victorian representations of childhood? Why is it so difficult for us to separate child play conceptually from the logic of play as *paideia*? Why do "Westerners" in particular, Sutton-Smith notes, have a tendency to "cherish" the notion that children "adapt and develop through their play"?[46] From middle-class common sense, through modern pedagogy, to early expressions of evolutionary psychology: Brontë confronts them all in her struggle to achieve critical distance from the all-encompassing modern ideology of child play. She shakes the normalizing foundations of modern consciousness and causes the cosmic vault to collapse upon her head. In the pages that follow, I explore the historical vicissitudes not of *actual* child play, which routinely subverts cultural expectations, but of its representations in pedagogical discourse over the last four centuries. It is against this backdrop that Brontë unleashes Heathcliff and Cathy.

We should resist the urge to project onto ancient and premodern child play prelapsarian authenticity. The belief that child play socializes children and trains them to be productive citizens is ubiquitous in educational treatises in early and late antiquity. In Latin, *ludus* mean "school" as well as "play" and "game." The Roman *ludus* is a site of physical and mental exercise, an institution of ludic development. Unlike modern educationalists, however, ancient pedagogues make no attempt to obfuscate the coercive, prescriptive quality of the ludic regimen to which children are subjected. Greek and Roman tutors *compel* productive and socially viable play in their pupils. In *The Republic*, Plato views the childish will to play as a mimetic impulse, which can and should be harnessed by a "system" of musical training and gymnastics for purposes of producing "well-conducted and virtuous citizens."[47] It is an impulse, however, which can just as easily be channeled by irresponsible guardians, or by "pantomimic gentlemen," toward less virtuous ends:

And when [children] have made a good beginning in play, and by the help of music have gained the habit of good order, then this habit of order, in a manner how unlike the lawless play of the others! will accompany them in all their actions and be a principle growth to them, and if there be any fallen places in the State will raise them up again.

From antiquity to the early modern period one sees the indelible handprint of a teacher, tutor, or mentor on the productive play of children. Although debates about when the modern child—and by extension the modern ideology of child play—first emerged are far from settled, when it comes to the English context, it seems likely that the modern child congealed as a subject at some point in the early seventeenth century: the product of the familial ideology of a nascent middle class, Puritan educational reforms, and an early Enlightenment culture of liberty.[48]

The story of child play since the early seventeenth century is the story of the gradual withdrawal of the pedagogue's hand from the child's productive play. By the late eighteenth century, the ludic child has become a potent symbol of human autonomy and dignity, irrefutable proof of the self-generating power of civilization, of the intrinsic productivity of man. The modern ideology of child play genializes self-discipline and renders innocuous the logic of socialization. As we shall see, nineteenth-century anthropologists, psychologists, and physicians—Herbert Spencer, Alexander Francis Chamberlain, Karl Groos, and Granville Stanley Hall, among others—biologize the productive play impulse in children, thereby naturalizing the capitalist tendencies that educational reformers had been detecting in child play for two hundred years. By the nineteenth century, the hand of the teacher all but disappears. The child takes himself in hand, and for that matter, takes humanity in hand.

In the seventeenth century the shift toward viewing child play as an act of spontaneous self-governance, as protowork, reaches its ideological apogee in John Locke's influential treatise, *Some Thoughts Concerning Education* (1693). Explaining how play forms a child's character, and how children who are given too great a variety of toys "are taught pride, vanity, and covetousness almost before they can speak," Locke offers exasperated parents the following advice:

> How then shall they have the play-games you allow them, if none must be bought for them? I answer, they should make them themselves, or at least endeavor it and set themselves about it; till then they should have none, and till then they will want none of any great artifice. A smooth pebble, a piece of paper, the mother's bunch of keys, or anything they cannot hurt themselves with, serves as much to divert little children as those more chargeable and curious toys from the shops, which are presently put out of order and broken. . . . Indeed, when they once begin to set themselves to work about any of their inventions, they should be taught and assisted, but should have nothing whilst they lazily sit still expecting to be furnished from others' hands without employing their own.[49]

While the hand of the pedagogue is still visible in Locke's account of child play, it is in the process of withdrawing, becoming less authoritarian: a self-effacing hand. The absence of the coddling parent spurs the child's innate industriousness, his entrepreneurial play impulse, inspiring him to govern himself. It is Lockean liberalism writ small. By refraining from giving the child a toy, forcing him to invent his own plaything, Locke successfully reconciles socialization and self-determination, development and enjoyment. Play serves as the cradle of liberty, the incubator of capitalism:

> Recreation belongs not to people who are strangers to *business* and are not wasted and wearied with the employment of their calling. The skill should be so to order their time of recreation that it may relax and refresh the part that has been exer-

cised and is tired, and yet do something which, besides the present delight and ease, may produce what will afterwards be *profitable*.[50]

A century later, another Enlightenment philosopher, Mary Wollstonecraft, insists even more emphatically that parents unhand their children's play. In *A Vindication of the Rights of Women* (1792), she claims that a future-producing sociality, a seed of liberalism, is intrinsic to child play—a seed that a parent crushes by "retir[ing] into a desert with his child," monopolizing the role of his child's "playfellow."[51] Parental attempts to partake of the child's play, and thereby control it, "stop[ ] the growth of every vigorous power of mind or body," instill in the child "a dash of fear," an antisocial leaning toward authoritarianism.[52] Enlightened society necessitates parental withdrawal from child play, for children must be free "to play and prattle with [other] children."

According to toy historian Kenneth Brown, Britain's indigenous toy and children's book industries emerged in the eighteenth century, products of the modern ideology of child play.[53] Manufacturers and printers marketed their wares to a middle class whose attitudes about childhood had been shaped, as we learned in Chapter One, by the confluent forces, to quote Davidoff and Hall, of Britain's "Evangelical and Enlightenment traditions," both of which "focused on children's character as the basis for reforming society."[54] Thus, the vast majority of toys, games, and books were instructional in nature, infused with a middle-class work ethic: "little sets of carpenter's tools, garden implements, cheap microscopes and plaster bricks for model making."[55] In the mid-eighteenth century, middle-class children learned geography while playing *A Journey Through Europe*, the first commercially successful board game; the first mass-produced jigsaw puzzles were also maps.[56] In addition to dolls and dollhouses, girls received "needlebooks and miniature work baskets."[57] "Both sexes," Davidoff and Hall note, participated in recreational "activities such as keeping pets and tending small gardens," but boys played with owls and planted trees and ferns, while girls cultivated flowers and played with rabbits. Middle-class child play is paradoxical. On the one hand, it indoctrinates children ideologically; on the other hand, it inspires intellectual and moral autonomy in them. When parents purchase an educational toy for their child, they purchase a proxy for themselves; but they also purchase the illusion of noncoercion, noninterference in a child's supposedly spontaneous cultural development. It would be inaccurate to suggest that middle-class parents in eighteenth-century Britain did not see themselves as active, even fervent, participants in their child's socialization. The modern ideology of child play, however, naturalizes socialization, masks its violence, suggests that socialization can be *fun*, that children, in the absence of direct adult supervision, instinctively socialize themselves and produce the future.

Consider Thomas Day's *Sanford and Merton* (1783–89), a classic work of children's literature from the eighteenth century. Coddled by his prosperous parents, young Tommy Merton must "sit still for fear of spoiling his clothes," must "stay in the house for fear of injuring his complexion," "[i]nstead of playing about, and jumping, and running like other children."[58] Fearful that his son's character is being compromised by this lack of ludic opportunity, Tommy's father arranges for him to play with a "hardy" and "honest" working-class boy named Harry Sanford. After instructing the boys in their daily lessons, their tutor, Mr. Barlow, encourages them to "go out and amuse yourselves."[59] Invariably, their play metamorphoses into some variety of rational work. Their efforts to make a "prodigious snow ball," for example, lead to their self-education about the physics of wedges, or, as Harry terms it, the "business" of wedges.[60] At one point, they build a small house, putting Mr. Barlow, "by Harry's direction," "to work" cutting lumber.[61] If *Sanford and Merton* pedagogically co-opts child play, then Harry and Tommy playfully co-opt pedagogy and subjugate, in the name of play, their susceptible teacher.

"Perfect play is the anticipation of perfect work."[62] So writes Mary Wright Sewell, mid-Victorian wife, mother, and advocate of domesticity, in a letter to a friend, recalling her child-rearing strategies from earlier in life. Even in the case of a toddler stringing beads, she advises, "there should be a degree of perfectness and even something approaching business habits encouraged and expected even in these little amusements to give a worth and interest to them." It is not that an innately unproductive child must be *made* productive through play; rather, the businesslike quality of play must be made palpable to that constitutionally productive toddler in order for her to find something of "interest" in those beads. In delving into nineteenth- and twentieth-century literature on child development, one descends into an ideological echo chamber. The logic of industrious play ricochets about one's ears. Take this quotation from

Pauline Kergomard, late nineteenth-century French education reformer: "Play is the child's labour, its trade, its life, its initiation into society."[63] Or consider Friedrich Froebel, the inventor of Kindergarten: "The plays of childhood are the germinal leaves of all later life; for the whole man is developed and shown in these, in his tenderest dispositions, in his innermost tendencies."[64] Or the assertion in 1863 by German psychologist Wilhelm Wundt that "play is the child of work."[65] Or nineteenth-century Italian child psychologist Paola Lombroso: "Play is for the child an occupation as serious, as important as study and work are for the adult."[66] Or the blunt pronouncement by early twentieth-century childhood expert Susan Sutherland Isaacs that "play is the child's work."[67] Or Jean Piaget's observation that "between ludic construction [in children] and work" "there are all shades of transitions."[68] Or the claim by child psychologists Jerome Bruner, Alison Jolly, and Kathy Sylva in 1976 that "play is the principal business of childhood," "the first carrier of rule systems through which a world of cultural restraint is substituted for the operation of impulse."[69] The notion that child play constitutes a form of protowork has ossified into fact. It wears a mantle of common sense, saturates the consciousness, and shapes the dinner-party small talk of more than a few parents. It structures and re-forms the memories of nearly everyone who once was a child, and it worms its way into Victorianist scholarship: "For young children," Thomas Jordan waxes sentimental in *Victorian Childhood*, "the business of life is play."[70] One finds the modern ideology of child play at work in Freud, of course, in his account in *Beyond the Pleasure Principle* (1920) of the so-called "*fort/da*" game, in which his infant grandson, by throwing and retrieving a wooden reel, does the important work of inventing symbolism, entering language, and therapeutically coming to terms with his mother's departure from the room.[71] This desire for power, this retentive impulse in his grandson, suggests to Freud that an "*economic motive*" "lead[s] children to play."[72] The modern ideology of child play trumpets forth in H.G. Wells's *Floor Games* (1911), in his assertion that the "British Empire will gain new strength from nursery floors."[73]

The modern ideology of child play can make malevolence disappear and lighten with a hint of productivity even the darkest shade of violence. In *The Criminal* (1890), Havelock Ellis considers the case of "a little Russian girl of five, a peasant's daughter, who having one day looked on with great interest while her father was engaged in killing a sheep, said to her younger brother a few days later, when the parents were away, 'Let us play at killing sheep', and making him lie on the floor proceeded to cut his throat from ear to ear, so that he died."[74] Despite the fact that she waited to play her game until after her parents departed, Ellis insists that "[w]e cannot say" for certain "that this was a genuinely criminal impulse." He might well be right. The modern ideology of child play is nevertheless at work in Ellis's insistence upon withholding judgment, as well as in our own willingness, indeed, eagerness, to accept his nonjudgment. It is nearly impossible to purge from our modern minds that intractable sense, an intuitive pang, that she was instinctively mimicking her father, training herself to kill sheep, and that the episode is but a tragic mishap in a little girl's otherwise productive march toward the future. And so we succumb, like sheep, to the modern ideology of child play.[75]

The question remains: How does the British middle class make the conceptual and ideological leap from conceiving of child play in the eighteenth century as spontaneous economic productivity, to conceiving of it in the nineteenth century as a biological impulse to perpetuate the species? How is ludic productivity corporealized? In other words, how does the *source* of cultural production in child play migrate from the pedagogue's hand in the seventeenth century, to the child's own hand by the early eighteenth century, coming to rest in the early nineteenth century *within* the child's hand, in the organic forces that animate life? One sees this urge to subsume child development in the logic of nature, to de-socialize socialization, in the English Romantic poets' cult of the child, in Wordsworth and Coleridge in particular. Romanticism "uncouples the link," Judith Plotz explains, "between schooling and childhood," "wrests children away from the female sphere" of socialization, "and sequesters them in a paternally circumscribed realm of permanent difference."[76] Wordsworth's famous injunction to "quit your books," to "Let Nature be your teacher," might seem, on the surface, a rejection of socialization, a renunciation of middle-class productivism and Enlightenment rationalism.[77] But Wordsworth actually naturalizes socialization, relocates "wisdom" and cognitive development in "Spontaneous" "impulse," conceives of human beings as innately future-oriented, as *organically* productive. In *The Prelude* (1805), he addresses nature as his "Playmate."[78] Devoid of nagging mothers and stern schoolmasters, the natural world becomes for Wordsworth a space of spontaneous self-parenting, where a child *fathers* his future self, poeticizes himself, "compose[s] [his] thoughts" through "boyish sports," "exercise and play," and "games / Confederate."[79] Far from freeing the modern child from the middle-class imperative to play productively, Wordsworth, by naturalizing the child's play impulse and by idealizing what it means to be a "productive" adult, raises the stakes tremendously for the ludic child, who has been promoted from mere "future doctor" or "future cotton merchant" to "spiritual visionary."

Late eighteenth-century aesthetic and poetic theories of play inspired Victorian scientific explanations of play behavior in humans. To put it another way, the Victorian logic of play as *paideia* co-opts the Romantic logic of play as imaginary. Consider Spencer, whom I discuss in Chapter One. In *Principles of Psychology* (1855), Spencer advances the theory that the play impulse and the cultural and aesthetic production that flows from it derive from surplus energy, a superabundant life force left over from a primordial period in the evolution of mankind, when the proto-human body required more brute strength to survive. According to Spencer, play expressions are evolutionary echoes of obsolete life-and-death activities on which we no longer need to expend energy. We play sports in lieu of killing our rivals. Courtship activities such as dance and poetry replace coerced mating. Play is a foreign currency we have no choice but to spend, the remnants of our journey. While play might be physically useless and biologically superfluous, it nevertheless performs the valuable *work* of culture. Spencer readily admits that his evolutionary theory of play was inspired by "a quotation from a German author" whose name he does "not remember."[80] The quotation is Schiller's. In *On the Aesthetic Education of Man* (1795), Schiller claims "the animal plays when superabundant life is its own stimulus to activity."[81] While his theory of the "play impulse" (*Spieltrieb*) is influenced in part by Henry Home and Kant, Schiller, more than any other eighteenth-century aesthetic philosopher, enshrines play at the center of human experience: "Man plays only when he is in the full sense of the word a man, and *he is only wholly Man when he is playing.*"[82] Spencer repackages Romantic aesthetics as Victorian science. One sees Spencer's theory of play at work in Burton's *Personal Narrative of a Pilgrimage to Al-Madinah and Meccah*:

in his ethnographic account of the Badawin warriors of the Arabian peninsula. "Even in his sports," Burton writes, "he affects those that imitate war," "[p]reserving the instinctive qualities which lie dormant in civilization."[83] Invoking the modern ideology of child play, Burton notes that Badawin "children," who are really "men in miniature," prefer to "play upon the backs of camels" rather than with unmanly "Egyptian plaything[s]."[84]

In *The Play of Animals* (1898), evolutionary psychologist Karl Groos advances an even more nakedly functionalist theory of child play. Play activities in humans and animals, he insists, *contra* Spencer, "are not imitative repetitions," nor are they physically useless, "but rather [they are] preparatory efforts" for "serious activity," that is to say, an anticipatory form of self-training, a survival instinct: "the dog . . . educates itself, by play, for fighting with other dogs."[85] Whereas Spencer sees child play as a superfluous biological impulse that performs cultural work, Groos sees it as a necessary "biological" "instinct" that performs cultural *and* biological work: "*[T]he very existence of youth*," he claims, "*is due in part to the necessity for play*; the animal does not play because he is young, he has a period of youth because he must play."[86] Caterpillars spin cocoons, grizzly bears hibernate, and children play in order to perpetuate themselves bodily. Though Groos is writing on the cusp of the twentieth century, he is essentially putting into scientific terms the widespread middle-class assumption in the nineteenth century that child play constitutes an uncanny physical foresight in the child. Groos has simply applied a patina of evolutionary psychology to Wordsworth's assertion that "The Child is Father of the Man."[87] In *Letters from London* (1808), an anonymously penned instructional pamphlet for children, we see the ideological linkage of child play, ninety years prior to *The Play of Animals*, to a survival instinct, to organic intuition in the child-organism. The narrator describes his visit to a London "School for the indigent Blind," where he observes "nineteen boys and nine girls" "not only at work," "manufactur[ing] baskets," but more tellingly, "at play": "it was surprising," he recalls, "how well they avoided running against any part of the building when at play."[88] Though decreasingly so after the Factory Acts of 1833, 1844, and 1867, children were an integral component of the workforce in nineteenth-century Britain. So natural, so instinctive, are the cross-pollinating activities of work and play, the pamphlet's author suggests, that English children engage in them to productive effect even with their eyes "closed."

But *real* historical children can be shockingly violent and ill-mannered in their play. How is the modern ideology of child play not continuously undermined by real-world experience? Ideology has a stomach of iron: an unnerving ability to reconcile all contradictions. With the modern ideology of child play, even destructive and antisocial ludic behavior appears developmentally redeemable. Consider the theory of late nineteenth-century American psychologist Granville Stanley Hall that child play constitutes a cathartic stage in human development during which primitive "congenital hereditary" impulses are purged and processed, tamed by the child through violent expression.[89] In child play, Hall claims, "we rehearse the activities of our ancestors, back we know not how far, and repeat their life work in summative and adumbrated ways."[90] Without access to his inner Neanderthal, to his "most bestial" "instincts," without ludic resistance to "regimentation" and "uniformitarianism," the modern boy becomes "a milk-sop, a lady-boy, or a sneak."[91] Bloody work, yes, but child play is work nonetheless; "[t]oo early distinction between play and work," Hall insists, "should not be taught."[92] What form does this cultural work take? Hall gleefully elaborates:

Noses are bitten, ears torn, sensitive places kicked, hair pulled, arms twisted, the head stamped on and pounded on stones, fingers twisted, and hoodlums sometimes deliberately try to strangle, gouge out an eye, pull off an ear, pull out the tongue, break teeth, nose, or bones, or dislocate jaws or other joints, wring the neck, bite off a lip, and torture in utterly nameless ways. . . . To be angry aright is a good part of moral education, and non-resistance under all provocations is unmanly, craven, and cowardly.[93]

In nineteenth-century Britain, the assumption that aggressive child play (at least among boys) instills virtue in the child is evident in the mid-Victorian cult of boy-sports, as I noted in Chapter One, in the football and rugby culture advocated by reformer Thomas Hughes, for instance, one of the founders of the Working Men's College, where muscle-pumping sports inspired a new character-building curriculum. Likewise, in Hughes's *Tom Brown's Schooldays*, moral strength arises from the middle-class boy's "education of his own body" through sportive, rebellious play, his avoidance of the muscle-atrophying life of the mind.[94] Hughes is Wordsworth on steroids. Subversive play, competitive play, even imaginative play: *paideic* play absorbs them all. While the violent play of working-class Victorian children might seem more difficult to assimilate ideologically, as it smacks of unruliness and sedition, successfully assimilated it repeatedly is. Historian Colin Heywood describes how "local employers" in Suffolk regularly observed area boys engaged in a violent type of football known as "Kicking Camp" in order to identify "the strongest and most courageous youths," future foremen and managers.[95]

More threatening to the Victorian middle-class ideal of childhood than violent or antisocial child play, which can easily be naturalized as competitiveness or individuality, more threatening even than *perverse* child play, which can be pathologized and exceptionalized, is the politically dispiriting sight of an *unludic* child: the child too damaged to play, too weary, whose lack of play is invariably couched in economic terms. Because I give an account of some of these children in Chapter One, a single example will suffice here. Recall, for a moment, the disturbing spectacle of Jenny Wren in Dickens's *Our Mutual Friend* (1864–65): the "weird," "queer" girl too overworked to play, whose backbreaking employment as a "dolls' dressmaker" precludes her playing with the very dolls she dresses.[96] She triggers in those who see her an uncanny sensation of temporal distortion: "a child—a dwarf—a girl—a something—sitting on a little low old-fashioned arm-chair, which had a kind of little working bench before it."[97] Young and old, cute and decrepit, Jenny Wren embodies the collapse of teleological causality, the death of time, of the middle-class dream of a better tomorrow. She is not so much a symbol of the cruelty of child labor, as of the cruelty of the wrong *kind* of child labor, for overworked Jenny Wren is less productive, in the end, than the future-producing child at play, whose ludic activity represents a more culturally profitable form of child labor.

To suggest that Emily Brontë alone of nineteenth-century thinkers recognizes the ideological nature of middle-class attitudes toward child play, that she pits herself in messianic fashion against history itself, would be to overstate the case. Plenty of her contemporaries felt uneasy about the ideological work demanded of child play. Many others, including parents, especially parents, felt ambivalent about it. In *Culture and Anarchy*, for instance, Arnold jabs with his stiletto wit the mind-numbing productivism, the future-oriented "Philistinism," that underlies "all the games and sports which occupy the passing generation of boys and young men."[98] "Culture," he slyly insists, "does not set itself against the games and sports": "it congratulates the future, and hopes it will make a good use of its improved physical basis; but it points out that our passing generation of boys and young men is, meantime, sacrificed." Rather than negate the future, however, Arnold seeks merely to lighten it, to sweeten it, to loosen the utilitarian chains that bind the present so tightly to a productivist end.

Brontë goes further. In *Wuthering Heights*, she attempts the impossible: to discover a ludic space *outside* futurity, where the child plays against the forces of production and becomes a vehicle of sacred destruction. In contrast to the character-building roughhousing of Hall's ideal boys, Heathcliff and Cathy's antisocial play cannot be culturally assimilated, rendered characterologically or politically redeemable. Neither, however, does she pathologize Heathcliff and Cathy, present them as mere bad children, run-of-the-mill moral weaklings, like the spoiled brats we encounter in Anne Brontë's *Agnes Grey* (1847). From the start, Brontë infuses Heathcliff and Cathy's mysterious play with cosmological profundity. She loosens child play from its domestic moorings and unfurls it into the tumultuous night sky. It rips a hole in the cosmos. Whereas Wordsworth makes a *home* for child play outside the middle-class home, in wholesome and hospitable nature, Brontë makes child play eternally *homeless*, irredeemable, morally uninhabitable. At Emily Brontë's feet, the great educational treatises of the West—from Plato's, through Locke's, to Froebel's—lie in ruins.

Brontë's Ethic of Destruction

If Heathcliff and Cathy's child play, their elliptical and paranarrative activity on the moors, resists representation, it is because it escapes the order of *things*. A social and epistemic void, their ludic world constitutes, in essence, an *un*world: the immanence of nothingness, a sublime state of no-*thingness*, where subject-object differentiations and even basic grammatical oppositions between "I" and "you" waver and become unfixed. In *Theory of Religion*, Bataille characterizes this sensation of violent continuity and intimacy with the cosmos as "animality," as being "on a level with the world in which [one] moves like water in water"; like great ravenous waves, spasms, mouths that taste their own collapse.[99] Brontë wrests sublimity from the manly brains of Romantic poets and places it in the sticky paws of children. Heathcliff and Cathy are not vessels of an inexpressible Coleridgean divinity: their version of the sublime is more naughty, an amalgamation of the logics of play as fate and play as subversion. They are agents of cosmic dissolution, of the demonic, undulant, infertile landscape on which they play. On the cusp of puberty, with adulthood just over the horizon, these rebel angels fall. On a midnight "ramble," their ludic oneness, their "oceanic" sense of self, crashes against the fixity of Thrushcross Grange, against the unyielding order of *things*. Heathcliff explains to Nelly what occurred:

> Both of us were able to look in by standing on the basement, and clinging to the ledge, and we saw—ah! It was beautiful—a splendid place carpeted with crimson, and crimson-covered chairs and tables, and a pure white ceiling bordered by gold, a shower of glass-drops hanging in silver chains from the centre, and shimmering with little soft tapers.... Edgar and his sister had it entirely to themselves.... And now, guess what your good children were doing? Isabella, I believe she is eleven, a year younger than Cathy, lay screaming at the farther end of the room, shrieking as if witches were running red hot needles into her. Edgar stood on the hearth weeping silently, and in the middle of the table sat a little dog shaking its paw and yelping, which, from their mutual accusations, we understood they had nearly pulled in two between them.... We laughed outright at the petted *things*, we did despise them![100]

The unassimilable play of unruly children confronts, from the outside, from the margins of the social, the proprietary play of ruling-class children, who, Midas-like, turn everything into a thing, an object to possess, and who are thus absorbed themselves into the order of things, reduced to mere "petted things." "When would you catch me," Heathcliff mocks, "wanting to have what Catherine wanted? or find us by ourselves, seeing entertainment in yelling, and sobbing, and rolling on the ground, divided by the whole room?"[101] Whereas Heathcliff and Cathy's play escapes the logic of instruction and evades the pedagogical grasp of Joseph, Edgar and Isabella perform in their self-centered play the alienating but socially mandated work of differentiation, of ownership: objectifying, demarcating, and dividing the world. In their "sobbing" and "yelling," in their psychic severance from each other, in their economic competition for the dog, Edgar and Isabella prepare themselves socially and intellectually for lifelong membership in the landed gentry, for the alienating sensation of ownership. Heathcliff and Cathy have caught Edgar and Isabella in the act of *producing* property, of training themselves for the future.

The production of things profanes the "immanent immensity," as Bataille terms it, of the cosmos, shatters the "indistinct continuity" of animality, rips from the timeless oneness of nothingness a discrete, isolated object, a "not-I," and by extension an "I," an alienated subject defined against the alterity of the emergent thing.[102] A rock becomes a primordial flint knife; a wild goat becomes livestock. In plucking the rock or the goat from the play of the cosmos, however, man plucks *himself* from his former oneness with the cosmos, shatters his animalistic intimacy with rocks and goats. In producing an object, he condemns himself to subjecthood. Human history, Bataille suggests, indeed, time itself, is the *effect* of things, for in becoming a knife, that rock becomes a utilitarian means to an *end*, a tool, a plan for the future. All *things* brim with futurity, with profanity, with the fallenness of time. What is most interesting, from our perspective, about Bataille's quasi-anthropological allegory of socialization, and what is particularly applicable to Brontë, is its economic nature. To turn something into a toy or plaything is to profane not only it, but play itself, to subordinate play to a utilitarian end, a productive future, to transform it into a tool of socialization. This explains why, when we first encounter Heathcliff, he emerges from Mr. Earnshaw's coat as a destroyer of toys, of Hindley's fiddle, as an animalistic force of ludic destruction. He also displaces Cathy's whip, a tool for taming animality. This also explains why, when we first encounter Edgar and Isabella, they are competing for a plaything, a dog whose animality has been debased by the creature's metamorphosis into a toy, a tool for ego-development. It is no coincidence that Heathcliff and Cathy have no toys. Their play precedes property. In Brontë's eyes, the modern ideology of child play profanes play, subordinates the very play of the cosmos to a *telos* of development, a trajectory of profit. Heathcliff stubbornly resists the unstoppable march of time, the victorious order of things. He watches helplessly as his childhood "playmate," injured on the Lintons' estate, is seamlessly absorbed by gentry domesticity, transformed into "a very dignified person," a doll whose "beautiful hair" the Lintons "dried and combed," and whom they "wheeled" dotingly, like a thing, to the fireplace.[103] They give her "a plateful of cakes." They give her a husband. They give her a future. But she loses, in effect, the cosmos.

There is a word in English for making something that has been profaned, or *thingified*, sacred, for making it continuous with the world once again. The word "sacrifice," Bataille reminds us, means "nothing other than the production of *sacred* things," that is, the destruction of the profane thing to which a person, animal, or inanimate object has been reduced.[104] Sacrifice plucks the sacrificed object from time, from its utilitarian movement toward a finite end, from its "real ties of subordination," and returns it to nothingness, to the unfathomable depths of "unintelligible caprice," to the sacred play of the universe.[105] Sacrifice, as terrible as it might be in the case of human or animal sacrifice, reestablishes a violent intimacy, a state of animality, between subject and object, which shatters, if only for a fleeting instant, the victim's "thingness" and hence the sacrificer's alienating subjectness. By killing the thing to which the victim has been reduced, you kill the thingness to which you, in opposition, have been relegated. Heathcliff and Cathy's child play constitutes an obscene ritual of sacrificial mutuality, in which their socialized selves, the profane vessels of their futures, are daily destroyed during their ineffable ventures on the moors. They kill each other's futures and turn each other "savage." Brontë has elevated child play, or degraded it, depending on how invested one is in the project of socialization, to a sacred and masturbatory act of future-negation: a childish suicide pact. Brontë exposes the sentimental logic of play as *paideia* as profane and egotistical; the logic of play as fate she makes sacred and obscene. Once Heathcliff and Cathy are essentially forced by the world to grow up, to succumb to the demands of socialization, once they become alienated from each other, first through Cathy's marriage to Edgar Linton and then through her death, Heathcliff embarks on an unrelenting campaign of destruction. He seeks to destroy two families, to lay waste to their ancient names. His maniacal acquisition of *things*, of houses, lands, and people, is not, as one might initially suspect, capitalistic in nature. Rather, it is sacrificial, for the goal of his acquisitiveness is not profit, self-perpetuation, or respectability, but sacred destruction at the altar of Cathy. He experiences the world of things as a vast collection of potential offerings to his dead playmate. Sacred in nature, his will to destroy, his cruelty to the profane order of things, reunites him with the fluid universe with which Cathy is now one.

To roll our eyes at Brontë's angsty privileging of the presocial over the social, to attempt to unearth, instead, political redemption, a flicker of usefulness, in Heathcliff and Cathy's destructiveness, is to partake of the very productivist logic against which the novel militates. To associate antiproductivism, as many people instinctively do, with nihilism, with the view that life has a value of *nil*, is to miss the point entirely. Brontëan child play has sacred rather than profane value. Brontë *revalues* child play by devaluing it economically, by making it profitless. Her sense of the sacred, however, is decidedly materialistic and antimetaphysical in nature. It is triggered by a simple act—simple for children, difficult for adults—of abandoning oneself to *presence*, to a cosmos unstructured by futurity, untrammeled by the profane logic of self-perpetuation: namely, that sense of direction, of moving always toward a goal, toward a *thing* that defines one's life. She turns the Victorian cult, the modern cult, of the future-producing child on its head; she transforms childhood into an atavistic blood cult, ritualistic annihilation. An impractical text, *Wuthering Heights* does not *teach* anything. Or rather, it teaches the value of *nothing*. The novel has no "mother." Brontë did not give birth to it. It is not a vessel of socialization. One must respect its author for the person she was and the person, years later, she remains: the great *antiparent* of nineteenth-century British literature.

CHAPTER 4

A Joy on the Precipice of Death

MUIR AND STEVENSON IN CALIFORNIA

My heart's in the Highlands, my heart is not here;
My heart's in the Highlands a-chasing the deer;
Chasing the wild deer, and following the roe,
My heart's in the Highlands, wherever I go.
—Robert Burns[1]

Two Weeks in San Francisco

John Muir and Robert Louis Stevenson never met. For two weeks in February 1880, however, the paths of these Scottish travel writers converged in San Francisco, where each awaited marriage to an American bride: Muir to Louie Wanda Strentzels on April 14th, Stevenson to Fanny Osbourne on May 19th. Wrapped in the same winter fog, they might have passed each other on Market Street, or on a hill bristled with houses, en route to their respective lodgings, where they spent their mornings writing about the American frontier. Stevenson lived at 608 Bush Street, on the southern slope of Nob Hill. He descended twice a day for meals at a coffee house on Sixth Street, south of Market. Homesick, he would have jumped at the sound of Muir's Scots brogue. But Muir disliked the bustle of urban life and kept to himself. Had Stevenson followed Market south, he would have arrived at the unassuming house where Muir resided. But Stevenson's health was poor, the foggy climate inflaming his already diseased lungs.[2] He was seldom in the mood for walks. For a fortnight, then, John Muir and Robert Louis Stevenson circled each other unawares, leaving in their wakes overlapping ripples of an encounter that never was.

Years later, Muir would "fill his personal library," biographer Donald Worster notes, with Stevenson's collected works, which he placed on a shelf beside his Burns and Scott.[3] It is the only evidence we have of anything approximating literary influence. Aside from Scotland, however, or their impending nuptials, or their distaste for San Francisco, Muir and Stevenson had little in common that February in 1880. Muir exuded rusticity and shyness, a monkish charm. Stevenson, with his easy air of shabby gentility, was often mistaken for a thespian or musician. The former was ascetic, the latter, aesthetic. Both were cosmopolites but different sorts, Muir more at home in the *cosmos* than the *polis*, reminding us in *The Mountains of California* (1894) that "trees and men" "travel the milky way together."[4] A hardworking immigrant from Dunbar, whose pious father, a shopkeeper, transplanted his family to a Wisconsin farm in 1849, Muir infuses his conservationist writings with a proselytizer's zeal, a mystical attachment to the natural world, describing himself, at one point, as a citizen of "Earth-planet, Universe."[5] Stevenson, a self-declared "amateur emigrant" from a prosperous Edinburgh family and a Bohemian proponent of "idleness," sketches the American landscape through which he passes with ironic detachment, focusing instead on the privations endured en route to meet his California bride, reminding us obliquely of the etymological connection between "amateur" and "amorous."

Yet, for all their temperamental and stylistic differences, an uncanny parallel exists between the post-Gold Rush California in Stevenson's travel narratives and the Sierra Nevada that Muir describes in his mountain journals, written and rewritten over a span of three decades. Muir and Stevenson experience the Golden State as simultaneous playground and graveyard: a joy on the precipice of death. It is a decidedly Romantic vision. It is an inescapably Scottish one. It is a vision that persists to this day. The "myth" of California "as an enchanted and transformed place" first emerged, historian Kevin Starr suggests, during the Spanish colonial era, gaining new ideological potency during the Gold Rush.[6] Muir and Stevenson invoke the old myth and update it in similar ways. They describe California somewhat predictably as a therapeutic place of recreation, an earthly paradise. At the same time, however, it embodies, in their eyes, *re*-creation, creative destruction, where American civilization meets a suicidal end, where self-congratulatory modernity feels its mortality, and where egoistical men die at the hands of their own latent boyishness. In the popular imagination today, it is California's sprawling urban and suburban landscapes wherein the confluence of death and play becomes most pronounced: decadent cities shaken by earthquakes; mansions licked by wildfires; overdoses and drive-bys beneath palm trees and smog. For Muir, however, who traveled to California to recuperate from malaria contracted in Florida, and for Stevenson, whose pulmonary disease positioned him perpetually on the cusp of death, it is the state's vast stretches of unspoiled wilderness, its status as "national playground," to quote Muir, wherein the simultaneity of death and play becomes most pronounced.[7] Muir and Stevenson detect in the ludic impulses inspired in them by California's topography—the childlike wonder, the recreational bliss—a barely repressed desire to fling themselves into the aleatory currents of the universe, to watch their Anglicized or Americanized egos disintegrate in the abyss. The proximity of death enchants California, buoys its mirth, makes it an ideal place of rest. In California, boys dance atop the graves of the men they once were.

The image of California that takes shape in Muir and Stevenson's travel writings draws its inspiration from several English and American literary sources: from Wordsworth's cult of the ludic nature-boy as spiritual visionary in an industrialized world, which we explored briefly in the previous chapter; from Ralph Waldo Emerson's transcendentalist vision of Nature, wherein "all mean egotism vanishes" in the face of "infinite space," the modern subject becoming "a transparent eye-ball," a sublime and life-affirming "nothing"; and from Mark Twain's homosocial ethos of comradeship, the uncivilized or partially socialized boy, Huck Finn or Tom Sawyer, serving as model for a more egalitarian social and political order.[8] One even detects in Muir and Stevenson's embrace of creative destruction intimations of the Brontëan sacred, the annihilation of self by a sadistic Heathcliffian cosmos. What most intrigues me about Muir and Stevenson's California writings, however, is their counterintuitive conflation of modernity with the natural world. To my mind, this is what makes them unique among Victorian representations of nature, with the possible exception of the neomedieval futurism depicted in Robert Jefferies's *After*

London (1885) and William Morris's *News from Nowhere* (1890). Indeed, they anticipate neo-Thoreauvian texts like John Krakauer's *Into the Wild* (1996), in which a Gen Xer discards his earthly possessions, takes a new name, and sets off for the Alaskan wilderness, where he ecstatically reunites with the universe. Muir and Stevenson are among the first writers to conceive of nature as a life-affirming expression of a reformed modernity, rather than as modernity's antithesis, its ancient or primitive Other. They reverse the nature-modernity opposition, aligning nature optimistically with futurity, the past with an antiquated and inflexible model of capitalist subjectivity. With its capricious lack of fixity and its collapsing boundaries, cosmopolitan nature ushers in the future, a more ethical and wholesome world in play. The natural world functions in this scenario as a more effective incubator for modern subjectivity, with its blurring signifiers and concomitant psychological flux, than the marketplace itself. Muir and Stevenson's nature-worship, or proto-environmentalism, should not be viewed, then, as antimodern, as a nostalgic retreat into pastoralism, a stable world *at* play; in truth, it is more "hyper-modern" than antimodern, more intensely modern than modernity itself, more *in play* than the Victorian world in play. Here, ludic nature displaces and outplays ludic capitalism. Nature is modernity taken to its extreme, its oscillating horizon. Though their accounts of California differ in tone and style, Muir and Stevenson are united in their efforts to reform modernity by turning the middle-class cult of recreation on its head. Just as Brontë revalues child play by purging it of its normalizing tendencies, Muir and Stevenson revalue recreation by purging it of its egoism and insularity, displacing the logic of play as self-creation, as well as the logic of competition that creeps into it, with the ego-shattering logic of *re*-creation and cosmic flux. Thus, the weekend warrior turns Thoreauvian nature tramp, a jester in the court of capitalism.

We typically associate nineteenth-century American modernity with the systematic conquest of the natural world, and the enterprising frontiersman's acquisitive march toward the West. But Muir and Stevenson redefine modernity, perhaps naïvely, as the psychological defeat of the frontiersman by the natural world, his humbling conversion to the joyful worship of nature. The natural splendor of California, its endless regeneration and unsettling fluidity, its geographical and geological lack of fixity, becomes, for Muir and Stevenson, a more powerful expression of modern life than the alienation induced by capitalism, by its endlessly circulating signifiers. The wild places in California, its shifting landscapes, sea fogs, and landslides, accelerate the cosmological motions of life more rapidly than the marketplace ever could. The middle-class sportsman, with his shiny gun and expensive hiking gear, is outmaneuvered at every turn by the natural world he strives to conquer. Nature proves too mischievously protean, too brutally creative, to be defeated in his game. In Muir and Stevenson's ideal account, modern man is made cognizant of the futility of his capitalist belligerence; he surrenders happily, gratefully, to California's cosmic caprice and learns to love nature as his trickster playmate, his boyhood friend. Put another way: if capitalist modernity creates the conditions whereby "all that is solid melts into air," then ludic California melts capitalism itself into air, increases the dizzying motions of the universe to such a point, that capitalism's very logic comes undone. Thus, earthquakes, glaciers, Pacific storms, and Sierra winters swallow the abandoned camps of greedy gold and silver prospectors. The miner's machinery for melting hillsides into money is itself melted by the mountain wind. Muir and Stevenson present their nature-worship as an extreme expression of the modern spirit; they co-opt modernity in the name of nature. They seek to transcend the industrious world in play, the egotistical game of acquisition, by throwing themselves recklessly into a more deadly and more capricious world.

The fleeting refuge from middle-class capitalism that Brontë discovers only in timeless, madness-inducing immanence, in the sacred destruction of one's future self, Muir and Stevenson discover—with minimal psychic damage to themselves and in great heaping amounts—in California in the ego-shattering futurity it unleashes in them. If they have more faith in the future than does fatalistic Brontë, who experiences temporality as constriction, as normalization, it is because Muir and Stevenson, who have no qualms about presenting the mischievous middle-class boy as a redemptive agent, as a symbol of possibility, have the masculine luxury of open space at hand, an ever-receding horizon with which to play. Ludic California is so welcoming that these peripatetic Scottish misfits begin to believe that modernity holds a place for them after all, that, despite their oddness and eccentricity, they might really find joy in the modern world and achieve ethical and political distance from within. In California Muir and Stevenson come to terms with modernity, learn how to be at play in a world in play.

Most Californians today have only a vague sense of the role played by Muir and Stevenson in shaping their state's mythologized identity. Having sat for hours on the freeway behind Sierra Club bumper stickers, or having driven past one of the many public schools named in Muir's honor, they probably associate him with the national parks system. In their pockets or purses, they have carried tiny monuments to the man, in the form of California's commemorative state quarter, which depicts Muir in Yosemite, an endangered California condor soaring overhead. The utter ridiculousness of placing Muir's likeness on *money*, of all things, was lost apparently on the U.S. Mint. The state, however, has honored him in more appropriate ways. For 211 miles, the John Muir Trail meanders along the crooked spine of the Sierra Nevada, from Yosemite Valley to Mt. Whitney in the south. And north of San Francisco, in Marin County, Muir Woods National Monument preserves a small forest of old-growth Coast Redwoods, some over a thousand years old and 250 feet tall, in the shadow of a region that is home to some 7.2 million people.

Stevenson's connection to California is less commonly known. He lived for a time in the Bay Area and has also been honored by the state. In fact, its primary tribute to Stevenson, visible every day to hundreds of thousands of people, captures best California's vision of itself as a far-fetched and capricious place. In the center of San Francisco Bay sits an artificial island two-thirds of a square mile in size that borrows its name from Stevenson's most famous novel. Created in 1936 and 1937 to house the 1939 World's Fair, Treasure Island celebrates the construction of the Golden Gate and San Francisco-Oakland Bay bridges. Palm trees, hangars, and athletic fields dot it today: a green and white mirage on a choppy blue-gray bay. A naval base from World War II to 1997, Treasure Island is built entirely on landfill. It is vulnerable, therefore, to liquefaction in the event of a major earthquake, such as a repetition of the seismic event of 1906, which destroyed 80 percent of San Francisco, including Muir's former residence. The name of this man-made island is a testament to the inspirational reciprocity between Stevenson and California. As Katharine Osbourne reminds us, Stevenson's descriptions of the fictional Treasure Island of his novel, its brambles and coves, its "sand-hills and lagoons," were inspired by another Northern California bay: Monterey, where he lay for hours on the beach, the roar of the Pacific in his ears, salt air in his lungs, thoughts of home catching his breath.[9]

In the pages that follow, I explore the subtle ways that two homesick Scotsmen shaped California's peculiar auto-iconography as a land of death and play, a cosmic playground on the knife-edge of apocalypse. Rather than depicting the Golden State as a refuge from modernity, as a sweet-natured world at play, Muir and Stevenson—the former, a nature zealot, the latter, a homeless dandy—envisioned the fledgling state as a whimsical yet lethal place, a world very much in play, where men died and boys leapt from their ashes, where modern life reached its apogee in its disintegration. For two weeks in 1880, mere blocks from each other, these two men dreamt of mountains, California's rugged terrain mingling in their sleep with ghosts from Caledonia. In the night sky above San Francisco, over an undulant forest of masts, their confected landscapes converged. And like a mountain of vapor, the idea of modern California amassed.

Dead Cities in the Hills

Stevenson makes a small but telling mistake at the end of *The Amateur Emigrant*, which contains his moving account, from the vantage of a railcar, of Nevada's "deadly" "desert scenes" giving way to California's "sea of mountain forests."[10] His health compromised by a transatlantic voyage in steerage, fever pangs punctuating his fitful crawl from the Rockies to the Sierra, he recalls that his "heart leaped" at the sight of otherworldly California, its "chill" "atmosphere," the "continuous plunge of a cascade," and the inexorable tug of "the Golden Gates" on his Oakland-bound train.[11] Golden *Gates*? Three years later, in "San Francisco: A Modern Cosmopolis," an essay written for the *Magazine of Art*, Stevenson again refers to the straits at the mouth of San Francisco Bay in the plural.[12] On the cusp of death, he confuses the Golden Gate, symbol of Manifest Destiny and California's promise, with the Pearly Gates. It is a mistake his editor never caught, nor his friends or literary agent, who, anxious for him to return from his life-threatening trip, viewed "California and California things" with disdain.[13]

Victorian writers described a variety of spiritual sensations—religious conversion, the overcoming of despair, the discovery of God—as a metaphorical journey from death to life, as being "recalled to life," as Dickens termed it.[14] Looking, he admits, like "a man at death's door," Stevenson invokes a very different metaphor to mark his entrance into California: a sickbed release into death. "I was dead sleepy," he recalls, "with a grateful mountain feeling at my heart."[15] "I had come home again," he muses, "from the unsightly deserts to the green and habitable corners of the earth." Mountainous California metamorphoses, in Stevenson's feverish eyes, into a Highlands afterlife, a postmortem homecoming. A Lowlands lad, born and raised in Edinburgh, Stevenson has returned to a Scottish home, however, that was never his, a fantasy of the Highlands. It is the mythic Scotland of *Kidnapped* (1886), culled, Barry Menikoff notes, from Stevenson's readings in Scottish history, rather than from his actual experience of the Highlands.[16] In California, Stevenson discards his Lowlands childhood, buries his biographical self, and adopts a contrived past, a ludic nostalgia, inspired by his boyhood readings. He *plays* at feeling nostalgic for the Highlands. In its staggering ravines, mischievous streams, and piney air, California makes him feel like the Highlands boy he never was, severing his psychological connection to his Lowlands family, his middle-class background; "every trouty pool along that mountain river," he insists, "was more dear to me than a blood relation."[17] The hyperbolic Highlands setting of *Kidnapped* reminds us, Jenni Calder suggests, of just how "estrange[d]" Stevenson was from Scotland's preindustrial "landscape" and "past."[18] California enables Stevenson to overcome this estrangement, for only there, biographer Claire Harman explains, did he "discover[ ] himself to be a Scot," experience those mythic Highlands, and cast aside his Anglicized Lowlands identity.[19] "When . . . at home," Stevenson confesses, "countless local patriotisms and prejudices," "innumerable forms of piety" and "many dialects," alienate him from his countrymen.[20] "Yet let us meet in some far country, and, whether we hail from the braes of Manor or the braes of Mar, some ready-made affection joins us on the instant" and stirs feelings for "the old land." In California, Stevenson relives a childhood that was not his, his invented Highlands persona becoming more real to him than his waking life or his actual past. Hence, his first act upon seeing the Golden State is to fall "dead" asleep. California is a joyful suicide.

A city boy, Muir visited the Highlands for the first time in 1893 at the age of fifty-five. It was his first trip to Scotland since his departure in 1849. In *My First Summer in the Sierra*, California's mountains trigger in Muir, as they did in Stevenson, a deathlike sleep, an elision of self: "Every morning, arising from the death of sleep, the happy plants and all our fellow animal creatures great and small, and even the rocks, seemed to be shouting, 'Awake, awake, rejoice, rejoice.'"[21] Muir presents his book, published in 1911, as his minimally revised journal from his 1869 Sierra expedition. According to Steven Holmes, no such journal exists. "[T]he handwritten notebooks upon which the book was based," Holmes explains, "date from 1887."[22] *My First Summer in the Sierra* was "undertaken for the specific purpose of *creating* an ideal model of a dramatic, transformative encounter with wilderness," which Muir then filtered through his emotional 1893 return to Scotland. Like Stevenson, then, Muir sees in California's mountains an opportunity to invent a past, to *play* at being Scottish, to shed his Lowlands skin. Muir even credits himself with having "Scotch Highland instincts," which strangers, he insists, instantly "[r]ecogniz[e]."[23] Scottish literature infiltrates Muir's Sierra. Burns and Scott echo in its canyons. Muir quotes Burns repeatedly in *My First Summer in the Sierra*, as well as in his other writings, conflating the ineffability of the natural world, California's sublimity, with the romance of preindustrial Scotland.[24] Dead Scotland and living California circle each other in a dialectical dance. With their auto-exoticizing Scottishness and their diasporic poignancy, Burns's lyrics function as multitasking signifiers for California's unspeakable grandeur, as well as for Muir's instinctive, subrational insistence that "going to the mountains is going home."[25]

I noted that Muir experiences in the Sierra a subjectivity-shattering sleep: "How deathlike is sleep in this mountain air," he muses in an entry dated, fictively, "July 14," "and quick the awakening into newness of life!"[26] Forest becomes "fir bed" where one slips into "death sleep."[27] In *The Mountains of California*, he gives a similar account of the peculiar "deathlike sleep of the tired mountaineer."[28] If Muir's sleep is more mystical than Stevenson's, it is partly because he was a more spiritual person, but also because the Highlands were for Muir an abstraction. Yosemite Valley brims with metaphysics. Standing before Cathedral Peak, which rises "eleven thousand feet above the sea," Muir jokes with truant insinuation:

"This I may say is the first time I have been at church in California, led here at last, every door graciously opened for the poor lonely worshiper."[29] If Muir's life as a young man took shape on his father's Wisconsin farm, where "plow and axe," Worster writes, devoured "wild and fecund nature," severing his childhood connection to Scotland, then California became for Muir a living afterlife, a wild temple where American egoism expired, where alienated manhood drowned in boyish dreams.[30]

For all their talk of the overwhelming aliveness of California, Muir and Stevenson detect death all around them: the death of their melancholic manhood, of sad mankind. They express a childlike exuberance at all things macabre, a thrill at the flimsiness of life, symbolized for Muir, for example, by the "black pillar" of a "dead pine," a "monument" to destruction, or by "the blood stains on the rocks from the unfortunate animals" that inspired the Mono Lake moniker "Bloody Cañon Pass."[31] A sleeping giant roused by the clamor of Lilliputian gold miners, who "dammed and tamed" its "streams," turned its "channels" into "slaves," "imprisoned" its waters "in iron pipes to strike and wash away hills," California quakes anthropomorphically with wakefulness, unleashing, to Muir's delight, its floods and storms and tremors, reminding humankind of the destructive power of nature.[32] Michael Cohen claims that Muir felt a "cold" disgust at the sight of the forty-niners' "dead towns," scattered like "monuments to the failure of wasted effort" and "get-rich-quick schemes."[33] And yet these "dead" "[m]ining-towns" simultaneously arouse, Muir admits, respect for the inexorable and healing motions of geological and astral time, "tree[s]," exempt from the "universal struggle for existence," facing their inevitable destruction with "an invincible gladness."[34] In *The Silverado Squatters* (1884), Stevenson notes that California, which sits at the forefront of America's future, surprises visitors with its myriad "antiquities" and "deserted places," the "whole neighborhood of Mount Saint Helena" in the Napa Valley, "now so quiet and sylvan," "once" having been "alive with mining camps and villages": "I suppose there are, in no country in the world, so many deserted towns as here in California."[35] Stevenson makes himself at home in the ruins of California, whether in "a ruined mission" in Monterey, perched on "unfinished hills," or in a "ruined" and "deserted" silver mine on Mount Saint Helena, near Calistoga, famous for its hot springs.[36] He spent his honeymoon squatting in this dilapidated mine. Death lurks around every corner. With its "railway," "telephones, and telegraphs," its trappings of modernity, Calistoga nonetheless "seems to repose," Stevenson observes, "on a mere film above a boiling, subterranean lake."[37]

Some might be tempted to chastise Muir for his liberal use or abuse of religious-architectural metaphors in his descriptions of the natural world. He titles an early essay "God's First Temples" (1876). Architectural imagery pervades four decades' worth of his nature writings. The "mighty Sierra" "rises," he declares, "the wall of some celestial city."[38] Muir recounts the Sierra's "spiry wall of pines," Yosemite's "domes and gables," "battlements and plain mural precipices."[39] Even cynical Stevenson, who brags that he is "usually calm over the displays of nature," steals an occasional crumb from this rhetorical feast, contrasting, in *The Amateur Emigrant*, "every spire of pine along the hill-top" with the abandoned "mining camps" below.[40] Are Muir and Stevenson guilty of anthropomorphism? Does Muir's claim, for instance, that mountains are "the grandest of God's terrestrial cities" suggest that nature has value only insofar as it reminds us of ourselves?[41] Do phrases like "mountain streets" and "mountain mansions" reduce the natural world to a human thing?[42] Muir's architectural metaphors certainly smack of what Lawrence Buell terms "homocentrism."[43] That said, these metaphors are more ecocentric than egocentric, for the Sierra looms with homicidal nonchalance, invokes man only to bury him, wiping him from the Earth. Muir's Sierra might have the jagged silhouette of a city skyline, but it is a city in ruins, devoid of human inhabitants, "masses of slate" "rising abruptly" "like ancient tombstones in a deserted burying-ground."[44] Muir's mountain-city is necropolitan, apocalyptic. The Sierra entombs civilization and mocks human architectural achievements. Nature functions for Muir as the city of the future, the *anticity* of a more ethical world. Muir's racist dismissals of the "dirty" Native Americans who intrude upon his idyll can be attributed in part to the way their easy subsistence on the land belies his claim that the Sierra is too sublime for human habitation, just as Coleridge would be irritated if Chamonix locals built a snowman on Mont Blanc.[45] In *The Mountains of California*, Muir dances atop his own grave: "[T]hese mountain mansions are decent, delightful, even divine, places to die in."[46] The Yosemite is a "page of mountain manuscript," he declares, "that I would gladly give my life ... to read."[47] Though Stevenson is referring to California's cities and towns, he, too, detects in the Golden State a giddy undercurrent of genocide, the destruction of mankind as we know it, although the "genocide" he imagines is of a humane variety. Describing the cosmopolitanism of California, the fact that the state is a crossroads for travelers "who belong," like himself, "to many countries," Stevenson suggests that the "scattered friendships" occasioned by the state "may prepare the euthanasia of ancient nations," nations embroiled in the nineteenth century in geopolitical brinkmanship, manly competition.[48] The modern world comes to California, then, expressly to die, to be recreated, to be made *more* modern.

The People's Playground

March was merciless. Stevenson's lungs began to hemorrhage. Alarmed, his fiancée Fanny, ten years his senior, moved him to an Oakland hotel, then to her cottage in East Oakland, where, for six uncertain weeks, fever and coughing fits nearly broke him. He prepared himself to die.[49] In her 1911 account of his California travels, Katharine Osbourne, Fanny's estranged daughter-in-law, declared that Stevenson's year in California marked "the dividing line between a reckless, intense, but indulgent youth and a deep and sincere manhood."[50] Nothing could be further from the truth. Stevenson rediscovered his boyhood in California. He grappled with death by bifurcating his subjectivity into chronological-geographical zones: a dying Lowlands man, on the one hand, an Anglicized shell of himself, and a playful Highlands boy, on the other hand, unabashedly Scottish. Health he pictured as an ascent into mountainous and mischievous boyhood; death, descent into the foggy depths of manhood, glimpses of which we catch six years later in the suffocating echo world of Jekyll's egocentric London. California's mountains exude a ludic Scottishness; thus, the "fine bulk of [Mount] Tamalpais," north of San Francisco, "look[s] down" on the city, Stevenson writes, "like Arthur's Seat on Edinburgh."[51] As a boy, Stevenson rambled on Arthur's Seat.

By mid-April, the worst had passed. Stevenson began to envision himself a triumphant boy-mountaineer in a new world, having discarded the burdensome corpse of adulthood. On April 16, 1880, he wrote his friend

Edmund Gosse: "I have come out of all this, and got my feet once more upon a little hill-top, with a fair prospect of life and some new desire of living. Yet I did not wish to die, neither, only I felt unable to go on farther with that rough horseplay of human life."[52] And again in May, this time to Sidney Colvin: "When ever I get into the mountains, I trust I shall rapidly pick up."[53] By "mountains," Stevenson means the Coastal Range, specifically Mount Saint Helena, with its "unexhausted soil," where Stevenson and Fanny moved shortly after May 19.[54] Mount Saint Helena mingles with the hilltop of Stevenson's second boyhood. Once there, he becomes a child at play, inspired, Robert Crawford speculates, by the presence of his eleven-year-old stepson, Lloyd, to whom Stevenson acted more as "playmate" than as disciplinarian.[55] He rechristens himself and his wife "the King and Queen of Silverado," and Lloyd, "the Crown Prince."[56] Stevenson spends his days "tak[ing] sunbaths and do[ing] calisthenics," exploring his improvised home.[57] He listens to the "idle" "song of the crickets," so like the "happy" "shout" of "children."[58] He drinks the "playful" wine of Napa; this "American cocktail" awakens in Stevenson a boyish Scottishness: "I am interested in all wines, and have been all my life, from the raisin wine that a schoolfellow kept secreted in his play-box up to my last discovery."[59] Stevenson wrote *The Silverado Squatters* in the Scottish Highlands and experiences California and Scotland as cross-pollinating daydreams. In the flyleaf of the copy he sent his California friends Virgil and Dora Norton Williams, he scrawled: "In the Pacific air it sprang," "[i]n the Scottish heather blossomed."[60]

Muir draws a more overtly causal connection between Caledonian child play and Californian mountaineering in his autobiography, *The Story of My Boyhood and Youth* (1913). Like Stevenson, he turns his attention as a boy to a desolate hill, a vestige of bygone Scotland, which rises above the urban bustle and "smooth cultivation" of his Lowlands home: "One of our best playgrounds was the famous old Dunbar Castle, to which King Edward fled after his defeat at Bannockburn.... We tried to see who could climb highest on the crumbling peaks and crags, and took chances that no cautious mountaineer would try."[61] Mountains and ruins, a robust California and a dead Scotland, his career as a conservationist and his boyhood play: the key to Muir's life, it would appear, can be found in Dunbar Castle. Invoking the logic of play as *paideia*, Muir recasts his child play as an adaptive and preparatory drive, a world-producing impulse; thus, his adult "mountaineering" was preordained, "destined," he insists, by his "rock-scrambling" as a boy, by "games of daring," "voyages around the world under the bed-clothing."[62] Lest anyone doubt that Muir views his child play as anticipatory of his life in California, he recounts how he used to "play[ ] with gunpowder" and "straw": "This we called making earthquakes."[63] Stevenson invokes the same developmental logic of child play in his autobiographical essay "Child's Play" (1878), claiming that children "anticipate and rehearse in their play hours" their adult "business."[64] Unlike Brontë, Muir and Stevenson believe in the future.

Just as death pervades their representations of California, so does play. The fledgling state's very landscape—with its "frequent earthquakes,"[65] "far likelier" than "rain,"[66] and its boom-and-bust construction, its "changeful and insecure" topography—is in play.[67] Noting the rapid growth of San Francisco, its "swiftness of increase" and "corresponding swiftness of destruction," Stevenson waxes philosophical: "In this busy, moving generation, we have all known cities to cover our boyish playgrounds, we have all started for a country walk and stumbled on a new suburb."[68] California's lack of fixity, the "unfinished look" of its "hills," the fact that it has "no very durable foundation," or the fact that the tremulous ground is literally in play, a *playground*, means that its past bumps awkwardly into its present, disorients residents and visitors alike, loosening their toehold in space and time. Stevenson deems the new city of South Vallejo "a blunder," an "untenable" "site," a historical stumble: "it has already begun to be deserted."[69] An unsettled and unsettling place, California provides Muir and Stevenson with mountaintop perches from which to spy, boyishly, on the vicissitudes and permutations of modernity. From the limits of the modern world, from the heave of its pacific breast, California puts unruly life in perspective: "mount[ing]" a "hill," Stevenson spots "the blue peak of Tamalpais" "stand[ing] sentry" "over the Golden Gates."[70] Again, with those *gates*!

Muir dedicates *My First Summer in the Sierra* to the organization he helped found: the Sierra Club, the "Defender of the People's Playground." Muir's Sierra brims with ludic energy, with "endless Godful play" of which "the lowlander never dreams."[71] Muir watches "[l]izards" "at their work and play," "as happy and companionable as the birds and squirrels."[72] "Butterflies," or "winged people" as he calls them, "are waltzing together high over head, seemingly in pure play and hilarious enjoyment," the "smaller flies" "danc[ing] in the sunbeams" "with no apparent lack of playful, joyful life."[73] An ouzel "indulge[s] in a little play"; a squirrel puts on a "harlequin gyrating show"; a "fat" "woodchuck who "cheerily" "pipes and whistles," proceeds "to fight and play"; even "the wild waters" rush past "in play."[74] These anthropomorphic animals, creatures plucked from children's fairytales, remind Muir of the "playful" "human-like horse" on his father's Wisconsin farm.[75] Just as Muir humanizes animals, he animalizes humans, refers affectionately to "baby boys," his Dunbar "playmates," as "wild beasts," and famously defines "Man" as "half animal, half angel."[76] Muir reframes the potentially alienating wildness of the natural world as mischievousness. He does not hide nature's deadliness from his readers. He parades it before them, depicts it walking hand-in-hand with play. He encourages his readers to confront death with boyish nonchalance, to let go their middle-class fears. Thus, were a man to wander into a hungry bear's territory and find himself *eaten*, "[t]his would be only fair play," Muir quotes a hunter as saying, "for we eat them."[77]

If the playground of California, the very ground on which Muir stands, seems in tectonic and meteorological play, "ever changing, ever beautiful," "pulling down, creating, destroying," then so does Muir's invocation of play, which, like California, is crisscrossed with fault lines and fissures.[78] While Muir's embrace of play might seem ideologically suspect to some readers, concealing a more complicated reality about the relationship between humans and the Earth, in truth, Muir, like Stevenson, is well aware of the conceptual instability and definitional multiplicity of play and the world-historical tensions it contains. Play is no panacea. Like Dickens, Tennyson, Arnold, and Brontë, indeed, like so many of the Victorian writers and thinkers discussed in this book, Muir and Stevenson pit play against play in the name of play. Idleness in particular functions for Muir and Stevenson as an ethical and political corrective to the consumerist and agonistic play impulses of the middle class. "Here," Muir declares, referring to the Sierra, "every day is a holiday, a jubilee ever sounding with serene enthusiasm."[79] "[N]ever, in all my life," Stevenson concurs, referring to another mountain range, "was [I] conscious of so strong an atmosphere of holiday."[80]

Stephen Arata makes the case that idleness functions for Stevenson not as "passivity" or "escapism," but as a "revolutionary energy," a renunciation of capitalist productivity.[81] Idleness is political. Its target, however, is not work or toil, but another logic of play: competition. Stevenson considers capitalist productivity a form of aggressive play, a sportive impulse to defeat an opponent: "The whole game of business is beggar thy neighbor; and though perhaps that game looks uglier when played at such close quarters and on so small a scale, it is none the more intrinsically inhumane for that."[82] In his essay, "An Apology for Idlers," Stevenson characterizes commercial modernity as a life lived always with one "eye on the medal."[83] Rather than "money-grubbing," he insists, "[t]here should be nothing so much a man's business as his amusements."[84] Muir and Stevenson set out to sever the psychological connection between leisure and competition, the utilitarian idea that the sole purpose of our hobbies, weekend excursions, touristic recreations, and lazy pastimes is to reenergize ourselves so that we return to work on Monday renewed, ready to compete in the capitalist game.

Some readers, I realize, will still find Muir and Stevenson's comparison of nature to a permanent holiday politically suspect, the reduction of nature to a pastoral toy, an object of touristic consumption. I would agree were it not for the fact that the holiday they imagine is *permanent*. A permanent holiday banishes capitalist competition from the universe, ushers in a future unstructured by workweeks and coffee breaks. It destroys human time. It exudes apocalypse. Competition, and hence capitalist time, all but disappears on Mount Saint Helena. Sport manifests itself only ironically in the "athletic opposition of the wind."[85] Stevenson notes that his neighbor, Rufe, a hunter who "loved all games" and who "lay long in bed in the morning," viewed "his own profession" "mainly as a sort of play."[86] Far from the "turbulent world," Mount Saint Helena—a "fine place, after all, for a wasted life to doze away in"—shatters one's sense of time, "hour melt[ing] insensibly into hour," "household duties" "dwindl[ing] into mere islets of business in a sea of sunny day-time."[87] Likewise, when Muir characterizes the Sierra as a place of "rest," a place he would like to stay for "all eternity," it is unclear whether Yosemite is a vacation destination or a sepulcher.[88] It is both. What dies in the Sierra, however, and lies buried, is the predatory instinct in mankind, the nagging need to win the contest, to triumph over others: "Up here all the world's prizes seem nothing."[89] Muir was opposed to competitive mountaineering, Cohen explains, to hunting, and to the "so-called sport" of fishing, which he likened to "church-goers" "pass[ing] the time fishing in baptismal fonts."[90] Muir is haunted by memories of "Yankee" boys hunting birds in Wisconsin; this "shameful sport" or "gory business," as he terms it, consisted of killing as many "unprotected" birds as possible, tearing off their heads, thrusting the severed heads into "bulging," "blood-stained" "game-bags," emblems of burgeoning manhood, of future moneybags.[91] The only hints of competition in Muir's Sierra are muscular junipers flexing their limbs "like stubborn wrestlers."[92]

Buell worries that Muir's rhetorical transformation of "the great outdoors" into "a vast playground" "threaten[s] to pull [him] back toward homocentrism."[93] It is true that Muir can sound at times like the overeager author of a guidebook for mountain climbers, pointing out "killer" hiking trails. Cohen is more forgiving. Muir's embrace of the "tourist business," he argues, was motivated by political pragmatism, a strategic desire to displace more insidious business interests: the water, "timber, agricultural, and sheep interests" eyeing Yosemite and its neighboring valleys.[94] Muir's mythologization of California as a cosmic playground was meant as a potent counternarrative to the state's Gold Rush reputation as a gritty arena of ruthless competition, where American masculinity tests its mettle. Muir wielded the logic of wholesome play as an ideological shield in his war with capitalists over the future of California's wilderness; hence, his defensive equation of nature with modernity, with the rhetoric of progress. He was not always successful. In his losing battle with former San Francisco mayor James Phelan over the fate of Hetch Hetchy Valley, which developers succeeded in damming and flooding, Muir suffered the indignity of seeing the logic of recreational play turned against him. In a 1909 letter to the *California Weekly*, Phelan paints Muir and his fellow Sierra Club members as leisure-class oppressors of the "toiling masses."[95] In a rhetorical flourish that must have irked Scottish Muir to no end, especially considering his opposition to hunting, millionaire Phelan compares the conservationists to "self-indulgent" English "fox hunters."[96] One San Francisco political cartoonist even depicted Muir in a dress, a bearded and broom-wielding maid up to her ankles in water, frantically "sweeping back the flood" of progress.[97]

Muir's detractors were correct in detecting something "unmanly" in his worship of nature; they misdiagnosed it, however, as femininity, European effeteness, and antimodern backwardness. The Otherness that Muir cultivates in opposition to Anglo-American manliness is Highlands boyishness. The nature-boy is Muir's new symbol of the future. Muir's autobiography concludes with his graduation from college. Boyhood *is* his life. An implicit critique of Frederick Jackson Turner's classic 1893 formulation that the American frontier is "productive" of a heroically "anti-social" "individualism," of unfettered manliness, Muir's nature writings advance an alternative wilderness paradigm.[98] "Homocentrism" is not the word to describe it. "Puerocentrism" comes closer: a shamelessly juvenile experience of the outdoors, a refusal to grow up. Hence, Muir's opposition to the type of rational recreation, the "utility of rest," advocated by Frederick Law Olmsted and other park designers, who "made recreation," Cohen argues, "the handmaiden of a growing urban industrial civilization," whereby weekend warriors emerged from the mountains "refreshed," ready "to do more duty, more business."[99] As we shall see, boyish caprice functions for Muir and Stevenson as the philosophical and ethical corrective to manly rationality.

The Boyish Sublime

Aesthetic philosophers traditionally align the beautiful with the feminine, the sublime with the masculine. In their Romantic representations of California, Muir and Stevenson complicate this tired binary by revealing the hidden presence within the sublime of another aesthetic player, a third sexual category, neither masculine nor feminine: a culturally and historically marginal figure who is Other to the manly mindfulness of the sublime and thus central, paradoxically, to its psychological operations. I am referring to the boy. Though male, the boy is excluded from the inner sanctum of masculinity, from its epistemological profundity and majesty; he lacks, too, the pleasing elegance and refinement traditionally associated with the feminine, though he is occasionally (if begrudgingly) relegated to the beautiful under our binary system. The boy is the sublime's other Other. Like Stevenson's Hyde, the boy is an unreasonable baby-beast, an arrested or transitional development, the horrifying state of being not-quite-ready, which every man—every middle-class man—feels compelled to deny in himself, against which he defines himself. Defenders of maligned boyhood, Muir and Stevenson recognize the danger of Calibanizing the boy within, hiding him, stunting or alienating him. As we have seen, they wholeheartedly celebrate the aesthetic and political efficacy of nonaggressive boyhood, of a boyhood distinct from protomanhood: from the eye-gouging, prepubescent masculinity advocated by evolutionary psychologist Granville Stanley Hall, for instance, in the previous chapter.

In the eighteenth and nineteenth centuries, expressions of masculinity reach their most ethereal and belletristic heights, pulsate most poignantly with metaphysical and epistemological profundity, in the concept of the sublime. Muir and Stevenson force the sublime to confront its unacknowledged boyishness, the suppression of which is integral to the *work* of the sublime, just as the master is beholden to the slave for his sense of mastery. Indeed, the English word "boy" originally meant "slave" or "servant." Positioning his California writings squarely within canonical representations of the sublime, Stevenson informs his reader in *The Silverado Squatters* that "Mount Saint Helena . . . is the Mont Blanc of one section of the Californian Coast Range."[100]

In his *Philosophical Enquiry* (1757), Burke makes a distinction between the pleasurable sensation produced by the beautiful and the "delight" produced by the sublime: a delight "blended with no small uneasiness," a bit of "terror," "which always produces delight when it does not press too close."[101] A delight that "turns" on "pain and danger," on its "idea," as opposed to its reality, the sublime triggers the exciting recoil of "self-preservation": the vertigo one experiences on the observation deck of a skyscraper, the thrilling thought of leaping to one's death, one's correspondent bodily refusal.[102] According to Burke, sublimity builds masculinity. One inoculates oneself against emasculation or destruction by pondering emasculating or destructive phenomena. One could even say that the subject *plays* at pain and danger. He flirts with powerlessness, just as the little boy in Freud's Oedipal narrative confects a sense of self, a defensively masculine identity, out of the *idea* of castration: his fear of the castrating father with whom he competes for his mother's affection. Burke compares the experience of the sublime to a powerless boy's fearful contemplation of, and erotic shudder of identification with, superior masculine power:

> Look at a man, or any other animal of prodigious strength, and what is your idea before reflection? Is it that this strength will be subservient to you, to your ease, to your pleasure, to your interest in any sense? No; the emotion you feel is, lest this enormous strength should be employed to the purposes of rapine and destruction.[103]

Hence, "young persons little acquainted with the world," Burke writes, "who have not been used to approach men in power, are commonly struck with an awe which takes away the free use of their faculties": "*When I prepared my seat in the street* (says Job) *the young men saw me, and hid themselves.*"[104] The psychosexual sensation of the sublime is akin to a boy's fearful delight in the presence of "*dread majesty*": a fleeting mental flirtation with castration followed by recoil into defensive masculinity; identification, in other words, with the threatening object, whether it be avalanche or hurricane or God. The sublime inoculates men against their boyishness. Integral to the workings of the sublime, its key player, the figure of the boy is at the same time its eternally abject Other.

Kant dematerializes the sublime in *The Critique of Judgment* (1790), transforms it from the idea of a potentially emasculating *thing* into the intellectual experience of a potentially emasculating Idea. He claims "no sensible form"—"the wide ocean," for example, "disturbed by the storm"—"can contain the sublime properly so-called."[105] However, the psychosexual vocabulary, the Burkean logic of inoculation against abject boyhood, remains unchanged. Hence, the "irresistibility" of conceptual "might," Kant insists, our fearful delight in the face of boundless Idea, "make[s] us recognize our own impotence."[106] The "humanity in our person remains unhumiliated," however, even "though the individual might have to submit to this domination."[107] Although he remains just as central to its psychological operations, the ludic boy recedes further into the conceptual shadows in the Kantian sublime, elbowed aside by the manly work of Reason; the sublime, Kant proclaims, can "be regarded as emotion,—not play, but earnest in the exercise of the Imagination."[108] When Coleridge or Shelley stand before Mont Blanc, feel its deep rumble expanding their interiority, we invariably catch snatches of boyish play on the wind, always distant, tremors from the past, accentuating in its very faintness the poet's newfound manliness, the intellectual work of the sublime. Coleridge imagines "wild goats sporting round the eagle's nest! / Ye eagles, play-mates of the mountain-storm!"[109] Shelley asks: "Is this the scene / Where the old Earthquake-daemon taught her young / Ruin? Were these their toys?"[110] The disembodied voice of the boy is far away, echoed in the antics of an imagined animal, detected in an anthropomorphic avalanche. His voice is never the poet's. He is fodder for the poet's experience of the sublime, his internal Other, just as Wordsworth's "sense sublime" at Tintern Abbey emerges from the displacement of his "thoughtless youth" by "something far more deeply interfused."[111]

Muir and Stevenson experience the sublime as boys do, not as "deeply interfused" Wordsworthian men. No sublimation occurs; they make no effort to distance or hide the boyish nature of their flirtation with the overpowering force of nature, to inoculate themselves against humiliation, to deny their own undignified boyish excitement. When Stevenson's train enters otherworldly California and plunges "through a sea of mountain forests," which "dropp[ed] thousands of feet toward the far sea-level," "not I only, but all the passengers on board," he recalls, "bawled like school boys."[112] It is difficult to imagine Burke *bawling*. Muir, too, upon seeing Yosemite for the first time, its "sublime mountain beauty," "shouted and gesticulated in a wild burst of ecstasy," "puzzl[ing]" his St Bernard and comically startling a "brown bear," who "ran away very fast, tumbling over the tops of the tangled manzanita bushes in his haste."[113] When did Kant ever scream like a lunatic? Muir and Stevenson reunite the sublime with its repressed childishness. This boyish sublime might lack the self-respect and mindfulness of Burke's and Kant's more manly versions, but that is only because it is devoid of castration anxiety or fear of humiliation. In the boyish sublime, the subject is always already "unmanned." Burke's manly self-consciousness and Kant's professorial self-regard give way to the boyish forgetfulness typically induced by games. In lieu of a threatening father or a bosomy pre-Oedipal mother, California's mountainous topography becomes a Caledonian playmate in a game of Becoming, creation *as* childish destruction. Here nature is akin to the Heraclitean cosmos: the confluence, Mihai Spariosu explains, of the "Homeric notion of play as agon," "strife" as "a fundamental cosmic principle," and the "arbitrary, spontaneous and unpredictable character" of "child's play."[114] Hence, "[l]ifetime (*aion*)," Heraclitus proclaims, "is a child at play, moving pieces in a game."[115] There is no winning in this game, for "[t]he river where you set your foot just now is gone—those waters giving way to this, now this."[116]

The Yosemite Creek strides "bravely forward" to a cliff of "shining granite," over whose translucent lip it tumbles "half a mile" down "to another world, to be lost in the Merced, where climate, vegetation, inhabitants, all are different."[117] Muir is standing beside a 2,000-foot waterfall. The boundless vista beneath his feet, the suicidal silence of the creek, the moan of foam below, the tendrils twitching on the ledge, toward windy nothingness: the scene from *My First Summer in the Sierra* is undeniably sublime. What makes it an expression of the boyish sublime, however, is what happens next:

> I took off my shoes and stockings and worked my way cautiously down alongside the rushing flood, keeping my feet and hands pressed firmly on the polished rock. . . . I had expected that the sloping apron would terminate with the perpendicular wall of the valley, and that from the foot of it, where it is less steeply inclined, I should be able to lean far enough out to see the forms and behavior of the fall all the way down to the bottom. Tufts of artemisia were growing in the clefts of the rock near by, and I filled my mouth with the bitter leaves, hoping they might help to prevent giddiness . . . Here I obtained a perfectly free view down into the heart of the snowy, chanting throng of comet-like streamers, into which the body of the fall soon separates.[118]

Up to his calves in icy water, Muir places his toes at the smooth juncture of creek and cataract, the cosmos egging him on, gravity coaxing him forward. He leans over, peers down the half-mile-long throat of his annihilation. The "nerve-straining" "exhilaration" causes him to "start[ ] up" in the "night in a nervous tremor" days afterward, "and again and again I dreamed I was rushing through the air above a glorious avalanche of water and rocks" in "glorious death."[119] In Muir's California, the person most receptive to sublime experience is the wily boy. In *The Mountains of California*, he clambers to the top of a 100-foot pine tree in the middle of a windstorm, "feasting" "on the delicious fragrance . . . streaming past," watching his "resiny" neighbors "bend forward in concentric curves," lashed "like sea-waves" in "silvery splendor."[120] The scene's sublimity arises precisely from its utter foolishness, though confident Muir, like all reckless children, insists his "tree-top" perch was "safe." In the midst of this storm, hundreds of miles from the Pacific coast, Muir suddenly smells the ocean, and is reminded of a moment in Florida, a decade earlier, when, for the first time in nineteen years, he encountered "a sea-breeze," "which at once awakened and set free a thousand dormant associations, and made me a boy again in Scotland, as if all the intervening years had been annihilated."[121] This is the boyish sublime.

Stevenson experiences it on Mount Saint Helena, coastal California's answer to Mont Blanc. Having chosen the mountain for its situation above the "poisonous fogs" that nearly killed him in San Francisco, Stevenson awakens one chilly morning to discover a "vast fog ocean" has crept into the Napa Valley, transforming hills into islands, having "already caught the sun," wrapping Mount Saint Helena in "huge" "stationary" "waves."[122] A hundred feet below, the mountain lies "buried" "in salt and poisonous air," the entire world having disappeared; only "a thin scattered fringe of bluffs" remains "unsubmerged" across the valley; a "dead pine beckon[s] out of the spray like the arm of a drowning man."[123] Concerned about his health but also thrilled at the prospect of being chased by the fog, Stevenson "ascended the mountainside" beyond the reach of his adversary, his deadly playmate grasping at his ankles:

> The imagination loves to trifle with what is not. Had this been indeed the deluge, I should have felt more strongly, but the emotion would have been similar in kind. I played with the idea, as the child flees in delighted terror from the creations of his fancy. The look of the thing helped me. And when at last I began to flee up the mountain, it was indeed partly to escape from the raw air that kept me coughing, but it was also part in play.

He imagines the fog is "seawater": "[W]ith what a plunge of reverberating thunder would it have rolled upon its course, disemboweling mountains and deracinating pines!" It is a moving scene, so un-Burkean in its embrace of unmanliness. California reveals its true face to the dying Stevenson: a cosmic child extending its hand in apocalyptic fellowship. It "came so beautifully," he writes, "that my first thought was of welcome."[124]

The Boy Who Cried "Sheep"

Does this image of California as a world in play, an idea first popularized by Muir and Stevenson, reinforce conservative talking points about the cultural immaturity, the Peter-Panism, of the so-called Left Coast? From an ecocritical perspective, how useful is Muir and Stevenson's ludic paradigm? Is it another example of the "sentimental pastoralism" of which Leo Marx famously warns, wherein the "tendency to idealize rural ways" becomes an escapist "impediment to clarity of thought"?[125] Concerned that Muir will be accused of "pastoral ideology," Terry Gifford preemptively rechristens Muir a "post-pastoral" thinker for the twenty-first century: a writer who anticipates current critiques of pastoralism.[126] While I sympathize with Gifford's protective impulse, I question whether Muir enjoyed such prescience. I worry, too, that suturing the prefix *post* to *pastoral*, as in *postadolescent* or *postpubescent*, equates theoretical sophistication with movement beyond a psychologically immature state. While Muir certainly believed in progress, his sense of futurity is interoperable with the cultivation of boyhood, with the modern subject's willingness to outgrow his manly capitalist impulses, to become immature once again. In his effort to redeem Muir, Gifford glosses over the "pushy adolescent impetuousness" of which Muir's contemporaries, Buell reminds us, often accused him.[127]

Just as Muir invokes the boy to critique the Romantic sublime from within the sublime, he invokes the boy to critique pastoral false consciousness from within, rather than from a position of presentist anteriority. Muir presents himself quite literally as a failed *pastor* or capricious shepherd. Muir intensely disliked sheep, the domestic variety, describing them as "a horde of hoofed locusts."[128] He also loathed shepherds, referring to them as "arch destroyers" and "*muttoneers.*"[129] Yet Muir first encountered the Sierra in the guise of a shepherd, having been hired in 1869 by sheep rancher and former forty-niner Pat Delaney to "drive 2050 sheep to the headwaters of the Merced and Tuolumne rivers" in Yosemite.[130] He played at being a shepherd. Muir's puckish refusal to play the part of shepherd well, to allow meadows and forests to be deformed into pasturage, was his means of bringing justice to nature, fair play to pastoral ideology. Muir repeatedly exposes the violence of pasture-making, of the pastoral life. He rejects the idyllic image of the shepherd as caretaker. The bad shepherd, he insists, who abandons his sheep, and who delights in their destruction, cares more. Muir's vision of California takes shape in this rejection.

According to Starr, in the wake of the Drought of 1862–1864, "sheep-raising" began to replace the once "flourishing" "cattle economy" of Northern California.[131] By 1876, 7.7 million sheep dotted California's Central Valley. To escape the sweltering summer, shepherds drove their flocks to the Sierra to grow fat on mountain grasses, which meant that "the wild gardens and meadows" were "trampl[ed]" "almost out of existence."[132] "In order to make easy paths and to improve the pastures," the sheepmen, Muir explains, set fires "everywhere to burn off the old logs and underbrush," destroying countless sequoia and "young trees."[133] Shepherds were responsible for "more than 90 per cent. of all destructive fires that [swept] the woods." Muir presents his 1869 hike to Yosemite as his road to Damascus. His nature writings are conversion narratives, only he turns his back on the Good Shepherd and turns the metaphor of the flock on its head. Describing the devastation wrought by sheep on the meadows at Shadow Lake, Muir laments, "[t]he money-changers were in the temple."[134] California's sheep remind Muir of materialistic Scottish Lowlanders. They look like fat pensioners or self-absorbed consumers. Their ovine invasion of the Sierra assaults his Highlands fantasy. He draws a sharp distinction between wild sheep, on the one hand, "bold" and "clean," true "mountaineer[s]" and "highlanders," who live in the Sierra's "highland castles," and his own "helpless" domestic sheep, on the other hand, who are "ruffled and dirty," mere "half alive" "lowlanders."[135] A domestic sheep, Muir concludes, "can hardly be called an animal"; it is "misbegotten," "semi-manufactured."[136]

We tend to think of Muir as the quintessential conservationist. What repulses him about sheep, however, is precisely their self-preservative instinct, their stubborn refusal, for instance, to cross a shallow creek. By trampling mountain meadows into tamed pastures or "artificial lawns," the sheep destroy nature's volatility and ephemerality, plucking it from the fluctuations of the cosmos.[137] Muir wants to preserve the Sierra, yes, but what he aims to preserve is creative destruction itself, cosmic caprice. Like their flocks, shepherds are motivated by self-preservation, by capitalist acquisition, the desire to arrest the aleatory motions of nature, to eternalize profit. These "destroying angels" want to banish death from life.[138] They kill death, for "[a]ll sheepmen," Muir explains, "carry strychnine to kill coyotes, bears, and panthers."[139] Sheep are bleating dollar bills. At night beside the orange crackle of the campfire, while Muir, their supposed protector, sinks into his Highlands death sleep, his paranoid

Lowlands flock remains vigilant: "the thousands of sheep eyes glow," a "bed of diamonds."[140] Humankind's "deadly habit of endless hoarding for the future," Muir laments, "smothers all real life," and reveals its lack of confidence in its own improvisational abilities to live off the land.[141] A bad shepherd, a Heathcliffian pastor, Muir thinks more like a wolf than a man, fantasizing, at one point, about seeing "hundreds" of "silly" sheep "gain the romantic fate of being swept into Yosemite over the highest waterfall in the world."[142] "Aside from money profit," Muir muses, "one would rather herd wolves than sheep."[143] In *A Thousand-Mile Walk to the Gulf* (1916), Muir confesses that he has "little sympathy for the selfish propriety of civilized man": "[I]f a war of races should occur between the wild beasts and Lord Man, I would be tempted to sympathize with the bears."[144] This is the form that Muir's pastoralism takes: it is the act of unleashing within one's heart a wolf or bear to creep amongst one's flock.

Apples from the Sea

"One thing," Stevenson insists in *The Amateur Emigrant*, "is not to be learned in Scotland, and that is the way to be happy."[145] He eventually does learn to be happy in Scotland, of course, an ocean away in California, where he frees himself at last from Lowlands respectability, and sinks into the Highlands embrace of Mount Saint Helena. If California's Scottish mountains remind Stevenson and Muir of the sea, "a sea of mountain forests," it is because the earth's uncanny oceans simultaneously separate them from home and link them to it. A reflective surface, a funhouse mirror, the ocean doubles the cosmos, makes one feel at home in all places. Clinging to the top of a wind-lashed pine in the Sierra, Muir detects in a pocket of Pacific storm the seaside scents of his boyhood. Likewise, Stevenson's first intimation of his new Californian home, of the sublime play of its unsteady ground, comes on "the moving desert of seas" on his Atlantic voyage out: "And yet this waste was part a playground for the stormy petrel; and on the least tooth of reef, outcropping in a thousand miles of unfathomable ocean, the gull makes its home."[146] Stevenson watches the ship's children, "as thick as thieves at a fair," play unself-consciously on the lurching deck, "while their elders were still ceremoniously manœuvering on the outskirts of acquaintance."[147] Like seabirds, children make a home for themselves in a world in play. Muir recounts a similar scene from his 1849 crossing, only, eleven years old at the time, he belongs to the ludic band: "[W]e were on deck every day, not in the least seasick," "playing games with other boys," "in stormy weather rejoicing in sympathy with the big curly-topped waves."[148] The California that Muir and Stevenson invent, the California that persists to this day, is no Eden. It is no world at play. No, the fruit that grows in a world in play, on the oscillating surface of the cosmos, tastes more sublime than any fruit in Eden. I conclude with an image from Muir's Dunbar childhood. A schooner "loaded with apples" founders one gray day on the craggy shore outside town: "I remember," Muir writes, "visiting the battered fragments . . . and finding unpitiful sport in rushing into the spent waves and picking up the red-cheeked fruit from the frothy, seething foam."[149] Standing in the North Sea, Muir bites into his briny spoils. It is his first taste of California.

CHAPTER 5

Wilde's Folly

> I am afraid I play no outdoor games at all, except dominoes. I have sometimes played dominoes outside French cafés.
> —Oscar Wilde[1]

Lawn Tennis and Strawberries

To the dismay of his fellow undergraduates, Oscar Wilde made no effort to conceal his disdain for athletics, for the manly games that absorbed the time and fired the imagination of so many Oxford students. The cult of the athlete—playing sports, watching them, engaging in heated debates about them—was central to the late Victorian Oxford experience and to the university's Hellenized curriculum. Sport determined one's place in the pecking order and foretold success in life. Wilde certainly did not lack the capacity to be sporty. Tall and powerfully built, he could be persuaded on occasion, biographer Richard Ellmann notes, to do "a little boxing" or "paddle[ ] a canoe."[2] Provisioned with whiskey, Wilde even enjoyed "fishing" and "hare-shooting," but confessed to William Ward in an 1877 letter: "mountain-climbing is not my *forte*."[3] Another friend encouraged him to join the crew team, from which he was promptly ejected for ignoring the coxswain's barked orders, rowing in "Greek fashion" at a leisurely pace: "I don't see the use of going down backwards to Iffley every evening," he sighed.[4] Drawn to Ruskin's denunciation of the agonistic impulse, of the "fruitless slashing of the river," of the self-indulgent "hit[ting]" of "a ball with a bat," Wilde joined the Slade Professor of History of Art in building a new country road in Ferry Hinksey, planting flowers along its border, accompanying his hero around the construction site, his wheelbarrow heaped with aesthetic dirt.[5]

Unlike Ruskin, however, Wilde never railed against sport. He delighted, instead, in playing sports in such a way, or observing the play of others in such a manner, that the ennobling heat of competition, the pitch of manly battle, was—to the frustration of sports enthusiasts—cooled, the game's intent thwarted, the sportive experience recast in an alien and unsporty light. Watching a star runner train for a race, for instance, Wilde announced to his fellow undergraduates: "His left leg is a Greek poem."[6] Wilde played *badly*, in a manner that smacked of studied or ironic incompetence, thereby making others self-conscious about the play activity they took so seriously and the sportive ethic structuring modern consciousness. All these years we have been told—and we have eagerly believed it, for we have an emotional investment in associating freedom with play—that Wilde is play's patron saint, a ludic martyr in a tragically unplayful age. The truth is far more complicated. Wilde's real sin was not that he appeared too playful but that he did not take play seriously enough in a Victorian epoch steeped in play. His unforgivable crime in the eyes of his contemporaries? He was a spoilsport: he spoiled sport in the name of play. Rather than break the rules of the game, however, Wilde laughed at them, a raucous and demystifying laughter, inducing in the world's players, his middle-class audience, embarrassed snickers at the seriousness of their own play. To a competitive middle class that screamed "Win! Win at any cost!" Wilde responded, "It is far more fun to lose." Hence, in *A Woman of No Importance* (1893), the dandiacal Lord Illingworth insists: "To win back my youth . . . there is nothing I wouldn't do—except take exercise, get up early, or be a useful member of the community."[7] Likewise, in *The Importance of Being Earnest* (1895), Algernon complains that "[t]here's such a lot of beastly competition about."[8] As with Stevenson and Muir, Wilde's reluctance to win, his visceral distaste for competition, is more than ludic laziness or a decadent aversion to expending energy. Even games that Wilde plays well, games he wins, he refuses to take seriously, finding a way to undermine his sporty authority after the fact, rendering clownish that middle-class hunger for victory. Writing to Reginald Harding in July 1876, Wilde draws his friend's attention to the bloody smudges on his stationery: "These horrid red marks are strawberries, which I am eating in basketfuls, during intervals of lawn tennis, at which I am awfully good."[9]

This is the essence of Wildean playfulness: he has fun at play's expense, at the expense of the intractable logic of contest. Wilde played the game of life because he had no choice, because he fully understood, and urged his readers to accept the idea, that the modern world is a world in play, a world embroiled, in his eyes, in sportive combat. If Wilde could not step outside this world, situate himself in a space anterior to competition, for such a space did not exist, he could, at the very least, refuse to play well. As we shall see, this refusal to take play seriously from *within* play, this acrobatics of mind, contortion of soul, is the psychological foundation on which Wilde builds his aestheticism, ethics, politics, and eroticism. Wilde's intellectual challenge, then, and his spiritual one, was to find a way to play noncompetitively in an intrinsically competitive world, in which all attempts to position oneself against agon, even ironic, mischievous, apathetic, or self-destructive attempts, can easily be construed as agonistic themselves, as adversarial efforts to contest the logic of contest. The starry-eyed fantasy of outplaying or defeating the logic of contest, a logic constitutive of middle-class capitalist consciousness, only bolsters, in the end, that very logic. Agon feeds on critique. Competition welcomes competitors. One awakens to the nightmare one escapes by awakening. If Wilde's philosophical mission appears difficult, that is because it is.

I realize that the reading of Wilde that follows may rankle those readers who have a vested interest in preserving the canonical image of Wilde as ludic critic of Victorian earnestness. Because Wilde has become a symbol, over the years, of anti-Victorianism, of the nascent stirrings of twentieth-century thought, even of the birth-shriek of postmodernity, we must ask ourselves whether his purported Otherness to the Victorian period, an Otherness we foster and feed, is not simply our means—his homoerotic dandyism, his unassimilable Irishness, his anti-Philistine cosmopolitanism—of "Othering" the Victorians, contrasting the supposed brittleness and paucity of their play, their ludic timidity and inelasticity, with his (and our) more sophisticated playfulness. Identifying with Wilde makes us feel modern in the face of the Victorian. Critical treatments of Wilde's life and works, in fact, sometimes reveal more about a twenty-first-century critic's emotional and ideological stance toward the Victorian period than about Wilde. When I present my map of the Victorian world in play, for instance, at various academic gatherings, trace for my audience the pervasiveness of this trope in Victorian representations of modernity, shine a light upon play's totalizing tendency, two or three people invariably put up a fight. They attempt to name some Victorian category, or some Victorian idea, or some Victorian impulse, which they insist is *intrinsically* antithetical to play, something that proves that not *all* the world, surely, was or could be viewed as "in play," a toehold of not-play on my slippery slope, an ember of unplay in my merciless storm, some remnant of antiplay that escapes the sweep of my net. I understand their frustration. As I noted in the Introduction, the world in play is a disturbing idea. The experience of writing this book has caused me to lose faith in play, a concept I once viewed somewhat naïvely as an innocuous and relatively happy one. At the same time, however, the experience has increased my respect for the protean concept of play, for the conceptual power it wields so self-effacingly.

If play is more monstrous in its dimensions than I ever imagined, it is also more fascinating, more in need of scrutiny and analysis than ever before. Our twenty-first-century impulse to locate a conceptual "outside" to play in the Victorian period, to clear some solid ground on which the bogeyman of Victorian hostility to play might be kept alive—telling us, to our mischievous delight, to get off his lawn—is not motivated, as I initially thought, by a desire to protect the Victorian period from the totalizing concept of the world in play. On the contrary, it is motivated by a sentimental desire to protect the concept of play from the taint of Victorianism, to preserve the reassuring illusion that the Victorians had, on some irreducible, visceral level, a problem with play, that play was under assault, even if obliquely or faintly, during the Victorian period, and that we who have no fear of play, who smirk at Victorian phobias, and who are more playful than they could ever be, are thereby more free. It is because we love play so much, cherish the intellectual freedom it represents, or that its most radical spokesman, Oscar Wilde, represents, that we flinch at the notion that the Victorians inhabited a world in play. We find it painful to accept the fact that the late Victorian criminal justice system, a repository of Philistinism, bigotry, and cruelty, *outplayed* Wilde.

Guess which Victorian phenomenon is cited most frequently as antithetical to play, the concept that colleagues present to me—in snatches of interpanel conversation over bad coffee and worse cookies—as incontrovertible proof that play had, in the end, its conceptual limitations, an outside, from which certain Victorians ruthlessly assailed it. What magic thread, when tugged, unravels the world in play, proves that play was, for all its resilience, under attack in the Age of Victoria, in need, therefore, of our protection? It is *earnestness*, the middle-class moral seriousness, the self-important gravity, that Wilde mocks so deliciously, so devastatingly, in nearly all of his works. Yes, earnestness, I am repeatedly informed, is the Victorian beachhead against which play impotently crashes, the category that resists being subsumed in play, that reminds play at every turn of its mortality. A vampire at dawn, my little world in play, I am told, bursts into flames of earnestness.

If only it were true! I have no love for the world in play. I do not deny that Wilde poked fun at earnestness. Earnestness is one of his favorite targets. But let us consider Wilde's definition of earnestness, voiced again by Lord Illingworth, his epigrammatic mouthpiece, in *A Woman of No Importance*: "One should never take sides in anything, Mr. Kelvil. Taking sides is the beginning of sincerity, and earnestness follows shortly afterwards, and the human being becomes a bore."[10] The fruit of contest, of pitting one side against another, earnestness can be traced to the agonistic impulse, to the need to win, to prevail morally or intellectually over others. In Wilde's eyes, earnestness is moral athleticism, the sport of Puritans. Etymologically, "earnest" means "struggle," a contest with self, with temptation, a wrestling match with devils. Earnestness necessitates taking sides, the seriously boring act of rowing backwards to Iffley in order to outpace a rival and equally preposterous team of rowers. The anticlimactic Iffley functions as a metaphor here for the moralistic striving for truth, the antisocial, tasteless pleasure of being "the best." In his classic reading of Victorian earnestness, Walter Houghton—no play theorist he—highlights the agonistic dimension to the Victorians' etymologically perceptive cult of moral earnestness: "Unless you are struggling, unless you are fighting with yourselves," John Henry Newman informs his flock, "you are no followers of those who 'through many tribulations entered into the kingdom of God.'"[11] Houghton quotes Arthur Stanley's account of Thomas Arnold: "Even slight acquaintances were 'struck by his absolute wrestling with evil, so that like St. Paul he seemed to be battling with the wicked one.'" What is Charles Kingsley's so-called muscular Christianity but a literalization of the athletic trope that structures Victorian moral earnestness? Kingsley simply demands correspondence between the inward and outward lives of men, insists that a young man's physique be as winning, as competitive, as his soul. Give Kingsley his due: for all his ideological crudity, he refused to deny the fact that earnestness is, at its core, sport.

The enemies aligned against Wilde, the enemies who made their move in the winter of 1895, led of course by the pugilistic Marquis of Queensberry, were not the forces of *unplay*. No, the earnestness that bore down on him, that sought his defeat, and that danced in the street when the terrible verdict was read, was sport. During his boyhood in Ireland, Wilde played on the beach one halcyon summer with another boy, Edward Carson, the same Carson who would convince an English jury, four decades later, that Queensberry had been justified in accusing Wilde of homosexual offenses. In the words of Michael MacLiammoir, "Oscar probably upset Edward's sandcastle."[12]

Playing to Lose

"The Soul of Man Under Socialism" (1890) is Wilde's most politically ambitious effort to diagnose and transcend the agonistic impulse in modern life. He imagines a postcapitalist world devoid of "the stress of competition," of "that sordid necessity of living for others," of subordinating one's personality to the fight to best one's neighbors in a conformist "struggle for place."[13] Once machines liberate workers from the degradation of labor, Wilde prophecies, and once socialism frees the rich from their poisonous and jealous thirst for "gain," everyone will become artists, cultivators of "delightful leisure," of pure individuality, a subjectivity defined by *being* rather than by *having*.[14] Echoing Arnold in *Culture and Anarchy*, Wilde argues that capitalism does not merely pit individuals against each other in a soul-crushing death-match: even worse, it pits the poor against the rich, the middle class against the working class, producing a tyrannical and vulgar form of class group-think, socioeconomic rivalry between selfish, money-grubbing teams. Wilde points to the angry mob, with its "ready-made paving-stones," its thirst for revenge, as proof that conformism *is* inherently agonistic, and that the need to belong to a team is, at its root, a proprietary and territorial drive, an aggressively anti-individualistic need to defeat Otherness: "the rage" of the "mushroom against" the "orchid."[15] "[D]emocracy," he insists, "means simply the bludgeoning of the people by the people for the people."[16] Hence, true individualism, as opposed to bourgeois egoism, is antithetical to class-based competition, the violence of the herd: "A red rose is not selfish because it wants to be a red rose," Wilde writes, but "[i]t would be horribly selfish if it wanted all the other flowers in the garden to be both red and roses."[17] Wilde envisions an anticommunitarian communism, where people have no desire to compete with difference, or to enforce uniformity, and where energy is not "wasted in friction," the garden growing tall with unclassifiable, individualistic flowers, artistic self-creations, oblivious to popular opinion. Artists play for no team. "[W]andering wonder-makers," they charm the world with their "vagrant personalities," fascinate us with their "marvellous," "flower-like" disinclination to "argue or dispute," so self-absorbed and peaceful are they.[18] That is the message of Wilde's artistic hero and peacemaker, Christ: "Be thyself."[19]

If Wilde seems to undermine his anticapitalist polemic with his irrepressible insouciance and flippancy, or with occasional eruptions of dandiacal boredom (as Jeff Nunokawa might say) at having to contemplate a thing as vulgar as politics, it is because he knows that nothing is as agonistic, and hence as passionately earnest, as polemic.[20] Thus, he punctuates his serious topic, for the lives of the poor are at stake, with amusing analogies and "lexical manoeuverings," which border, in the words of Lawrence Danson, on "silliness," and which seem, for all Wilde's wisdom, "breezily inconsequential."[21] Adopting a morally serious tone in a critique of competition, however, undermines that critique, Wilde knows, even more than inappropriate bursts of glibness, for earnestness is rooted in competition. At the level of content as well as form, then, Wilde struggles in "The Soul of Man Under Socialism" with the will to struggle, with the seriousness constitutive of, demanded of, the modern agonistic self, the modern political thinker. His essay is not merely a critique of capitalism; it is a critique of polemic, of the Carlylean school of discursive warfare, which arises from the same discordant corner of the soul as capitalism. Thus, Wilde critiques the middle-class race to "accumulat[e] things," which destroy one's individualism, make one a slave to "endless industry," even as he strategically dilutes the polemical power of his own argument with his jaunty generalizations, with his bracing refusal to sentimentalize suffering, with effete bursts of wit, and with the self-indulgent and self-parodic manner in which he airs pet grievances against art critics, the press, and the world's Philistines.[22] If Wilde seems to be playing the game of polemic badly, feigning obliviousness to the tonal and moral conventions required of political writers, it is because he knows that being too convincing means winning the very contest he does not wish to win. Wilde's famous assertion that "a truth ceases to be true when more than one person believes in it" suggests a reluctance on his part to convince others to join his side, for taking sides is precisely the problem.[23] He does not want disciples; he wants every individual to be his or her own Christ. Because wanting others to adopt one's worldview is an inherently competitive desire, Wilde—in his ongoing struggle against struggle, his unsporty sportiveness—finds himself in the awkward intellectual position of "always [having to] be a little improbable," of making it difficult if not impossible for his power-hungry middle-class audience to take him seriously. He refuses to give them discursive tools with which to strengthen and expand their industrious thoughts, even as he attempts to inspire in them a noncompetitive spirit, laughter at their own earnest desire for control. Lest he be subsumed in the game he abhors, or begin to take himself too seriously, he makes sure that his success always seems slightly fraudulent, retains a trace of improbability. "My dear Jimmy," he writes to Whistler in 1882 from America, standing on the threshold of his fame, "They are 'considering me *seriously.*' Isn't it dreadful?"[24]

The only people more competitive than competitive people, of course, are those who claim not to be competitive at all. Refusing to compete in the game of life can be construed as the most aggressive maneuver of them all, a snobbish insistence that one is above the petty urge to be on top: that one is *above* above. Even cheating at the game of life is less competitive, in the end, than refusing to compete altogether, for the successful cheater does not flaunt his or her aggression toward the other players, but eludes detection, maintains the social illusion of agonistic cooperation. Likewise, there is something profoundly earnest, call it negative asceticism or moralistic dandyism, about avoiding seriousness altogether, about calling for an end to the political violence implicit in taking oneself too seriously. Here, irony or self-deprecation becomes another form of wrestling with one's demons, only the primary demon is earnestness itself. One can compete, after all, to be the least competitive.

Even the most cursory glance at his journalism and personal correspondence reveals how competitive a man Wilde truly was. He loved to mock; he loved to brag. Upon being awarded a First in classical moderation in 1876, Wilde confesses to Harding: "I *am* really a little pleased at getting it, though I swaggered horribly and pretended that I did not care a bit."[25] To Ward he brags about receiving a complimentary note from Walter Pater, transcribing for his friend, in fact, the entire letter, adding: "You won't think me snobbish for sending you this? After all, it *is* something to be honestly proud of."[26] His lecture tour of America uncorked a torrent of self-regard, a twenty-seven-year-old Wilde informing his friend Norman Forbes-Robertson about his "[g]reat success here": "nothing like it since Dickens, they tell me. I am torn in bits by Society."[27] Wilde craved success. To the same friend, he announces that he can see, from the window of his hotel room in Montreal, his name "printed" in "blue and magenta" letters "six feet high" "on the placards": "[I]t is fame, and anything is better than virtuous obscurity."[28] He proceeds to sketch the placard in question, so that his friend might enjoy the view he enjoys, capturing in loving detail a slender lamppost, dwarfed by a typographically beefy OSCAR. The only thing Wilde loved more than bragging, in fact, was the art, or the sport, of the witty putdown, at which he excelled. Henry James, he purrs in "The Decay of Lying" (1889), "writes fiction as if it were a painful duty."[29] Of George Meredith he writes: "As a writer he has mastered everything except language: as a novelist he can do everything, except tell a story."[30] And yet on the very next page, Wilde insists with a flourish of Arnoldian disinterestedness that "[w]e should, at any rate, have no preferences, no prejudices, no partisan feeling of any kind."[31] In "The Soul of Man Under Socialism," Wilde takes Thackeray to task for "mocking" "the public," for engaging in precisely the kind of petty squabbling, the rhetorical slugfest, at which he himself excels.[32]

Wilde's understanding of the psychological and spiritual violence of competition, of the fact that agon leaves one emptied of self, derives, then, from his deep and longstanding familiarity with the competitive impulse, from his myriad insecurities and jealousies, not from a delusional or self-congratulatory sense of being above it all. The game has no outside. Competition forms us. Wilde seeks a path to enlightenment *within* competition, not beyond it. He implicates himself in the game he condemns, admits that we are all trapped in the quicksand of strife: the more we struggle against struggle, the more we sink into the muck in which we hope not to sink. I agree with Amanda Anderson that Wilde roots his radical vision of the artist-critic, his Christlike peacemaker, in an "ideal of disinterestedness" and "reflective distance," in an Arnoldian "stance of cultivated detachment," wherein "the free play of the mind" displaces, to quote Wilde, "the sordid and stupid quarrels of second-rate politicians or third-rate theologians."[33] Wildean detachment, however, is not escapist. He detaches himself from the game precisely by submitting to it, not by resisting it, but by purposefully losing at it, playing to lose, accepting in a Christlike manner the ethical beauty of loss, the fruitlessness of competition. Thus, Wilde's claim that the "quarrels" of "second-rate politicians and third-rate theologians" are "sordid and stupid" is funny precisely because it is an example of the kind of pettiness and cattiness it critiques. Wilde's mockery makes mockery look bad, shamelessly naughty, inviting us to laugh at the sordid game of mockery. What are Wilde's comedies, with their myriad scenes of verbal fencing and backhanded compliments, in which High Society, with its matchmaking, marriages, and power plays, is exposed as sport: what are these comedies but opportunities for the bourgeoisie to laugh at its own pettiness, and for ambitious Wilde to laugh at himself? He undermines himself joyfully when he mocks, revels in his own unseriousness, pokes fun at his own competitiveness. This is why we never think of Wilde as mean-spirited, even though his tongue is so barbed.

To struggle earnestly against the urge to mock, Wilde knows, would only reinforce, indeed, valorize as a virtue, the agonistic impulse that underlies mockery. All resistance is violent and ultimately self-destructive. One of Wilde's favorite paradoxes, "I can resist everything except temptation," might sound like hedonistic nonsense to some; in truth, the statement communicates a message of radical pacifism, a pleasure in yielding, a sweet-natured detachment from the will to fight.[34] In order to avoid strengthening the agon, Wilde's struggle against struggle must take the form of an unselfish and hence noncompetitive contentment in loss, a self-conscious pleasure in playing to lose, a pleasure in failing to be above the urge to mock, to be a "better person." It cannot be a passive-aggressive pleasure, the insidious thrill of winning by losing. One must play with the intent of losing for the sake of losing. "A cigarette is the perfect type of a perfect pleasure," Wilde insists in *The Picture of Dorian Gray* (1890), for "it leaves one unsatisfied."[35] Thus, the "exquisite" sensation of self that the cigarette induces leaves one empty-handed, with only a pleasurable and slightly lugubrious rush, a nothingness, one's individuality unfurling in undulant wisps of smoke.

After Johan Huizinga and Roger Caillois, the twentieth century's most provocative theorist of the contestive or adversative dimension to human life, indeed, to all life, is Walter Ong, whose detailed investigation of the ubiquity of contest, of its pervasiveness "in the evolution of consciousness," reminds us just how daunting and utopian a project Wilde has undertaken in his ethical quest to play to lose.[36] "A map of the world," however, "that does not include Utopia," Wilde reminds us, "is not worth even glancing at."[37] Not only is sexuality inherently combative, according to Ong, "particularly male sexual identity," the agonistic nature of which enables the species to evolve biologically, he argues, but so too is logic, dialectical reasoning, indeed, the human search for knowledge, the "adversativeness" of which the ancient Greeks "formalized" "as no other culture had done."[38] The inherently and, from Ong's perspective, *productively* combative nature of academia, with its obsessively hierarchical and endlessly evaluative culture, is underwritten by what Peter Sloterdijk terms the "idyll" of the "dialogue of enlightenment," which is "nothing other than a laborious wrestling with opinions and an exploratory dialogue among persons who submit, a priori, to rules of peace because they emerge from the confrontation only as winners, winners in knowledge and solidarity."[39] In the game of Reason, losers receive a consolation prize: "the acceptance of the better position and the discarding of the previous opinion." As if Wilde's political and epistemological challenge were not difficult enough, Ong goes on to argue that all tension or opposition, even the force of gravity itself, can be construed as contestive:

We all have suffered from dreams in which we feel ourselves plummeting through space. Such dreams can be terrifying, for bodily existence is such that it requires some kind of againstness. Gravity is reassuring; it establishes fields where adversativeness can work and where it functions as a central element in all physical existence.[40]

There you have it. Wilde must achieve nothing less than the defiance of gravity. What is Wildean aestheticism, in the end, however, but a new culture built upon *levity*, a model of living devoid of any fear of falling?

In the Wildean dialogue, reason loses its footing; Socrates falls down, decides to stay put. In "The Critic as Artist" (1890), for instance, Wilde inverts the Arnoldian and Platonic search for truth, Gilbert convincing his friend Ernest that the "aim of the critic is to see the object as in itself it really is not."[41] That Wilde puts his words in the mouth of a cocky young dandy, who lacks the requisite gravitas of an Enlightenment pedagogue; that Gilbert is a reluctant participant in the dialogue, claiming that he is "not in the mood for talking to-night," preferring to smoke cigarettes and play the piano; indeed, that he implores Ernest not to agree with him at dialogue's end, for "[w]hen people agree with me I always feel that I must be wrong;" that Wilde makes all these unreasonable authorial choices demonstrates his penchant for playing to lose, for refusing to be taken seriously in the game of reason.[42] To get into the spirit of the Wildean dialogue requires lightheartedness. As with Nietzsche's *gaya scienza*, one must be content to lose the ground of truth on which one stands. Wilde teaches us how to be at peace with nothing: "[t]o do nothing at all is the most difficult thing in the world."[43] He sets thought free from its quest for victory, from its utilitarian aim. The free play of thought—the ethical mingling of minds, the joy of intellectual collusion—can only begin once one commits oneself to losing in the brutal sport of truth.

In *The Portrait of Mr. W.H.* (1889), Wilde plays the game of poetic exegesis just as ham-fistedly, as *badly*, as he plays the Enlightenment game of dialectic in "The Critic as Artist" and "The Decay of Lying," turning a close reading of same-sex desire in Shakespeare's *Sonnets*, the marriage of true minds, into an elaborate fictional conspiracy theory about the secret identity of Shakespeare's dedicatee, replete with a forged painting and a faked suicide by an obsessed proponent of the theory. Wilde uses his reading of Shakespeare to demonstrate that literary interpretation is essentially a monomaniacal projection on the part of the literary critic, and that scholarly dialogue amounts to mutual seduction, intellectual coercion, and delusion. The fictional format in which Wilde chooses to present his theory of Willie Hughes, Shakespeare's supposed boy toy, guarantees that he loses the scholarly debate even before he joins it, even though much of his text consists of relatively innocuous close readings of Shakespearean wordplay, some of which, in a different context, could be taken seriously. A tease, Wilde frustrates his readers' desire to take his theory seriously. As a result, however, he triggers in us, once we relinquish our agonistic will to truth, something infinitely more valuable than moral or epistemological clarity. Call it the free play of thought, or imagination: it is the thrilling sense not that we have discovered Shakespeare's secret but that we have been taught the art of love: how to connect with another person, whether a writer or a lover, without being in control, without needing to triumph.

The Hideous Game of Hate

He lost his wife and his children. He lost his house, furniture, and even his china. He lost all his "charming things," his "Burne-Jones drawings," his Whistlers, his entire library: his "collection of presentation volumes from almost every poet" of his "time," the "beautifully bound editions" of his "father's and mother's works."[44] To the auction block he even lost his "wonderful array of college and school prizes." Who would want them? No matter, they are *his*, and so they are his no longer. He lost all but his most loyal friends. He lost his freedom, his career, his name, his boundless future. His robust health dwindles steadily, 750 pieces of it stolen by 750 restless nights, and again in the morning by the hungry day. His fame has turned to infamy. Alone in Block C, on Floor 3, in Cell 3 of Her Majesty's Prison, Reading, where he suffers from chronic diarrhea and engages, according to prison officials, in compulsive masturbation, Wilde, his mane shorn as a precaution against head lice, is the ultimate loser.[45] Forced to fight for his life in the criminal justice system, Wilde, so terrible at fighting, so temperamentally unsuited for the middle-class game of winning, lost. As any historical account of his trials shows, Wilde made some careless mistakes under cross-examination, answering with insolence, for instance, when asked by Carson if he had ever kissed a servant named Walter Grainger: "Oh no, never in my life; he was a peculiarly plain boy."[46]

We have arrived at an ethically thorny question in our study of Wilde: What do his defeat and imprisonment teach us, if anything, about his art? The image of Wilde alone in his prison cell naturally angers and saddens us, causes our stomachs, more than a century later, to clench, our moods to grow sour. It makes us want to fight. How do we as Wilde scholars process this tragedy? At moments like this, Wildeans measure their words with more care than usual, knowing that anything they say can and will be used against them in the court of academic opinion, will matter more than their flimsiest theories about "The Canterville Ghost."

The problem with canonical explanations for why Wilde made the disastrous choices he made, and from a strategic perspective, they were pretty poor choices, is that they approach the problem from a purely agonistic and thus un-Wildean perspective, failing to see that, for Wilde, agon is precisely the problem. Certain psychoanalytic readings of Wilde, for instance, that present him as gloriously masochistic or as sexually self-destructive, or that detect in same-sex desire a rebellious death drive, go to extreme lengths to make lemonade out of Wilde's lemon of a fate; a lemonade, however, clouded with undercurrents of homophobia and sugarcoated fantasies of gay suicide. Here the idea is that Wilde essentially got what he unconsciously wanted, that he won in the end. Crying on the outside, he was laughing on the inside at having defeated his opponent in life: his own life. Are we so conditioned, I wonder, to crave victory at all costs, to fear loss in all its forms, and to see human behavior through a prism of gain, that we would happily grant Wilde victory in death? As Richard Kaye explains, to view Wilde as a martyr—for homosexuality, for Ireland, for art—is equally problematic, for it also suggests that Wilde wins by losing, that he allowed himself to be destroyed for a political or aesthetic cause greater than himself.[47] He lost so that future generations could win. Then there is the most viscerally agonistic explanation of them all: the idea that Wilde, blind to the gravity of his situation because of his ludic disposition, did not fight hard *enough*, did not rage, rage, against the dying of the light, and that we who have the benefit of hindsight have a duty to carry on (in his name and in our own) the fight he lost, railing against the injustice of it all.

There is, of course, another explanation, a perfectly good explanation, actually, one that everyone all but ignores, for its nonagonistic logic, its decidedly unwinning way, means that it passes unseen, more often than not, beneath our agonistic gaze. What is it? It is Wilde's *own* explanation in *De Profundis* (1897), the remarkable epistolary essay written to and for that supposed instrument of his downfall, his lover "Bosie," Lord Alfred Douglas. Penned in prison over a span of three months, it overflows with recrimination, self-pity, and ultimately and most crucially with *love*: "At all costs I must keep Love in my heart. If I go into prison without Love what will become of my Soul?"[48] *De Profundis* is Wilde's most personal and heartfelt critique of the logic of *sport*, his moving attempt to adopt as a style of ethical life, as a mode of existence, the experience of beauty in loss, the choice *not* to win, which he experienced, prior to his disastrous trials, only in theory, on the literary playground of his ideas. In *De Profundis*, however, Wilde's life finally imitates his art.

Wilde accuses his lover of dragging him into an ugly family dispute, a messy Oedipal competition between Douglas and his father, thereby forcing Wilde, against his good judgment, his "good-nature" and his "Celtic laziness," to fight on Douglas's behalf, "to wrestle with Caliban."[49] Because many of the witness accounts of homosexual activity that Queensberry presented at trial were, Wilde notes, "the actions and doings of someone else," in other words, of Douglas himself, Wilde "could have," as his attorney "earnestly advised, begged, entreated," "walked out of Court with my tongue in my cheek, and my hands in my pockets, a free man": "But I refused."[50] In the name of love, Wilde refused; he knowingly and willingly played to lose, against the earnest, agonistic pleading of his counsel. Is it revisionist history? Perhaps. The important thing, however, is that Wilde defines love in *De Profundis* as a nonagonistic impulse; love can never be a means to an end; it is the antithesis of greed and self-interest. It is the antidote to sport. One gains nothing, wins nothing, in love, and that is the point. Love is unselfish and thus profoundly unreasonable. Self-referential, unconcerned with what others think, love is supremely individualistic, like those unclassifiable, nonconformist flowers in "The Soul of Man Under Socialism," flowers that grow beautiful at the expense of power, the need to triumph:

But Love does not traffic in a marketplace, nor use a huckster's scales. Its joy, like the joy of the intellect, is to feel itself alive. The aim of Love is to love: no more, and no less. You were my enemy: such an enemy as no man ever had. I had given you my life, and to gratify the lowest and most contemptible of all human passions, Hatred and Vanity and Greed, you had thrown it away. In less than three years you had entirely ruined me from every point of view. For my own sake there was nothing for me to do but to love you.[51]

Wilde views himself in *De Profundis* as a philosopher of love; he discovers retrospectively what he knew on an instinctive level all along, what he taught his sons in "The Selfish Giant" and "The Happy Prince," and in his other Christian socialist fairytales: namely, that his lifelong distaste for competition, for the vulgar earnestness of the middle class, for the will to truth, for the dialogue of Enlightenment, for rowing backwards to Iffley, for the myriad ways in which agon manifests itself in quotidian life, indeed, for gravity itself, can be traced to his loving nature, to his incompetence at hatred. "Anybody can sympathise with the sufferings of a friend," Wilde notes in "The Soul of Man Under Socialism," but "it requires" "a true Individualist," a person incapable of hate, "to sympathise with a friend's success."[52] Prison teaches Wilde, reassures him to his soulful delight, that he is far better at love than at hate, even in a place as heartless as Reading Gaol, a world that fosters bitterness and coddles resentment. Sport is hate. Reason is hate. Truth is hate. Seriousness is hate. Property is hate. Hierarchy is hate. All desire for gain, all striving, all struggling, the drive to be the best, it is all, Wilde realizes, *hate*. His heart brimming with love, with a love he waters daily with the tears of loss, with the art of yielding, Wilde is freer in his captivity than globetrotting Douglas, who, in his Italian villa, flute of French wine in hand, is shackled by hate.

In his effort to teach Douglas how to love, Wilde contrasts the unselfish play of his own artistic mind, his willingness to lose, to defy gravity, with Bosie's stubborn sportiveness and intransient thirst for power, his insistence upon besting his sportsman father at every turn. Wilde accuses Douglas of bringing "the element of Philistinism into" his "life," a life "that had been a complete protest against it."[53] Devoid of individuality, of flowerlike self-absorption, Douglas suffers from a middle-class "incapacity of being alone," a greedy neediness, an inability "to play gracefully with ideas," "arriv[ing]" "merely" at a conformist "violence of opinion."[54]

Wilde depicts Douglas as consummate playboy and jock. Wilde describes in excruciating detail the enormous sums he spent to maintain Douglas in style, like the manager of a star athlete or prizefighter; he recounts the debt he incurred for their champagne lunches and "reckless dinners," for which Douglas shows no appreciation.[55] Meanwhile, Douglas spends his time sporting: "play[ing] golf" "for ten days," "gambling in some Algiers Casino," "fighting" his "mother's battles" against her estranged husband, the dread Queensberry.[56] Wilde portrays himself as the hapless plaything of Doom, drawn irrevocably into the "hideous game of hate," "the prize for the victor" in a "contemptible contest" between an equally egotistical father and son: "[Y]ou had both thrown dice for my soul, and you happened to have lost. That was all."[57] "In you," Wilde writes, "Hate was always stronger than Love."[58] Douglas's primary motivation in life, then, is to "score off" people: "I remember quite well your saying to me with your most conceited air that you could beat your father 'at his own trade.' Quite true. But what a trade! What a competition!"[59]

Thus, Wilde finds himself, to his dismay, drawn into a tragic contest of world-historical proportions, watching himself fight, as if from afar, not only Queensberry, or the British criminal justice system, or middle-class moralism, but Hate itself, punching away at a spirit of negation that grows stronger with each blow it absorbs. As Wilde queasily informs Ada Leverson in March 1895, he must prepare himself "to fight with panthers."[60] What is so tragic, from Wilde's perspective, about his lamentable fate is not that he lost in the Old Bailey but that he was forced to *want* to win in the first place, forced to fight with all his strength for life, thereby degrading that life, depleting that strength in the process. "I remember as I was sitting in the dock on the occasion of my last trial," Wilde writes, "listening to Lockwood's appalling denunciation of me," "and being sickened with horror at what I heard."[61] "Suddenly it occurred to me," he adds, "*How splendid it would be, if I was saying all this about myself!*" An agonistic reader will interpret this statement to mean that Wilde wants to deprive his oppressors of victory, to win masochistically, by seizing the power to destroy himself for himself, like some court-martialed sailor-martyr out of nautical melodrama. Such a reading misses the point. Wilde fantasizes about putting an end to the insufferable contest by losing, by refusing to hate his opponents, freeing them from the soul-crushing responsibility of having to be his opponents in the first place, thereby teaching them in a Christlike manner how to let go, how to love one's enemies by not taking oneself so seriously, by levitating playfully above the ethical quicksand of earnestness. Wildean detachment takes the form of a willingness to lose, an ethical detachment, call it cosmopolitanism if you prefer, from parochial hate, from the endless middle-class game played ferociously beneath his feet. The image from Christ's crucifixion that touches Wilde most deeply is the inartistic sight of those "soldiers gambling and throwing dice for his clothes," the bitter sport beneath Christ's feet.[62] Incapable of love, Douglas joins their game, hates the hate that destroyed his lover, attempts to outplay those soldiers, clutching at the fragments of Wilde's frayed reputation. Thus, after Wilde's defeat, melodramatic Douglas pens bombastic letters to "halfpenny newspapers," "appeal[ing] to the '*English sense of fair play*,' or something very dreary of that kind, on behalf of '*a man who was down*.'"[63]

Bosie's competitive nature prevents him from seeing the ethical power inherent in male same-sex love, its revolutionary potential in this brutally capitalist world of ours to defuse violence between men. Because Douglas's consumerist "soul" is "monopolise[d]" by "[b]oys, brandy, and betting," because it is mired in selfish appetite, because he treats people, young working-class men in particular, as trophies, and because the lesson he learns from Wilde's defeat is, tragically, to double down in his *fight* for "the love that dare not speak its name," Douglas fails to see that loving another man means freeing oneself, at least in theory, from the heteronormative imperative to compete with him, to view him defensively, reactively, as a threat to one's masculinity, as a potential source of humiliation or emasculation.[64] Wilde presents male same-sex love as an antidote to competition, just as Muir and Stevenson present the boyish sublime as an antidote to rational recreation. Permitting oneself to love the physique of another man, to take pleasure in his physical strength, in "the play of beautiful muscles and the moulding of fair flesh," means letting go of one's agonistic instinct to feel threatened, to measure oneself against that musculature, against the intellectual, social, or economic power it symbolizes.[65] Likewise, Wilde's sweet-tempered claim at Oxford that an athlete's "left leg" was "a Greek poem" undermines the psychosexual violence, the homosocial tension, that sport often fosters:

the melancholic intimacy between rivals, a fraternal regret at the impossibility of love.

Wilde's most homoerotic moments, and his most politically and ethically powerful, are not his critically fetishized "Bunbury" moments, his manic, nervous laughter at the decentered and double lives of men, but his fusion of Christianity, socialism, and aestheticism in the fearless logic of love, in his relatively straightforward but paradigm-shifting refusal to hate other men. I have never understood the impulse by some queer theorists to find coded expressions of same-sex desire, or sly, wistful allusions to homosexuality, *everywhere* in Wilde's writings, as if the political power of love between men, or between women, derives from its frequency of expression, its quantity, rather than from its ethical quality, as if homosexuality, as Douglas believed, must compete with heterosexuality, at every turn, to be the most interesting, the most epistemologically subtle, or the loudest expression of eros. In *The Importance of Being Earnest* (1895), Wilde invites his middle-class audience to laugh at the ridiculous spectacle of men competing with men, women competing with women, men and women competing with each other, self-important families competing with other self-important families, in the loveless sport of bourgeois marriage-making. By some absurd miracle, equilibrium is established in the world of the play between supply and demand in the marital marketplace. In the end, everyone wins and no one loses. What Wilde so humorously captures, then, is the ethically empty capitalist fantasy of love without loss, a vision of marriage as strategic acquisition in an erotic economy, an endless trafficking in names. Wilde has exposed the soulless sport, the refusal to lose, underlying middle-class moral earnestness.

Let's not be sexual partisans. Wilde does not believe, remember, in taking sides. In theory, the true artist plays for no team. Neither does true love. Wilde teaches *love*, not same-sex love merely. Love comes in many forms. And hate, Bosie proves, is an equal opportunity employer. Just as same-sex-oriented Douglas cannot bring himself to lose in love, to embrace the ethical beauty in loss, so plenty of Wilde's heterosexual (for lack of a better term) heroines seem joyously incapable of succumbing to competitive hate, to the quest for power that infects everyone else: whether it is Vera in Wilde's early play, *Vera, or the Nihilists* (1880), who chooses love over the political fight, or even, to a lesser degree, Salomé, who, oblivious to the political maneuverings around her, decides to silence the moralistic voice of judgment not by fighting it, like her mother Herodias, but by loving it, enveloping pugnacious Jokanaan in a mutually fatal and decidedly unreasonable embrace: an embrace that undermines Herod's imperial brinksmanship, his attempt to outplay Fate. In *The Picture of Dorian Gray*, Sibyl Vane's love for Dorian takes the form of an unselfish pleasure in loss, the loss of her trade, her ability to act beautifully and thus to triumph, as she once did, on the stage. She interprets the loss of her ability to act, her love for Dorian, as a sign of her moral growth. Acquisitive Dorian, however, who only worships her because she is the best, and because he wants to flaunt her before the envious eyes of men, hates her for her love, her pleasure in playing to lose: "You have thrown it all away. You are shallow and stupid. My God! how mad I was to love you!"[66] Dorian embodies the agonistic spirit, the refusal to lose, to release even a tiny wrinkle or a single gray hair to time. What is his violent relationship with his own portrait, his hateful bifurcation of self, but a taking of sides, a maniacal need to pit himself triumphantly against an opponent, any opponent, even himself? "Time is jealous of you," Lord Henry teases him, "and wars against your lilies and your roses."[67] Rather than learn to love time and hence himself, finding beauty in loss, in letting go of youth, Dorian becomes "jealous of everything whose beauty does not die": "I am jealous of the portrait you have painted of me," he informs Basil.[68] Jealous of himself, he experiences spiritual *agony*. Competition eventually kills the soul, of course, as he learns one evening in the lofty room in his London townhouse where he hides his ugly painting. Once his "play-room," this storeroom for his soul contains, among other things, a "ragged" "tapestry," on which "a faded king and queen," appropriately enough, "play[ ] chess."[69]

For all its denunciation of fighting, *De Profundis* is a decidedly agonistic text. Wilde crushes Douglas, humiliates him, brandishes before posterity his lover's vices and flaws. We avert our eyes. Wilde exaggerates, distorts, and omits. He attempts to make Douglas jealous by contrasting his selfish behavior with the loving behavior of another young man, Wilde's ex-lover, Robbie Ross, who dutifully visits Wilde in prison when Bosie will not, and who doffs his hat to the fallen Wilde when other men jeer and spit. Wilde transforms the spoiled Douglas, whom he was complicit in spoiling, into a veritable monster. Over a three-month period,

Wilde methodically slays, from his prison cell, the boy-monster he helped create, and twists and tears his monstrous flesh. On the cusp of triumph, however, his victory over his "enemy," as he calls him, in reach, Wilde pulls back in the final pages of *De Profundis* and gives up the fight. The agon collapses. Wilde professes his love for Douglas, and concedes: "At the end of a month, when the June roses are in all their wanton opulence, I will, if I feel able, arrange through Robbie to meet you in some quiet foreign town like Bruges, whose grey houses and green canals and cool still ways had a charm for me, years ago."[70] Wilde's critique of hate, of Bosie's stubborn competitiveness, threatens, he knows, to devolve into hate, to become the very thing it critiques. Wilde stops himself from winning the "hideous game of hate," from delivering the deathblow. He chooses loss. A loser, a fool in love, only now does Wilde become what he had always hoped to be: a philosopher of love.

Wilde the Fool

Intriguing work has been done in the last twenty-five years on Wilde's idiosyncratic views on Christianity. Hilary Fraser, for instance, has investigated the interoperability of Wilde's aestheticism and his interest in Christianity, his understanding of Christ as "a work of art."[71] Ellis Hanson has compellingly documented how Wilde's attraction to Catholicism interconnects with his attraction to the male body.[72] In this section, I would like to build on the ground cleared by these projects and explore how Wilde roots his understanding of Christian love in an ethic of folly, in foolishness itself. Because practitioners of Christianity traditionally view their faith as antithetical to foolishness, and because even sophisticated religious scholars presuppose that faith is by definition *serious*, critics who focus on the religious dimension to Wilde's work tend to downplay Wilde's vision of himself as a fool. Thus, despite the fact that she detects traces of "sincerity" in Wilde's early references to Christ, Fraser claims that his dandiacal "profanity," his "witty and ironic tongue," "complicate[ ]" her argument, suggest an "ambiguous reconciliation" at best between Christianity and aestheticism, at least until Wilde writes *De Profundis*, which she characterizes as a "profoundly serious work."[73] Hanson, too, takes critics to task who "deny the seriousness of Wilde's interest in

Christianity," or who "regard" him as an "aesthetic clown, whose writings on religion are all shallow and insincere."[74] But Wilde's clownishness, I suggest, his embrace of the logic of play as subversion, is precisely where his Christianity manifests itself most powerfully, and where his world-transforming vision of love takes shape.

Near the beginning of *De Profundis*, Wilde draws a sharp contrast between two types of fool: "the fool in the eyes of the gods and the fool in the eyes of man."[75] "The real fool," Wilde explains to Douglas, "such as the gods mock or mar, is he who does not know himself": "I was such a one too long. You have been such a one too long." Wilde repeatedly invokes the figure of the profane fool, spiritually blind and self-alienated, in his account of his disastrous relationship with Douglas. Wilde bemoans, for example, "the froth and folly" of their life together; he recalls the "foolish letters" Douglas sent when Wilde dared to "question" "the artistic value" of the young man's "translation of *Salome*"; he grapples with the fact that, "wherever I go" for the rest of "my life," "people will" "know" of "my . . . follies"; he chastises Douglas for his "foolish bravado" in wanting to dedicate a book of poems to him.[76] The fool in the eyes of the gods, then, is a vain or greedy person, devoid of a flowerlike sense of peace. It is the second kind of fool, however, "the fool in the eyes of man," the loser in the game of life, who triggers in Wilde a sensation of proximity to Christ, for this sacred or unworldly fool is "entirely ignorant of the modes of Art in its revolution or the moods of thought in its progress, of the pomp of the Latin line or the richer music of the vowelled Greek," and yet he or she is nevertheless "full of the very sweetest wisdom."[77] Those worldly sophisticates who turn art into a status symbol and education into a mark of distinction, who degrade beauty by reducing it to a competitive sport, and who mock the ignorant and simpleminded as fools, fail to understand that the peace constitutive of art, its refusal to struggle or to judge, its flowerlike and Christlike grace, is a celebration of beauty *in* loss and is therefore, from a capitalist or utilitarian perspective, utter foolishness. Thus, the ignorant and the clownish, those who were never trained in the art of discursive combat, in the game of Reason, those who are content therefore to yield, *because that is all they know how to do*, might appear fools in the eyes of agonistic man but they are wise, Wilde insists, in the eyes of the gods.

all times heavyhearted. It is the weaponization of gravity. In *The Ballad of Reading Gaol* (1898), Wilde's protest against capital punishment, in which he diagnoses the modern condition as a state in which "each man kills the thing he loves" in agonistic fits of jealousy or greed, Wilde literalizes the idea of gravity as a weapon in his description of the "hangman close at hand," his realization that a condemned man has "got to swing."[82] Christ teaches Wilde the difficult and divine art of foolishness, of defying gravity by forgiving one's oppressors, refusing to feel tense and defensive, refusing to fight with all one's strength against the unbearable weight threatening to break one's heart. The genius of Christ lies, then, in the fact that he was a fool: he possessed a stunningly unreasonable and gravity-defying ability to love his oppressors, to remain lighthearted, devoid of hate, even with all the sins of the world piled atop his human heart.

As Harvey Cox has documented, the image of Christ as a holy fool or a "clown" "has deep historical roots" in late antiquity: "One of the earliest representations of Christ in Christian art depicts a crucified human figure with the head of an ass."[83] As Elizabeth-Anne Stewart contends, in her theological exploration of the foolish dimension to Christ, early Christians saw in the figure of the fool intimations of otherworldly wisdom: a charismatic willingness to be humiliated, to embrace one's status as loser or bumpkin, as outsider; a tendency to speak incomprehensibly or nonsensically, to reveal truths that sound ridiculous to the worldly; and a tricksterlike or harlequinesque skill at entertaining people, distracting them from their quotidian lives with parables, riddles, and thought-provoking paradoxes, many of which playfully undermine the legitimacy of the powers that be.[84] Indeed, Cox points out that early Christians, a "wretched band of slaves, derelicts, and square pegs," were often dismissed in the Roman world as "fools for Christ," suggesting that Christianity emerges from a willingness to play to lose, to find ethical beauty in folly, in a faith that made a virtue of loss.[85] Christ and the first generation of Christians take pride in the fact that they appear fools in the eyes of man, for foolishness bespeaks wisdom. In the face of terrible oppression, they maintain their lightheartedness, their ability to laugh at themselves, painting on the wall of a catacomb their beloved divinity with the head of an ass.

Wilde finds it relatively easy to wear his folly as a badge of honor when the forces of oppression consist solely of insecure book reviewers and uptight Philistinism. In prison, however, his ethic of folly is put to the test. His foolishness threatens to turn bitter, his ability to achieve levity crushed along with his ability to love: "Our very dress make us grotesques. We are the zanies of sorrow. We are clowns whose hearts are broken. We are specially designed to appeal to the sense of humour."[86] In *The Ballad of Reading Gaol*, for instance, Wilde describes with barely suppressed bitterness the amusing spectacle of his fellow prisoners and himself, with "shaven head and feet of lead," taking their exercise in the prison yard: "With slouch and swing around the ring / We trod the Fool's Parade!"[87] In *De Profundis*, Wilde recounts his most humiliating episode:

On November 13th 1895 I was brought down here from London. From two o'clock till half-past two on that day I had to stand on the centre platform of Clapham Junction in convict dress and handcuffed, for the world to look at. I had been taken out of the Hospital Ward without a moment's notice being given to me. Of all possible objects I was the most grotesque. When people saw me they laughed. Each train as it came up swelled the audience. Nothing could exceed their amusement. That was of course before they knew who I was. As soon as they had been informed, they laughed still more. For half an hour I stood there in the grey November rain surrounded by a jeering mob. For a year after that was done to me I wept every day at the same hour and for the same space of time.[88]

Though it takes a year, Wilde eventually realizes that his broken heart, his oppression, can only be alleviated through a recognition of the wisdom implicit in appearing foolish in the eyes of competitive man: acceptance of oneself as always already a loser in the game of life. One's ability to perceive aesthetic and ethical beauty, to be artistic, comes from choosing not to win this ugly game. Just as he learns to love Douglas, his "enemy" in love, Wilde learns, like Christ, to love the jeering mob: "Well, now I am really beginning to feel more regret for the people who laughed than for myself."[89]

The Loser at the End of the World

Those who insist upon being the best, who define themselves in opposition to losers, have much in common with the countless Victorians, especially middle-class Victorian men, those modern capitalist subjects, who reacted to Wilde with visceral distaste, who experienced a shiver of disgust at his unmanly pleasure in not hating, in not distrusting, or in not outplaying other men. They instinctively recoiled from his refusal to compete in this world in play, to pit himself in soul-crushing combat against a world of opponents. Writing in 1882 from Boston to Mrs. George Lewis, the wife of Wilde's London solicitor, playwright Dion Boucicault worries that the managers of Wilde's American tour, in collusion with the American press, have transformed the naïve Wilde, with his long hair and silk stockings, into "a popular fool," have worked surreptitiously to market him to the public as a figure of "ridicule," a "caricature[ ]" of an Aesthete, in order to "advertise him in connection" with Gilbert and Sullivan's *Patience* and the emasculated Bunthorne, the effete and fleshly poet parodied in the opera.[90] "Oscar is helpless," Boucicault laments, "because he is not a practical man of business." After bragging to Mrs. Lewis about his own financial "success" in the United States, about having made "by far the most profitable sweep I have ever made," Boucicault turns his attention once again to pitiful Wilde, worrying that future lecture tours are now out of the question, so unmanned is Wilde, managers "tell[ing] me they would not be able to touch him." In the world of male capitalist competition, of endless strife and eternal maneuvering, in the Victorian world in play, Oscar Wilde is from the very beginning untouchable: the kid picked last in gym class, the odd man out. To Boucicault's avuncular entreaties, Wilde responds: "Let me gather the golden fruits of America that I may spend a winter in Italy and a summer in Greece amidst beautiful things." "Oh dear," an exasperated Boucicault exclaims, "if only he would spend the money and the time amongst six-per-cent bonds!"

Nearly two decades after Boucicault's masculine handwringing on behalf of his uncompetitive countryman, in the wake of Wilde's ignominious defeat and his subsequent immortalization as the last great loser of the Victorian Age, its biggest fool, legions of terrified same-sex-oriented men join their middle-class heterosexual counterparts in the Wilde-bashing game, defining themselves in paranoid fashion against him, internalizing as their sexual essence the capitalist consciousness of the male Philistine: an erotic consumerism and competitiveness, the unloving friction of *against*, an insistence upon being a winner, upon having the upper hand against all men. Of the numerous personal accounts of sexual inversion that Victorian sexologist Havelock Ellis collected in the 1890s, one case study in particular stands out.[91] "H.C.," as Ellis dubs him, recalls an erotic nightmare he suffered "[s]oon after" "the Oscar Wilde case was bruiting about": "I dreamed that Oscar Wilde" "approached me with a buffoon languishment and perpetuated *fellatio*."[92] "For a month or more, recalling this dream," H.C. confesses, "disgusted me." Wilde the unsporty clown, the happy fool, the perennial loser, made a name for himself playing eternal Other to middle-class man. To the Victorian world in play, to a world built upon a foundation of illusion, Wilde must have seemed, if nerve-wracked H.C. is any indication, the Angel of the Apocalypse, the big-mouthed harbinger of cosmological collapse, of modernity's apotheosis. Wilde did not, however, *end* the game of modern life. Neither did he outplay it. Nor did he flee emotionally into another world altogether, a new world, an old world, a cosmos buried deep inside. What Wilde did was infinitely more threatening. He proclaimed, with storm clouds of wit, with the forked fire of his love, that this game called modernity is not worth winning.

Notes

INTRODUCTION

1. William Makepeace Thackeray, *Barry Lyndon*, ed. Andrew Sanders (Oxford: Oxford University Press, 1984), 128–29.
2. Karl Marx and Friedrich Engels, *The Communist Manifesto*, trans. Samuel Moore, ed. David McLellan (Oxford: Oxford University Press, 1992), 6.
3. J. Jeffrey Franklin, *Serious Play: The Cultural Form of the Nineteenth-Century Realist Novel* (Philadelphia: University of Pennsylvania Press, 1999), 4.
4. See Mihai I. Spariosu, *Dionysus Reborn: Play and the Aesthetic Dimension in Modern Philosophical and Scientific Discourse* (Ithaca and London: Cornell University Press, 1989) and James S. Hans, *The Play of the World* (Amherst: University of Massachusetts Press, 1981).
5. See Brian Sutton-Smith, *The Ambiguity of Play* (Cambridge, MA: Harvard University Press, 1997).
6. Rudyard Kipling, *Kim*, ed. Zohreh T. Sullivan (New York and London: W.W. Norton, 2002), 143.

CHAPTER 1

1. George Eliot, *Daniel Deronda*, ed. Graham Handley (Oxford: Oxford University Press, 1988), 5.
2. Walter Besant, *All Sorts and Conditions of Men* (Oxford: Oxford University Press, 1997), 259.
3. George Meredith, *Modern Love*, ed. Gillian Beer (London: Syrens, 1995), 18.
4. Gerhard Joseph and Herbert Tucker, "Passing On: Death," in *A Companion to Victorian Literature and Culture*, ed. Herbert Tucker (Malden, MA: Blackwell, 1999), 110.
5. Eugen Fink, "The Oasis of Happiness: Toward an Ontology of Play," trans. Ute and Thomas Saine, *Yale French Studies* 41 (1968), 22.
6. Edward Gross, "A Functional Approach to Leisure Analysis" *Social Problems* 9:1 (Summer 1961), 2. Emphasis in original.
7. Kipling, *Kim*, 43.
8. Ibid., 182.

9. George R. Sims, *How the Poor Live* (Gloucester, UK: Dodo Press, 2009), 50.

10. See George Gissing, *The Nether World*, ed. Stephen Gill (Oxford: Oxford University Press, 1992), 123, 148, 154, 324.

11. Nancy Morrow, *Dreadful Games: The Play of Desire in the Nineteenth-Century Novel* (Kent, OH: Kent State University Press, 1988), 6–7. Emphasis in original.

12. Charles Dickens, *Hard Times*, ed. Fred Kaplan and Sylvère Monod (New York: W.W. Norton, 2001), 51.

13. Charles Dickens, *A Christmas Carol*, in *The Christmas Books*, ed. Michael Slater, vol. 1 (New York: Penguin, 1971), 46–47.

14. The following summary of Sutton-Smith's original rhetorics of play subjoins some of the academic disciplines he associates with each. The rhetoric of play as animal progress, prevalent in biological, psychological, and educational analyses, often informs the work of primatologists and developmental psychologists: see Robert Fagen, *Animal Play Behavior* (New York: Oxford University Press, 1981); L.S. Vygotsky, *Mind in Society: The Development of Higher Psychological Processes*, ed. Michael Cole, Vera John-Steiner, Sylvia Scribner, and Ellen Souberman (Cambridge, MA: Harvard University Press, 1978); and Jean Piaget, *Play, Dreams and Imitation in Childhood*, trans. C. Gattegno and F.M. Hodgson (New York: W.W. Norton, 1962). The rhetoric of play as fate is at the heart of many mathematical, economic, and philosophical approaches to play: see Don Handelman and David Shulman, *God Inside Out: Śiva's Game of Dice* (New York: Oxford University Press, 1997); Edmund Bergler, *The Psychology of Gambling* (New York: Hill and Wang, 1957); and Vicki Abt, J.F. Smith, and E.M. Christiansen, *The Business of Risk* (Lawrence: University Press of Kansas, 1985). Many sociological and historical students of play invoke the rhetoric of play as power: see Johan Huizinga, *Homo Ludens: A Study of the Play Element in Culture* (Boston: Beacon, 1950); Roger Caillois, *Man, Play and Games*, trans. Meyer Barash (Urbana: University of Illinois Press, 1961). Anthropologists and folklorists often rely heavily upon the rhetoric of play as identity, while the rhetoric of play as imaginary tends to be privileged by literary and cultural critics: see Bernard De Koven, *The Well-Played Game* (Garden City, NY: Doubleday, 1978); Clifford Geertz, *The Interpretation of Cultures* (New York: Basic Books, 1973); James S. Hans, *The Play of the World*; Wolfgang Iser, *The Fictive and the Imaginary: Charting Literary Anthropology* (Baltimore, MD: Johns Hopkins University Press, 1993); Mikhail Bakhtin, *Rabelais and His World*, trans. Hélène Iswolsky (Bloomington: Indiana University Press, 1984); and Jacques Derrida, *Writing and Difference*, trans. Alan Bass (Chicago: University of Chicago Press, 1978). The rhetoric of play as self is prevalent in psychiatry, e.g. in Mihaly Csikszentmihalyi, *The Evolving Self* (New York: HarperCollins, 1993). In pop culture stud-

ies and in cultural studies, also among liberal theologians, one finds the rhetoric of play as frivolity: see Lewis Hyde, *Trickster Makes This World: Mischief, Myth and Art* (New York: North Point Press, 1998); Harvey Cox, *The Feast of Fools: A Theological Essay on Festivity and Fantasy* (Cambridge, MA: Harvard University Press, 1969).

15. Ludwig Wittgenstein, *Philosophical Investigations*, 3rd ed., trans. G.E.M. Anscombe (New York: Macmillan, 1958), 31–32.

16. Herbert Spencer, *The Man Versus the State*, in *Political Writings*, ed. John Offer (Cambridge: Cambridge University Press, 1994), 127–29.

17. Samuel Smiles, *Self-Help*, ed. Peter W. Sinnema (Oxford: Oxford University Press, 2002), 262.

18. Donald E. Hall, "On the Making and Unmaking of Monsters: Christian Socialism, Muscular Christianity, and the Metaphorization of Class Conflict," in *Muscular Christianity: Embodying the Victorian Age*, ed. Donald E. Hall (Cambridge: Cambridge University Press, 1994), 46.

19. José Ortega y Gasset, *History as a System and Other Essays Toward a Philosophy of History*, trans. Helene Weyl (New York: W.W. Norton, 1941), 29–32.

20. Friedrich Nietzsche, "Homer's Contest," in *The Portable Nietzsche*, ed. and trans. Walter Kaufmann (New York: Penguin, 1954), 38.

21. Walter Pater, *Greek Studies: A Series of Essays* (London: Macmillan, 1911), 279.

22. Walter Pater, *The Renaissance*, ed. Adam Phillips (Oxford: Oxford University Press, 1986), 133–34.

23. Robert Knox, *The Races of Men: A Fragment* (Philadelphia: Lea and Blanchard, 1850), 45–47.

24. Charles Darwin, *The Descent of Man, and Selection in Relation to Sex*, ed. James Moore and Adrian Desmond (London: Penguin, 2004), 245.

25. Ibid., 408.

26. See, for instance, George Levine, *Darwin and the Novelists: Patterns of Science in Victorian Fiction* (Chicago: University of Chicago Press, 1988), 13–20, and *Darwin Loves You: Natural Selection and the Re-enchantment of the World* (Princeton, NJ: Princeton University Press, 2006), 202–51. See, too, Alfie Kohn, *No Contest: The Case Against Competition* (New York: Houghton Mifflin, 1986), 19–24, which includes personal correspondence between Kohn and Gould.

27. Anthony Trollope, *The Bertrams*, ed. Geoffrey Harvey (Oxford: Oxford University Press, 1991), 5.

28. Wilkie Collins, *Man and Wife*, ed. Norman Page (Oxford: Oxford University Press, 1995), 5–7.

29. John Ruskin, "Traffic," in *Unto This Last and Other Writings*, ed. Clive Wilmer (London: Penguin, 1985), 237.

30. Charles Dickens, *Nicholas Nickleby* (London: Penguin, 1994), 41.

31. For an excellent analysis of the history of the weekend, see Witold Rybczynski, *Waiting for the Weekend* (New York: Viking, 1991).

32. For a classic analysis of the Victorian "rational recreation" movement, see Peter Bailey, *Leisure and Class in Victorian England: Rational Recreation and the Contest for Control, 1830–1885* (London: Routledge, 1978), 35–55.

33. Charles Dickens, *Sketches by Boz*, ed. Dennis Walder (London: Penguin, 1995), 127.

34. Ibid., 119.

35. Hugh Cunningham, *Leisure in the Industrial Revolution, 1780–1880* (New York: St. Martin's, 1980), 140–87; Thorstein Veblen, *The Theory of the Leisure Class* (New York: Penguin, 1967).

36. Jacky Bratton and Ann Featherstone, *The Victorian Clown* (Cambridge: Cambridge University Press, 2006), 3–36.

37. Robert Surtees, *Mr. Facey Romford's Hounds*, ed. Jeremy Lewis (Oxford: Oxford University Press, 1984), 120.

38. Elizabeth Gaskell, *Mary Barton*, ed. Edgar Wright (Oxford: Oxford University Press, 1987), 327.

39. Charles Dickens, *A Tale of Two Cities*, ed. Richard Maxwell (London: Penguin, 2003), 31.

40. Thomas Carlyle, *The French Revolution*, ed. K.J. Fielding and David Sorensen (Oxford: Oxford University Press, 1989), 170.

41. Ibid., 225.

42. Knox, *Races of Men*, 213–14.

43. Rudyard Kipling, "The Man Who Would Be King," in *The Man Who Would Be King and Other Stories*, ed. Louis Cornell (Oxford: Oxford University Press, 1987), 255.

44. Richard Burton, *Personal Narrative of a Pilgrimage to Al-Madinah and Meccah*, ed. Isabel Burton (New York: Dover, 1964), 1:11–12.

45. Alexander Francis Chamberlain, *The Child: A Study in the Evolution of Man* (London: Walter Scott, 1900); Granville Stanley Hall, *Adolescence, Its Psychology and Its Relations to Physiology, Anthropology, Sociology, Sex, Crime, Religion and Education*, vol. 1 (London: Appleton, 1908; orig. pub. 1904); Friedrich Froebel, *The Education of Man*, trans. W.N. Hailmann (Mineola, NY: Dover, 2005; orig. pub. 1826); and Karl Groos, *The Play of Animals: A Study of Animal Life and Instinct*, trans. Elizabeth L. Baldwin (London: Chapman and Hall, 1898).

46. Besant, *All Sorts and Conditions of Men*, 107.

47. Charles Dickens, *Sunday Under Three Heads*, in *The Plays and Poems of Charles Dickens, With A Few Miscellanies in Prose*, ed. Richard Herne Shepherd (London: W.H. Allen, 1885), 2:251, 283.

48. Leonore Davidoff and Catherine Hall, *Family Fortunes: Men and Women of the English Middle Class, 1780–1850* (Chicago: University of Chicago Press, 1987), 343; Judith Plotz, *Romanticism and the Vocation of Childhood* (New York: Palgrave, 2001), 1–40.

49. Thomas Hughes, *Tom Brown's Schooldays*, ed. Andrew Sanders (Oxford: Oxford University Press, 1989), 96.

50. Ibid., 238.

51. Dickens, *Hard Times*, 99.

52. Huizinga, *Homo Ludens*, 11.

53. Thomas Babington Macaulay, "Milton," in *Critical and Historical Essays Contributed to "The Edinburgh Review"* (Leipzig: Bernhard Tauchnitz, 1850), 1:9.

54. Spariosu's wonderfully comprehensive discussion of the trope of play in Kantian and Nietzchean philosophies is too complex to rehearse here. See Mihai Spariosu, *Dionysus Reborn: Play and the Aesthetic Dimension in Modern Philosophical and Scientific Discourse*, 33–53, 68–99. See also Mark Johnson, *The Body in the Mind: The Bodily Basis of Meaning, Imagination, and Reason* (Chicago: University of Chicago Press), 147–72.

55. Pater, *The Renaissance*, 2; Matthew Arnold, *Culture and Anarchy and Other Writings*, ed. Stefan Collini (Cambridge: Cambridge University Press, 1993), 128, 37.

56. For a fascinating reading of Victorian realism through the lens of the logic of play as imaginary, see Franklin's *Serious Play: The Cultural Form of the Nineteenth-Century Realist Novel*. Informed primarily by a Romantic-Derridean model of play as liberatory or anticonservative, Franklin deconstructs what he sees as a false opposition between Victorian realism and postmodern theories of "free play," identifying in literary realism a ludic undecidability that is traditionally associated with the antirealist impulse (8–33).

57. Friedrich Schiller, *On the Aesthetic Education of Man*, trans. Reginald Snell (Mineola, NY: Dover, 2004), 133.

58. Herbert Spencer, *Principles of Psychology* (New York: D. Appleton and Co., 1890), 630.

59. Spencer, *The Man Versus the State*, 75, 80.

60. Charles Dickens, *Pictures from Italy*, ed. Kate Flint (London: Penguin, 1998), 85.

61. Ibid., 77–78.

62. Charles Dickens, *The Mystery of Edwin Drood*, ed. David Paroissien (London: Penguin, 2002), 7.

63. Robert Louis Stevenson, *An Inland Voyage* (Northridge, CA: Aegypan Press, 2005), 17.

64. Charles Dickens, *Barnaby Rudge: A Tale of the Riots of 'Eighty*, ed. John Bowen (London: Penguin, 2003), 5.

65. Eric Hobsbawm, "Introduction: Inventing Traditions," in *The Invention of Tradition*, ed. Eric Hobsbawm and Terence Ranger (Cambridge: Cambridge University Press, 1983), 1–14.

66. John Manners, *A Plea for National Holy Days*, 2nd ed. (London: Painter, 1843), 8.

67. Ibid., 7.

68. Ibid., 9.

69. Ibid., 9, 7.

70. Joseph Strutt, *The Sports and Pastimes of the People of England*, ed. J. Charles Cox (Detroit, MI: Singing Tree, 1968), li.

71. John Ruskin, *The Stones of Venice* (New York: Cosimo, 2007), 3:130.

72. Ibid., 2:164. For a provocative discussion of the gendered nature of Ruskin's ethic of aesthetic passivity and its function as a moral corrective to the impulse to compete, see Sharon Aronofsky Weltman, *Performing the Victorian: John Ruskin and Identity in Theater, Science, and Education* (Columbus: Ohio State University Press, 2007), 48–61.

73. E.P. Thompson, *Customs in Common: Studies in Traditional Popular Culture* (New York: New Press, 1993), 377, 404–27.

74. Celia Haddon, *The First Ever English Olimpick Games* (London: Hodder and Stoughton, 2004), 168–73.

75. T.J. Jackson Lears, *No Place of Grace: Antimodernism and the Transformation of American Culture, 1880–1920* (Chicago: University of Chicago Press, 1981), 63.

76. Dickens, *Pictures from Italy*, 45.

77. Lafcadio Hearn, *Glimpses of Unfamiliar Japan* (Rutland, VT: Charles Tuttle, 1976), 499.

78. Philip Meadows Taylor, *Confessions of a Thug*, ed. Patrick Brantlinger (Oxford: Oxford University Press, 1998), 177–78.

79. John Ashton, *The History of Gambling in England* (Montclair, NJ: Patterson Smith, 1969), 2.

80. Ibid., 2, 245, 275.

81. Gaskell, *Mary Barton*, 454.

82. Caillois, *Man, Play and Games*, 17.

83. Thomas Hardy, *The Collected Poems of Thomas Hardy*, ed. Michael Irwin (Ware, Hertfordshire: Wordsworth Poetry Library, 2006), 5.

84. Elaine Freedgood, *Victorian Writing About Risk: Imagining a Safe England in a Dangerous World* (Cambridge: Cambridge University Press, 2000).

85. Ian Hacking, *The Taming of Chance* (Cambridge: Cambridge University Press, 1990), 1–10.

86. For an analysis of Alan Leo's impact on modern astrology, see Patrick Curry, *A Confusion of Prophets: Victorian and Edwardian Astrology* (London: Collins and Brown, 1992), 122–59.

87. Heraclitus, *Fragments*, trans. Brooks Haxton (New York: Penguin, 2001), 51.

88. Dickens, *Edwin Drood*, 23.

89. Stevenson, *An Inland Voyage*, 19.

90. Edward FitzGerald, *The Rubáiyát of Omar Khayyám* (New York: Dover, 1990), 15.

91. Dante Gabriel Rossetti, *Selected Poems and Translations*, ed. Clive Wilmer (Manchester: Carcanet, 1991), 58. For an excellent analysis of the interconnectedness of the logics of play as imaginary and play as fate in Rossetti's vision of modern art, see Jerome McGann, *Dante Gabriel Rossetti and the Game that Must Be Lost* (New Haven, CT, and London: Yale University Press, 2000).

92. For a superb introduction to the ludic dimension to seventeenth-century English culture, see Anna K. Nardo, *The Ludic Self in Seventeenth-Century English Literature* (Albany: State University of New York Press, 1991).

93. Arnold, *Culture and Anarchy*, 128.

94. Ibid., 72, 85, 89, 105.

95. Alfred Tennyson, *Idylls of the King and a Selection of Poems*, ed. Glenn Everett (New York: Signet, 2003), 273.

96. Gregory Bateson, *Steps to an Ecology of Mind* (Chicago: University of Chicago Press, 2000), 182.

97. Nardo, *The Ludic Self in Seventeenth-Century English Literature*, 10.

98. Bateson, *Steps*, 185.

99. Stephen Nachmanovitch, "This Is Play" *New Literary History* 40 (Winter 2009), 19.

100. Nardo, *The Ludic Self*, 10–11.

101. Nachmanovitch, "This Is Play," 19.

102. Handelman and Shulman, *God Inside Out*, 38.

103. Bateson, *Steps*, 190.

104. Ibid., 191.

105. Handelman and Shulman, *God Inside Out*, 44.

106. Ibid., 4–5.

107. Gilles Deleuze and Félix Guattari, *Anti-Oedipus: Capitalism and Schizophrenia*, trans. Robert Hurley, Mark Seem, and Helen R. Lane (Minneapolis: University of Minnesota Press, 1983), 23.

108. Kipling, *Kim*, 125.

109. See Margaret Livingstone, *Vision and Art: The Biology of Seeing* (New York: Abrams, 2002), 12–35.

CHAPTER 2

1. George Bernard Shaw, "Boiled Heroine," in *Victorian Dramatic Criticism*, ed. George Rowell (London: Methuen, 1971), 215.

2. Isobel Armstrong, *Victorian Glassworlds: Glass Culture and the Imagination, 1830–1880* (Oxford: Oxford University Press, 2008), 99.

3. Jane Moody, *Illegitimate Theatre in London, 1770–1840* (Cambridge: Cambridge University Press, 2000), 152.

4. Armstrong, *Victorian Glassworlds*, 99.

5. Quoted in Jim Davis and Victor Emeljanow, *Reflecting the Audience: London Theatregoing, 1840–1888* (Hatfield, UK: University of Hertfordshire Press, 2001), 35.

6. Quoted in Moody, *Illegitimate Theatre*, 152.

7. Elaine Hadley, *Melodramatic Tactics: Theatricalized Dissent in the English Marketplace, 1800–1885* (Stanford, CA: Stanford University Press, 1995), 4.

8. Hadley, *Melodramatic Tactics*, 4–5.

9. Peter Brooks, *The Melodramatic Imagination: Balzac, Henry James, Melodrama, and the Mode of Excess* (New Haven, CT: Yale University Press, 1976), 36, 12, 15.

10. Ibid., 20.

11. Ibid., 36.

12. Edmund Burke, *Reflections on the Revolution in France* (Amherst, NY: Prometheus, 1987), 197.

13. Ibid., 174, 197.

14. For an informative account of the emergence of the myth of Merry England in the early seventeenth century, see Ronald Hutton, *The Rise and Fall of Merry England: The Ritual Year 1400–1700* (Oxford: Oxford University Press, 1994), 153–99.

15. Thompson, *Customs in Common*, 101–2.

16. Frances Power Cobbe, "Wife-Torture in England," in *Crime and Horror in Victorian Literature and Culture*, ed. Matthew Kaiser (San Diego, CA: Cognella, 2010), 1:413.

17. See Thompson, *Customs in Common*, 370–82.

18. Elaine Scarry, *On Beauty and Being Just* (Princeton, NJ: Princeton University Press, 1999), 91, 95.

19. Michael Booth, *Theatre in the Victorian Age* (Cambridge: Cambridge University Press, 1991), 155.

20. Edward Fitzball, *A Sailor's Legacy; or, The Child of a Tar* (London: Dicks, 1888), 13.

21. See Geoffrey J. Marcus, *Heart of Oak: A Survey of British Sea Power in the Georgian Era* (London: Oxford University Press, 1975), 167.

22. "*The Morning Chronicle*, April 5th, 1836," in *The Golden Age of Melodrama: Twelve 19th Century Melodramas*, ed. Michael Kilgarriff (London: Wolfe Publishing, 1974), 201.

23. Ibid., 202.

24. "*The Times*, April 5th, 1836," in *The Golden Age of Melodrama: Twelve 19th Century Melodramas*, ed. Michael Kilgarriff (London: Wolfe Publishing, 1974), 201.

25. "*The Morning Chronicle*," 202.

26. Quoted in Gillian Russell, *The Theatres of War: Performance, Politics, and Society, 1793–1815* (Oxford: Clarendon, 1995), 16.

27. See Marc Baer, *Theatre and Disorder in Late Georgian London* (Oxford: Clarendon Press, 1992).

28. Robert Fagen, "Play, Five Evolutionary Gates, and Paths to Art," in *Play: An Interdisciplinary Synthesis*, ed. F.F. McMahon, Donald E. Lytle, and Brian Sutton-Smith (Lanham, MD: University Press of America, 2005), 27.

29. Ibid., 25.

30. Ibid., 31.

31. Ibid., 27.

32. Ibid., 31.

33. On the relationship between play and love, see Nachmanovitch, "This Is Play," 19; Fagen, "Play," 31.

34. George Daniel, "Remarks" to *Shipwreck of the Medusa; or, The Fatal Raft!* by William Thomas Montcrieff (London: Thomas Richardson, 1830), viii.

35. William Thomas Montcrieff, *Shipwreck of the Medusa; or, The Fatal Raft!* (London: Thomas Richardson, 1830), 22.

36. Douglas Jerrold, *Black-Ey'd Susan; or, "All in the Downs,"* ed. George Rowell (Oxford: Oxford University Press, 1972), 18.

37. Edward Fitzball, *The Red Rover; or, The Mutiny of the Dolphin* (London: John Cumberland, 18--), 13.

38. William H. Williams, *The Wreck; or, The Buccaneer's Bridal* (London: H. Davidson, 18--) 34.

39. Jerrold, *Black-Ey'd Susan*, 17.

40. John Thomas Haines, *Breakers Ahead!; or, A Seaman's Log* (London: J. Duncombe & Co., 18--), 16.

41. See Jerrold, *Black-Ey'd Susan*, 18.

42. Douglas Jerrold, *The Mutiny at the Nore* (London: John Cumberland, 18--), 14.

43. John Thomas Haines, *My Poll and My Partner Joe*, in *Hiss the Villain: Six English and American Melodramas*, ed. Michael Booth (New York: Benjamin Blom, 1964), 97.

44. See John Russell Stephens, *The Profession of the Playwright, British Theatre 1800–1900* (Cambridge: Cambridge University Press, 1992), 15–16.

45. Jean Baudrillard, *Fatal Strategies*, trans. Philip Beitchman and W.G.J. Niesluchowski (New York: Semiotext(e), 1990), 54.
46. Haines, *Breakers Ahead!* 14–15.
47. Ibid., 16.
48. Ibid., 30.
49. Ibid., 11.
50. Thackeray, *Barry Lyndon*, 272.
51. Andrew Leonard Voullare Campbell, *Bound 'Prentice to a Waterman; or, The Flower of Woolnich* (London: J. Cumberland, 1836), 26.
52. Campbell, *Bound 'Prentice*, 27.
53. See Jeffrey N. Cox, "The Ideological Tack of Nautical Melodrama," in *Melodrama: The Cultural Emergence of a Genre*, ed. Michael Hays and Anastasia Nikolopoulou (London: Macmillan, 1999), 172–73.
54. Jerrold, *Black-Ey'd Susan*, 35.
55. Edward Fitzball, *The Pilot; or, A Storm at Sea* (London: Simpkin and Marshall, 1825), 52.
56. William Richardson, *A Mariner of England*, ed. Spencer Childers (London: John Murray, 1908), 292–93.
57. Haines, *My Poll and My Partner Joe*, 111.
58. Jerrold, *Black-Ey'd Susan*, 37, 32.
59. Haines, *My Poll and My Partner Joe*, 110.
60. Frederick Fox Cooper, *Black-Eyed Sukey; or, All in the Dumps* (London: Thomas Richardson, 18--), 33.
61. George Dibdin Pitt, *The Eddystone Elf* (London: Thomas Hailes Lacy, 18--), 25–26.
62. Andrew Leonard Voullare Campbell, *Rule Britannia* (London: John Cumberland, 18--), 17.
63. Campbell, *Rule Britannia*, 27.
64. Haines, *Breakers Ahead!* 18.
65. Ibid., 43.
66. Ibid., 24.
67. Haines, *My Poll and My Partner Joe*, 111, 107–8.
68. Jerrold, *Black-Ey'd Susan*, 18.
69. Ibid., 34.
70. Haines, *Breakers Ahead!* 24–25.
71. Fitzball, *The Red Rover*, 33.
72. See Gilles Deleuze, *Coldness and Cruelty*, in *Masochism*, trans. Jean McNeil (New York: Zone, 1991), 81–90.
73. Jerrold, *The Mutiny at the Nore*, 48.
74. Moody, *Illegitimate Theatre*, 105.
75. Jerrold, *The Mutiny at the Nore*, 47.

76. Jerrold, *Black-Ey'd Susan*, 34.
77. Fitzball, *A Sailor's Legacy*, 15.
78. Montcrieff, *Shipwreck of the Medusa*, 14.
79. Henri Bergson, *Laughter: An Essay on the Meaning of the Comic*, trans. Cloudesley Brereton and Fred Rothwell (Copenhagen: Green Integer, 1999), 28, 39.
80. Bergson, *Laughter*, 56, 34–35.
81. John Thomas Haines, *The Ocean of Life: or, Every Inch a Sailor* (London: Thomas Hailes Lacy, 1850), 38.
82. Fitzball, *A Sailor's Legacy*, 14.
83. John Bernard, *Retrospections of the Stage* (London: 1830), 2:129.
84. Jerrold, *Black-Ey'd Susan*, 19.
85. Isaac Pocock, *For England Ho!* 19. I quote from Pocock's handwritten script, which is now at the Huntington Library in San Marino, California.
86. Montcrieff, *Shipwreck of the Medusa*, 13.
87. Campbell, *Rule Britannia*, 18–19.
88. Haines, *The Ocean of Life*, 14.
89. Haines, *Breakers Ahead!* 43.
90. Louis Althusser, "Ideology and Ideological State Apparatuses (Notes Towards an Investigation)," in *Lenin and Philosophy*, trans. Ben Brewster (New York: Monthly Review, 1971), 175.
91. Jerrold, *Black-Ey'd Susan*, 36.
92. Ibid., 39.
93. Ibid., 39–40.
94. Fitzball, *A Sailor's Legacy*, 14.
95. Bergson, *Laughter*, 46, 20.
96. Pocock, *For England Ho!* 36; Haines, *Breakers Ahead!* 15.
97. Bergson, *Laughter*, 106.
98. Haines, *Breakers Ahead!* 20–21.
99. Fitzball, *The Pilot*, 2.
100. Jerrold, *Black-Ey'd Susan*, 18.
101. Campbell, *Rule Britannia*, 32.
102. Haines, *Breakers Ahead!* 23.
103. Ibid., 22.
104. Fitzball, *The Pilot*, 38.
105. Marcus, *Heart of Oak*, 227.
106. Haines, *My Poll and My Partner Joe*, 100.
107. Ibid., 122.
108. Pitt, *The Eddystone Elf*, 17–18.
109. Haines, *Breakers Ahead!* 21.
110. Fitzball, *The Pilot*, 5.

111. Shaw, "Boiled Heroine," 215–16. The review was originally published in *The Saturday Review*, 28 March 1896.
112. Ibid., 217.

CHAPTER 3

1. Emily Brontë, "Why ask to know the date, the clime?" in *Poems of Solitude*, ed. Helen Dunmore (London: Hesperus, 2004), 78.
2. See Mrs. Ellis H. Chadwick, *In the Footsteps of the Brontës* (London: Sir Isaac Pitman and Sons, 1914), 124.
3. Lee Edelman, *No Future: Queer Theory and the Death Drive* (Durham, NC: Duke University Press, 2004), 3–5.
4. Terry Eagleton, *Myths of Power: A Marxist Study of the Brontës* (Houndmills, UK: Palgrave Macmillan, 1975), 102.
5. Q.D. Leavis, "A Fresh Approach to *Wuthering Heights*," *Collected Essays*, vol. 1, ed. G. Singh (Cambridge: Cambridge University Press, 1983), 229.
6. Georges Bataille, *Literature and Evil*, trans. Alastair Hamilton (London: Marion Boyars, 1973; orig. pub. 1957), 19–29.
7. See, for instance, Leo Bersani, *A Future for Astyanax: Character and Desire in Literature* (New York: Columbia University Press, 1984); Sandra M. Gilbert and Susan Gubar, *The Madwoman in the Attic: The Woman Writer and the Nineteenth-Century Literary Imagination*, 2nd ed. (New Haven, CT: Yale University Press, 1984), 248–308; James Kavanagh, *Emily Brontë* (Oxford: Blackwell, 1985); Michael D. Reed, "The Power of *Wuthering Heights*: A Psychoanalytic Examination," *Psychocultural Review* 1 (1977): 21–42.
8. Elizabeth Gaskell, *The Life of Charlotte Brontë*, ed. Elisabeth Jay (London: Penguin, 1997), 69.
9. Carol Bock, "'Our plays': the Brontë juvenilia," *The Cambridge Companion to the Brontës*, ed. Heather Glen (Cambridge: Cambridge University Press, 2002), 35. Emphasis mine.
10. Polly Teale, *Brontë* (London: Nick Hern, 2005), 29.
11. Gaskell, 62.
12. Ibid., 149, 46, 79.
13. Sydney Dobell, "Currer Bell," *The Life and Letters of Sydney Dobell*, vol. 1, ed. Emily Jolly (London, 1878), 165–71.
14. F.R. Leavis, *The Great Tradition* (New York: Doubleday, 1948), 38.
15. See Lyn Pykett, *Emily Brontë* (Savage, MD: Barnes and Noble, 1989), 73.
16. Edward Chitham, *The Birth of Wuthering Heights: Emily Brontë at Work* (Houndmills, UK: Palgrave, 2001), 3.
17. Quoted in Gilbert and Gubar, *Madwoman in the Attic,* 257–58.
18. Gilbert and Gubar, *Madwoman in the Attic,* 258.

19. J. Hillis Miller, *The Disappearance of God: Five Nineteenth-Century Writers* (Urbana: University of Illinois Press, 2000), 160. Emphasis mine.

20. Emily Brontë, *Wuthering Heights*, ed. Diane Long Hoeveler (Boston: Houghton Mifflin, 2002), 58.

21. Only once, in fact, are we given specific details of their secret life on the moors. Heathcliff informs Nelly that Cathy, who lies injured at Thrushcross Grange, lost "her shoes in the bog" during a "race" to the Grange. He makes clear, however, that the race was not the *primary* aim of their "escape[ ]" to the moors. It was merely an extemporaneous expression of playfulness during their "ramble." Ibid., 59.

22. D.H. Lawrence, "Pornography and Obscenity," *Selected Literary Criticism*, ed. Anthony Beal (New York: Viking Press, 1956; orig. pub. 1929), 32. I am indebted to Daniel Donoghue for this etymology.

23. In her wonderfully suggestive lecture, "Better Left Unsaid: Dickens's Narrative Refusals," delivered to much acclaim at the Dickens Universe at the University of California at Santa Cruz in August 2006, Robyn Warhol outlined the narratological significance of various types of ellipsis, or "unnarration," as she termed it. I am grateful for her insights.

24. Brontë, *Wuthering Heights*, 58.

25. Ibid., 85.

26. Ibid., 61–62, 156.

27. Ibid., 26.

28. Ibid., 39.

29. Wolfgang Iser, "Interaction between Text and Reader," *The Reader in the Text: Essays on Audience and Interpretation*, ed. Susan Suleiman and I. Crosman (Princeton, NJ: Princeton University Press, 1980), 112.

30. Brontë, *Wuthering Heights*, 51.

31. Ibid., 52.

32. Ibid., 96.

33. Ibid., 37–38.

34. Ibid., 38, 40.

35. Ibid., 42.

36. Ibid., 43.

37. Ibid., 42.

38. Ibid., 62.

39. Althusser, "Ideology and Ideological State Apparatuses (Notes towards an Investigation)," 175.

40. Brontë, *Wuthering Heights*, 48.

41. Pykett, *Emily Brontë*, 102. Emphasis in original.

42. Brontë, *Wuthering Heights*, 92.

43. Gilbert and Gubar, *Madwoman in the Attic*, 291. See Deleuze, *Coldness and Cruelty*, 86–90.

44. Brontë, *Wuthering Heights*, 50.
45. Ibid., 105.
46. Sutton-Smith, *The Ambiguity of Play*, 9.
47. Plato, *The Republic and Other Works*, trans. Benjamin Jowett (New York: Anchor Books, 1973), 86, 113–14. See also 92 and 296.
48. See, for instance, Colin Heywood, *A History of Childhood: Children and Childhood in the West from Medieval to Modern Times* (Cambridge, UK: Polity, 2001); Philippe Ariès, *Centuries of Childhood: A Social History of Family Life*, trans. Robert Baldick (New York: Vintage, 1962); Davidoff and Hall, *Family Fortunes: Men and Women of the English Middle Class, 1780–1850*; Kenneth D. Brown, *The British Toy Business: A History since 1700* (London: Hambledon Press, 1996).
49. John Locke, *Some Thoughts Concerning Education; and, Of the Conduct of the Understanding*, ed. Ruth W. Grant and Nathan Tarcov (Indianapolis: Hackett, 1996), 100.
50. Ibid., 155. Emphases mine.
51. Mary Wollstonecraft, *A Vindication of the Rights of Women* (Buffalo, NY: Prometheus, 1989), 169.
52. Ibid., 169–70.
53. See Brown, *British Toy Business*, 11–40.
54. Davidoff and Hall, *Family Fortunes*, 343.
55. Brown, *British Toy Business*, 15.
56. See ibid., 16.
57. Davidoff and Hall, *Family Fortunes*, 344.
58. Thomas Day, *History of Sanford and Merton* (Philadelphia: J.B. Lippincott, 1887), 10–11.
59. Ibid., 234.
60. Ibid., 234, 237.
61. Ibid., 129.
62. Quoted in Davidoff and Hall, *Family Fortunes*, 281.
63. Quoted in Chamberlain, *The Child: A Study in the Evolution of Man*, 16.
64. Froebel, *The Education of Man*, 55.
65. Quoted in Groos, *The Play of Animals: A Study of Animal Life and Instinct*, 9.
66. Quoted in Chamberlain, *The Child*, 17.
67. Quoted in Peter K. Smith, "Play, Ethology, and Education: A Personal Account," *The Future of Play Theory: A Multidisciplinary Inquiry into the Contributions of Brian Sutton-Smith*, ed. Anthony T. Pellegrini (Albany: State University of New York Press, 1995), 11.
68. Piaget, 144–45.
69. Jerome S. Bruner, Alison Jolly, and Kathy Sylva, *Play: Its Role in Development and Evolution* (New York: Penguin, 1976), 20.

70. Thomas E. Jordan, *Victorian Childhood: Themes and Variations* (Albany: State University of New York Press, 1987), 195.

71. See Sigmund Freud, *Beyond the Pleasure Principle*, trans. James Strachey (New York: W.W. Norton, 1989), 13–16.

72. By "economic," Freud is referring, of course, to a *psychic-physical* economy of pleasure and unpleasure. However, in his 1908 essay, "Character and Anal Eroticism," Freud suggests that adult "character-traits" of "parsimony and obstinacy" "are prominent in people who were formerly anal erotics" as infants, and that people who resist letting go of their valuables experience in a sublimated form the fecal retentiveness of their babyhood. The child's retentiveness with regards to its mother, therefore, is proprietary, a desire to possess. Sigmund Freud, "Character and Anal Eroticism," trans. James Strachey, *The Freud Reader*, ed. Peter Gay (New York: W.W. Norton, 1989), 294–95.

73. H.G. Wells, *Floor Games* (Alexandria, VA: Skirmisher, 2006), 4.

74. Havelock Ellis, *The Criminal* (London: Walter Scott, 1901), 383–84.

75. Readers might be interested to learn that Cesare Lombroso, the so-called father of criminology and the scholar on whose work Ellis models his own, appears in his classic *Criminal Man* (1876–84) defiantly immune to the modern ideology of child play. Going against the grain of nineteenth-century European thought, Lombroso—the father of Paola Lombroso, a passionate proponent, as we have seen, of productivist readings of child play—draws an explicit connection between criminals and children, claiming not only that criminals are childlike but that children possess innate criminality. Like criminals, he contends, children are "more cruel than kind," sneaky, vain, lazy, wrathful, vengeful, dishonest, amoral, prone to "masturbation" and vice, and insincere: "When you believe they love you," he stunningly complains, "you discover that children are just like prostitutes." Cesare Lombroso, *Criminal Man*, trans. Mary Gibson and Nicole Hahn Rafter (Durham, NC: Duke University Press, 2006), 188–92.

76. Plotz, *Romanticism and the Vocation of Childhood*, 31, xvi.

77. William Wordsworth, "The Tables Turned," in *The Major Works*, ed. Stephen Gill (Oxford: Oxford University Press, 1984), 130–31.

78. Wordsworth, *The Prelude*, in *Major Works*, ed. S. Gill, 382.

79. Ibid., 382, 386–87.

80. Spencer, *Principles of Psychology*, 533.

81. Schiller, *On the Aesthetic Education of Man*, 133.

82. Ibid., 80. Emphasis in original.

83. Burton, *Personal Narrative of a Pilgrimage*, 2:103.

84. Ibid., 103–4.

85. Groos, *Play of Animals*, 7.

86. Ibid., xx. Emphasis in original.

87. Wordsworth, "My Heart Leaps up When I Behold," in *The Major Works*, ed. S. Gill, 246.
88. Anonymous, *Letters from London* (London: Darton and Harvey, 1808), 15.
89. Granville Stanley Hall, *Adolescence: Its Psychology and Relations to Physiology, Anthropology, Sociology, Sex, Crime, Religion and Education,* vol. 1 (London: Appleton, 1908), 233.
90. Ibid., 202.
91. Ibid., 216, 230, 217.
92. Ibid., 231.
93. Ibid., 217.
94. Hughes, *Tom Brown's Schooldays*, 255.
95. Colin Heywood, *A History of Childhood*, 114.
96. Charles Dickens, *Our Mutual Friend*, ed. Michael Cotsell (Oxford: Oxford University Press, 1989), 223.
97. Ibid., 222.
98. Arnold, *Culture and Anarchy and Other Writings*, 72.
99. Georges Bataille, *Theory of Religion*, trans. Robert Hurley (New York: Zone, 1992), 23, 25.
100. Brontë, *Wuthering Heights*, 59–60. Emphasis mine. With "oceanic" I allude to Freud's characterization in *Civilization and Its Discontents* (1929) of the spiritual "sensation of 'eternity'" as "a feeling as of something limitless, unbounded—as it were, 'oceanic,'"—which he attributes to the subject's pre-Oedipal nostalgia. Sigmund Freud, *Civilization and Its Discontents*, trans. James Strachey (New York: W.W. Norton, 1989), 11.
101. Brontë, *Wuthering Heights*, 60.
102. Bataille, *Theory of Religion*, 42, 27.
103. Brontë, *Wuthering Heights*, 74, 62.
104. Bataille, "The Notion of Expenditure," in *Visions of Excess: Selected Writings, 1927–1939*, ed. Allan Stoekl, trans. Stoekl, Carl R. Lovitt, and Donald M. Leslie, Jr. (Minneapolis: University of Minnesota Press, 1985), 119.
105. Bataille, *Theory of Religion*, 43.

CHAPTER 4

1. Robert Burns, *Collected Poems of Robert Burns*, ed. Tim Burke (London: Wordsworth Editions, 2008), 340.
2. For a poignant account of Stevenson's ill health in California, see his stepdaughter's autobiography: Isobel Field, *This Life I've Loved: An Autobiography* (Lafayette, CA: Great West Books, 2005), 110–21.
3. Donald Worster, *A Passion for Nature: The Life of John Muir* (Oxford: Oxford University Press, 2008), 14.

4. John Muir, *The Mountains of California* (Stilwell, KS: Digireads, 2008), 97.
5. See Worster, *A Passion for Nature*, 122.
6. Kevin Starr, *California: A History* (New York: Modern Library, 2005), xi.
7. John Muir, "Hetch Hetchy Invaders," *New York Times* 21 July 1913: 6.
8. Ralph Waldo Emerson, *Nature; Addresses and Lectures*, in *Ralph Waldo Emerson: A Critical Edition of the Major Works*, ed. Richard Poirier (Oxford: Oxford University Press, 1990), 6.
9. Katharine D. Osbourne, *Robert Louis Stevenson in California* (Chicago: A.C. McClurg, 1911), 28.
10. Robert Louis Stevenson, *The Amateur Emigrant*, in *Travels with a Donkey in the Cévennes and The Amateur Emigrant*, ed. Christopher MacLachlan (London: Penguin, 2004), 212, 226. Though an abridged version of Part 2 of *Amateur Emigrant* was published in 1883, including the portion discussed in this section, the text was not published in its entirety until 1895, a year after Stevenson's death.
11. Ibid., 226, 224.
12. Robert Louis Stevenson, "San Francisco: A Modern Cosmopolis," in *The Works of Robert Louis Stevenson*, vol. 11 (New York: Davos Press, 1906), 86.
13. William Ernest Henley to Sidney Colvin, in *The Letters of Robert Louis Stevenson: August 1879–September 1882*, vol. 3, ed. Bradford A. Booth and Ernest Mehew (New Haven, CT: Yale University Press, 1994), 41.
14. I am referring to Book I, "Recalled to Life," of *A Tale of Two Cities*.
15. Stevenson, *Amateur Emigrant*, 206, 226.
16. See Barry Menikoff, *Narrating Scotland: The Imagination of Robert Louis Stevenson* (Columbia: University of South Carolina Press, 2005), 28–48.
17. Stevenson, *Amateur Emigrant*, 226.
18. Jenni Calder, "Figures in a Landscape: Scott, Stevenson, and Routes to the Past," in *Robert Louis Stevenson: Writer of Boundaries*, ed. Richard Ambrosini and Richard Dury (Madison: University of Wisconsin Press, 2006), 132.
19. Claire Harman, *Myself and the Other Fellow: A Life of Robert Louis Stevenson* (New York: HarperCollins, 2005), 201.
20. Robert Louis Stevenson, *The Silverado Squatters* (Northridge, CA: Aegypan Press, 2005), 25.
21. John Muir, *My First Summer in the Sierra* (Mineola, NY: Dover, 2004), 37.
22. Steven J. Holmes, *The Young John Muir: An Environmental Biography* (Madison: University of Wisconsin Press, 1999), 7.
23. Muir, *Mountains of California*, 38.
24. See Muir, *My First Summer*, 26, 121.
25. John Muir, "The Wild Parks and Forest Reservations of the West," in *John Muir: Nature Writings*, ed. William Cronon (New York: The Library of America, 1997), 721.
26. Muir, *My First Summer*, 59.

27. Ibid., 73.
28. Muir, *Mountains of California*, 15.
29. Muir, *My First Summer*, 139.
30. Worster, *A Passion for Nature*, 48.
31. Muir, *My First Summer*, 24, 118–19.
32. Ibid., 31.
33. Michael P. Cohen, *The Pathless Way: John Muir and American Wilderness* (Madison: University of Wisconsin Press, 1984), 227.
34. Muir, *Mountains of California*, 7, 95–96.
35. Stevenson, *Silverado Squatters*, 31.
36. Stevenson, *Amateur Emigrant*, 223; *Silverado Squatters*, 55.
37. Stevenson, *Silverado Squatters*, 13.
38. Muir, *Mountains of California*, 5.
39. Muir, *My First Summer*, 12, 63.
40. Stevenson, *Amateur Emigrant*, 226.
41. Muir, "Wild Parks," 743.
42. Muir, *Mountains of California*, 6.
43. Lawrence Buell, *The Environmental Imagination: Thoreau, Nature Writing, and the Formation of American Culture* (Cambridge, MA: Belknap-Harvard University Press, 1995), 155.
44. Muir, *Mountains of California*, 7.
45. Muir, *My First Summer*, 114.
46. Muir, *Mountains of California*, 33.
47. Muir, *My First Summer*, 56.
48. Stevenson, *Silverado Squatters*, 18.
49. See Harman, *Myself and the Other Fellow*, 193.
50. Osbourne, *Stevenson in California*, 3.
51. Stevenson, "San Francisco," 87.
52. Stevenson to Edmund Gosse, in *Selected Letters of Robert Louis Stevenson*, ed. Ernest Mehew (New Haven, CT: Yale University Press, 1997), 167–68.
53. Stevenson to Sidney Colvin, *Selected Letters*, 168.
54. Stevenson, "San Francisco," 88.
55. Robert Crawford, *Scotland's Books* (London: Penguin, 2007), 496.
56. Stevenson, *Silverado Squatters*, 51.
57. Ibid., 100.
58. Ibid., 102.
59. Ibid., 46, 19.
60. Quoted in Osbourne, *Stevenson in California*, 81.
61. John Muir, *The Story of My Boyhood and Youth*, in *John Muir: Nature Writings*, ed. William Cronon (New York: Library of America, 1997), 7, 14.
62. Muir, *Boyhood and Youth*, 17, 12, 14, 15, 16.

63. Ibid., 24.

64. Robert Louis Stevenson, "Child's Play," in *Virginibus Puerisque and Other Papers* (New York: Elibron, 2006), 111.

65. Stevenson, "San Francisco," 88.

66. Stevenson, *Silverado Squatters*, 95.

67. Stevenson, "San Francisco," 88.

68. Ibid., 87–88.

69. Stevenson, *Silverado Squatters*, 6.

70. Stevenson, *Silverado Squatters*, 7.

71. Muir, *My First Summer*, 118.

72. Ibid., 23.

73. Ibid., 88–89, 130.

74. Muir, *Mountains of California*, 107; *My First Summer*, 39, 96; *Mountains of California*, 99.

75. Muir, *Boyhood and Youth*, 56.

76. Ibid., 11; "Wild Parks," 723.

77. Muir, *My First Summer*, 16.

78. Ibid., 131.

79. Ibid., 42.

80. Stevenson, *Silverado Squatters*, 35.

81. Stephen Arata, "Stevenson, Morris, and the Value of Idleness," in *Robert Louis Stevenson: Writer of Boundaries*, ed. Richard Ambrosini and Richard Dury (Madison: University of Wisconsin Press, 2006), 6.

82. Stevenson, *Silverado Squatters*, 48.

83. Robert Louis Stevenson, "An Apology for Idlers," in *Virginibus Puerisque and Other Papers* (New York: Elibron, 2006), 57.

84. Robert Louis Stevenson, *An Inland Voyage* (Northridge, CA: Aegypan Press, 2005), 19.

85. Stevenson, *Silverado Squatters*, 37.

86. Ibid., 60, 66.

87. Ibid., 79, 96.

88. Muir, *My First Summer*, 34, 129.

89. Ibid., 85.

90. See Cohen, *The Pathless Way*, 84–85; Muir, *My First Summer*, 105.

91. Muir, *Boyhood and Youth*, 83. Holmes argues that Muir's resistance to "Americanization," which he associated with "Anglo-Saxon" aggression, can be traced to his opposition to the Civil War. The war alienated Muir from his fellow Americans and made him feel more Scottish. See Holmes, *Young John Muir*, 97.

92. Muir, *Mountains of California*, 79.

93. Buell, *Environmental Imagination*, 194.

94. Cohen, *Pathless Way*, 206.

95. Quoted in Worster, *A Passion for Nature*, 420. See James Phelan, "Hetch Hetchy and the Wealth-Producers," *California Weekly* 18 (26 March 1909): 283–84.

96. Worster, *A Passion for Nature*, 420.

97. See ibid., 434.

98. Frederick Jackson Turner, "The Significance of the Frontier in American History," in *Rereading Frederick Jackson Turner: "The Significance of the Frontier in American History" and Other Essays*, ed. John Mack Faragher (New Haven, CT: Yale University Press, 1994), 53.

99. Cohen, *Pathless Way*, 219.

100. Stevenson, *Silverado Squatters*, 5.

101. Edmund Burke, *A Philosophical Enquiry into the Origin of our Ideas of the Sublime and Beautiful*, ed. James T. Boulton (Notre Dame, IN: University of Notre Dame, 1958), 46.

102. Burke, *Philosophical Enquiry*, 51.

103. Ibid., 65.

104. Ibid., 67; emphases in original.

105. Immanuel Kant, *The Critique of Judgment*, trans. J.H. Bernard (Amherst, NY: Prometheus Books, 2000), 103.

106. Ibid., 125.

107. Ibid., 126.

108. Ibid., 102.

109. Samuel Taylor Coleridge, "Hymn Before Sun-Rise, In the Vale of Chamouni," in *The Major Works*, ed. H.J. Jackson (Oxford: Oxford University Press, 1985), 120.

110. Percy Bysshe Shelley, "Mont Blanc," in *Shelley's Poetry and Prose*, ed. Donald H. Reiman and Neil Fraistat (New York: W.W. Norton, 2002), 99.

111. Wordsworth, "Lines Written a Few Miles above Tintern Abbey," in *Major Works*, ed. S. Gill, 134.

112. Stevenson, *Amateur Emigrant*, 226–27.

113. Muir, *My First Summer*, 63.

114. Mihai I. Spariosu, *God of Many Names: Play, Poetry, and Power in Hellenic Thought from Homer to Aristotle* (Durham, NC: Duke University Press, 1991), 66–67.

115. Quoted in Spariosu, *God of Many Names*, 66.

116. Heraclitus, *Fragments*, trans. Brooks Haxton (New York: Penguin, 2001), 27.

117. Muir, *My First Summer*, 64.

118. Ibid., 64–65.

119. Ibid., 65–66.

120. Muir, *Mountains of California*, 95.

121. Ibid., 96. He describes this same moment in his posthumously published *A Thousand-Mile Walk to the Gulf*, ed. William Frederic Badè (Gloucester, UK: Dodo Press, 2008), 61.

122. Stevenson, *Silverado Squatters*, 70–71.

123. Ibid., 72–73.
124. Ibid., 71.
125. Leo Marx, *The Machine in the Garden: Technology and the Pastoral Ideal in America* (Oxford: Oxford University Press, 2000), 7–8.
126. Terry Gifford, *Reconnecting with John Muir: Essays in Post-Pastoral Practice* (Athens: University of Georgia Press, 2006), 28–36.
127. Buell, *Environmental Imagination*, 192.
128. Muir, *Mountains of California*, 47.
129. Ibid., 129, 76.
130. Worster, *A Passion for Nature*, 159.
131. Starr, *California*, 111.
132. Muir, *Mountains of California*, 40.
133. John Muir, "God's First Temples," in *John Muir: Nature Writings*, ed. William Cronon (New York: Library of America, 1997), 632. "God's First Temples" was first published in the *Sacramento Daily Union* on February 5, 1876.
134. Muir, *Mountains of California*, 47.
135. Ibid., 113–19.
136. Muir, *My First Summer*, 62, 52.
137. Ibid., 112.
138. Muir, "Wild Parks," 741.
139. Muir, *My First Summer*, 115.
140. Ibid., 116.
141. Ibid., 98.
142. Ibid., 62.
143. Ibid., 142.
144. Muir, *Thousand-Mile Walk*, 60.
145. Stevenson, *Amateur Emigrant*, 134.
146. Ibid., 114.
147. Ibid., 109.
148. Muir, *Boyhood and Youth*, 31.
149. Ibid., 23.

CHAPTER 5

1. Quoted in E.F. Benson, *As We Were: A Victorian Peep Show* (London: Longmans, Green and Co., 1930), 212.
2. Richard Ellmann, *Oscar Wilde* (New York: Vintage, 1987), 39.
3. Oscar Wilde to William Ward, in *The Complete Letters of Oscar Wilde*, ed. Merlin Holland and Rupert Hart-Davis (New York: Henry Holt, 2000), 60.
4. Quoted in Ellmann, *Oscar Wilde*, 39.
5. Ibid., 49. Ruskin biographer Tim Hilton suggests that "road" might have been a euphemism for "sewer." See Tim Hilton, *John Ruskin* (New Haven, CT: Yale University Press, 2002), 549.

6. Quoted in Ellmann, *Oscar Wilde*, 39.

7. Oscar Wilde, *A Woman of No Importance*, in *The Complete Works of Oscar Wilde* (New York: Harper and Row, 1989), 458–59.

8. Oscar Wilde, *The Importance of Being Earnest*, in *The Portable Oscar Wilde*, ed. Richard Aldington and Stanley Weintraub (New York: Penguin, 1974), 440.

9. Wilde to Reginald Harding, in Holland and Hart-Davis, *Complete Letters*, 21.

10. Wilde, *A Woman of No Importance*, 437.

11. Walter E. Houghton, *The Victorian Frame of Mind, 1830–1870* (New Haven, CT: Yale University Press, 1957), 233.

12. Quoted in Ellmann, *Oscar Wilde*, 19.

13. Oscar Wilde, "The Soul of Man Under Socialism," in *The Artist as Critic: Critical Writings of Oscar Wilde*, ed. Richard Ellmann (Chicago: University of Chicago Press, 1969), 286, 255, 286.

14. Wilde, "Soul of Man," 261, 269.

15. Ibid., 273, 274.

16. Ibid., 266.

17. Ibid., 285.

18. Ibid., 282, 263.

19. Ibid., 263.

20. See Jeff Nunokawa, *Tame Passions of Wilde: The Styles of Manageable Desire* (Princeton, NJ: Princeton University Press, 2003), 71–89.

21. Lawrence Danson, *Wilde's Intentions: The Artist in His Criticism* (Oxford: Oxford University Press, 1997), 151–52.

22. Wilde, "Soul of Man," 262, 264.

23. Oscar Wilde, "Phrases and Philosophies for the Use of the Young," in *The Artist as Critic: Critical Writings of Oscar Wilde*, ed. Richard Ellmann (Chicago: University of Chicago Press, 1969), 434.

24. Wilde to James McNeill Whistler, in Holland and Hart-Davis, *Complete Letters*, 139.

25. Wilde to Harding, in ibid., 21.

26. Wilde to William Ward, in ibid., 59.

27. Wilde to Norman Forbes-Robertson, in ibid., 127.

28. Ibid., 168.

29. Oscar Wilde, "The Decay of Lying," in *The Artist as Critic: Critical Writings of Oscar Wilde*, ed. Richard Ellmann (Chicago: University of Chicago Press, 1969), 295.

30. Ibid., 298.

31. Ibid., 299.

32. Wilde, "Soul of Man," 280.

33. Amanda Anderson, *The Power of Distance: Cosmopolitanism and the Cultivation of Detachment* (Princeton, NJ: Princeton University Press, 2001), 152–53; Oscar Wilde, "The Critic as Artist," in *The Artist as Critic: Critical Writings of Oscar Wilde*, ed. Richard Ellmann (Chicago: University of Chicago Press, 1969), 406.

34. Oscar Wilde, *Lady Windermere's Fan*, in *The Complete Works of Oscar Wilde*, 388.

35. Oscar Wilde, *The Picture of Dorian Gray*, ed. Norman Page (Peterborough, Ontario: Broadview, 1998), 116.

36. Walter J. Ong, *Fighting for Life: Contest, Sexuality, and Consciousness* (Ithaca, NY: Cornell University Press, 1981), 28.

37. Wilde, "Soul of Man," 269.

38. Ong, *Fighting for Life*, 25, 22.

39. Peter Sloterdijk, *Critique of Cynical Reason*, trans. Michael Eldred (Minneapolis: University of Minnesota Press, 1987), 13.

40. Ong, *Fighting for Life*, 15.

41. Wilde, "Critic as Artist," 369.

42. Ibid., 343, 401.

43. Ibid., 381.

44. Oscar Wilde, *De Profundis* (New York: Modern Library, 1992), 37.

45. See Neil McKenna, *The Secret Life of Oscar Wilde* (New York: Basic Books, 2005), 398–409. According to McKenna, the first person to become concerned about Wilde's compulsive masturbation, which was then considered a possible symptom of insanity, was W.D. Morrison, the prison chaplain at Wandsworth Prison, where Wilde was incarcerated before his transfer to Reading.

46. Quoted in McKenna, *Secret Life*, 370.

47. See Richard Kaye, "Oscar Wilde and the Politics of Posthumous Sainthood: Hofmannsthal, Mirbeau, Proust," in *Oscar Wilde and Modern Culture: The Making of a Legend*, ed. Joseph Bristow (Athens: Ohio University Press, 2008), 110–32.

48. Wilde, *De Profundis*, 38.

49. Ibid., 9, 93.

50. Ibid., 38–39.

51. Ibid., 39.

52. Wilde, "The Soul of Man," 286.

53. Wilde, *De Profundis*, 92.

54. Ibid., 6.

55. Ibid., 9.

56. Ibid., 7, 8, 29.

57. Ibid., 35, 107, 35.

58. Ibid., 31.

59. Ibid., 37, 94.

60. Wilde to Ada Leverson, in Holland and Hart-Davis, *Complete Letters*, 635.

61. Wilde, *De Profundis*, 105.

62. Ibid., 74.

63. Ibid., 36.

64. Wilde to Robert Ross, in Holland and Hart-Davis, *Complete Letters*, 1192; Lord Alfred Douglas, "Two Loves," in *Aesthetes and Decadents of the 1890's: An Anthology of British Poetry and Prose*, ed. Karl Beckson (Chicago: Academy Chicago, 1981), 82.

65. Wilde, *De Profundis*, 62.

66. Wilde, *Dorian Gray*, 124.

67. Ibid., 62.

68. Ibid., 66.

69. Ibid., 155–56.

70. Ibid., 115–16.

71. Hilary Fraser, *Beauty and Belief: Aesthetics and Religion in Victorian Literature* (Cambridge: Cambridge University Press, 1986), 225.

72. See Ellis Hanson, *Decadence and Catholicism* (Cambridge, MA: Harvard University Press, 1997), 229–96.

73. Fraser, *Beauty and Belief*, 206, 210, 222.

74. Hanson, *Decadence and Catholicism*, 233, 231.

75. Wilde, *De Profundis*, 4.

76. Ibid., 14, 5, 64, 50.

77. Ibid., 4.

78. Ibid., 83.

79. Oscar Wilde, "Impressions of America," in *The Artist as Critic: Critical Writings of Oscar Wilde*, ed. Richard Ellmann (Chicago: University of Chicago Press, 1969), 9.

80. Wilde, *De Profundis*, 69.

81. Ibid., 61.

82. Oscar Wilde, *The Ballad of Reading Gaol*, in *The Complete Works of Oscar Wilde*, 844, 849, 843.

83. Harvey Cox, *The Feast of Fools: A Theological Essay on Festivity and Fantasy* (New York: Harper and Row, 1969), 140.

84. See Elizabeth-Anne Stewart, *Jesus the Holy Fool* (Franklin, WI: Sheed and Ward, 1999), 6, 27–33.

85. Cox, *The Feast of Fools*, 140.

86. Wilde, *De Profundis*, 90.

87. Wilde, *Ballad of Reading Gaol*, 848.

88. Wilde, *De Profundis*, 90–91.

89. Ibid., 91.

90. Dion Boucicault to Mrs. George Lewis, in Holland and Hart-Davis, *Complete Letters*, 135.

91. Christopher Craft analyzes H.C.'s dream in *Another Kind of Love: Male Homosexual Desire in English Discourse, 1850–1920* (Berkeley: University of California Press, 1994), 106–11.

92. Havelock Ellis, *Studies in the Psychology of Sex*, Volume II: *Sexual Inversion* (Charleston, SC: BiblioBazaar, 2006), 211.

Index

alea, 37–38, 57, 72, 98, 141. *See also* gambling
Althusser, Louis, 80, 99
Anderson, Amanda, 153
animal play, 30, 43, 47, 63, 87, 109. *See also paideia*
Arata, Stephen, 132
Ariès, Philippe, 186n48
Armstrong, Isobel, 51–52
Arnold, Matthew, 5, 30, 32–33, 40, 111–12, 131, 149, 152–53, 155
Arnold, Thomas, 148–49
Arts and Crafts Movement, 35
Ashton, John, 37

Bailey, Peter, 27, 176n32
Bakhtin, Mikhail, 174n14
Bataille, Georges, 87–88, 112–15
Bateson, Gregory, 43–44, 47, 63, 67
Baudrillard, Jean, 66
Bergson, Henri, 78, 80
Bersani, Leo, 184n7
Besant, Walter, 13, 30
Bock, Carol, 89
Booth, Michael, 60
Boucicault, Dion, 170
Bratton, Jacky, and Ann Featherstone, 28
Brontë, Anne, 89, 92, 112
Brontë, Charlotte, 87, 89–91
Brontë, Emily, 4, 7–8, 30, 42, 45–46, 85–102, 111–16, 119–21, 130–31; Gondal, 46, 89, 91–93; *Wuthering Heights*, 7, 86–88, 91–102, 112–16, 185n21
Brooks, Peter, 55, 57–58
Brown, Kenneth, 104, 186n48

Bruner, Jerome, and Allison Jolly and Kathy Sylva, 106
Buell, Lawrence, 127, 133, 140
Bulwer-Lytton, Edward, 25, 38
Burke, Edmund, 57, 135–37
Burns, Robert, 117–18, 125
Burton, Richard, 29–30, 108–9

Caillois, Roger, 37–38, 154, 174n14
Calder, Jenni, 124
Carlyle, Thomas, 29, 150
Campbell, Andrew, 67, 74–75, 79–81
Carroll, Lewis, 2; *Alice's Adventures in Wonderland*, 2, 4, 47
Chamberlain, Alexander Francis, 30, 103
chance, 37–39, 74. *See also alea*
Chaplin, Charlie, 81
child play, 5, 86, 93–116, 128–30, 138–39, 142; and cosmic caprice, 38–39, 112–16, 137–39, 143; modern ideology of, 31–32, 87, 90–91, 99–112; and pedagogy, 7–8, 30–32, 42, 89–90, 92, 101–11
Chitham, Edward, 92
Christianity, 23, 42, 55, 150, 153, 161–62, 164–66, 168–69
Cobbe, Frances Power, 59
Cohen, Michael, 126, 133–34
Coleridge, Samuel Taylor, 107, 113, 127, 136–37
Collins, Wilkie, 25
competition, 8, 18–19, 22–25, 28–29, 33–34, 37, 40–42, 56, 72, 110–11, 128, 131–33, 145–46, 149–66 *passim*, 169–71
consumerism, 26, 51–52, 131–32, 161, 170

Index

Cooke, Thomas Potter, 79, 83–84
Cooper, Frederick, 73
Copernicus, Nicolaus, 47
cosmic play, 3, 7, 38, 42, 44–48, 52, 99, 101, 112–16, 119, 133, 137, 141–43
Cox, Harvey, 168, 175n14
Cox, Jeffrey, 69
Crawford, Robert, 129
Crick, Francis, 47
Cunningham, Hugh, 27
custom, 6, 23, 34, 42, 57–59, 64, 66

Daniel, George, 64
Danson, Lawrence, 150
Darwin, Charles, 14, 24, 47
Davidoff, Leonore, and Catherine Hall, 31, 104, 186n48
Day, Thomas, 105
death, as play, 9, 15, 39, 130
Deleuze, Gilles, 5, 76, 100; and Félix Guattari, 45–46
De Quincey, Thomas, 34
Derrida, Jacques, 5, 174n14, 177n56
Dickens, Charles, 5, 19, 30, 124, 131, 152; *Barnaby Rudge*, 34; *A Christmas Carol*, 18–19, 31, 34; *Great Expectations*, 26, 32; *Hard Times*, 17–18, 28, 31–32; *A House to Let*, 31; *Martin Chuzzlewit*, 15, 33; *Mrs. Lirriper's Lodgings*, 31; *The Mystery of Edwin Drood*, 34, 38; *Nicholas Nickleby*, 25, 28, 31; *The Old Curiosity Shop*, 28; *Oliver Twist*, 15; *Our Mutual Friend*, 31, 111; *Pictures from Italy*, 33, 36; *Sketches by Boz*, 26–27; *Sunday Under Three Heads*, 30; *A Tale of Two Cities*, 29, 189n14
Disraeli, Benjamin, 35
Dobell, Sydney, 91

Eagleton, Terry, 87
earnestness, 8–9, 42, 146, 148–52, 158–59, 161–62, 166–67
Edelman, Lee, 86, 88
Einstein, Albert, 47

Eliot, George, 13
Ellis, Havelock, 106–7, 170–71
Ellmann, Richard, 144
Emerson, Ralph Waldo, 119
Epimenides, 43

Fagen, Robert, 63, 174n14
fair play, 6, 25, 41–42, 57–59, 63–66 *passim*, 71–72, 75, 84, 131, 140, 161
fate, as play, 37–39. *See also* cosmic play
festivity, 15, 18–19, 34–37, 41. *See also* custom
Feyerabend, Paul, 5
Fink, Eugen, 15
Fitzball, Edward, 62; *The Pilot*, 70, 81–83 *passim*; *The Red Rover*, 64, 76, 83; *A Sailor's Legacy*, 60, 77–78, 80
FitzGerald, Edward, 39
folly, 8, 42, 138, 145, 153, 155, 164–71
Foucault, Michel, 26, 86
Franklin, J. Jeffrey, 2, 177n56
Fraser, Hilary, 164
Freedgood, Elaine, 38
freedom, as play, 5, 17–18, 32–33, 145, 147, 155–56. *See also* imagination
Freud, Sigmund, 45, 94, 106, 135, 187n72, 188n100
Froebel, Friedrich, 30, 106, 112

Gadamer, Hans-Georg, 5
Galileo (Galileo Galilei), 47
gambling, 1–2, 37, 39, 46, 57, 98, 160–61. *See also* alea
Gaskell, Elizabeth, 29, 37, 89–91
Gifford, Terry, 140
Gilbert, Sandra, and Susan Gubar, 92, 100, 184n7
Gilbert, W.S., and Arthur Sullivan, 61, 84, 170
Gissing, George, 16
Gould, Stephen Jay, 24, 175n26
Groos, Karl, 30, 103, 109
Gross, Edward, 15–16
Grossmith, George and Weedon, 27

Index 201

Hacking, Ian, 38
Haddon, Celia, 36
Hadley, Elaine, 53, 66, 69
Haines, John Thomas, 61–62; *Breakers Ahead!* 65–66, 75–76, 80–83 *passim*; *My Poll and My Partner Joe*, 65, 67, 70–71, 73, 75–76, 82–83; *The Ocean of Life*, 70, 78, 80, 83
Hall, Donald, 23
Hall, Granville Stanley, 30, 103, 110, 112, 135
Handelman, Don, and David Shulman, 44–46, 174n14
Hans, James, 5
Hanson, Ellis, 164–65
Hardy, Thomas, 38
Harman, Claire, 124
Hearn, Lafcadio, 36
Heraclitus, 3, 38, 45, 137–38
Heywood, Colin, 111, 186n48
Hobsbawm, Eric, 34
Holmes, Steven, 125, 191n91
Home, Henry, 108
Houghton, Walter, 148
Housman, A.E., 23
Hughes, Thomas, 14, 30–31, 110
Huizinga, Johan, 23, 32, 154, 174n14
Husserl, Edmund, 5
Hutton, Ronald, 180n14
Hyde, Lewis, 175n14

idleness, 13, 28–30, 33, 118, 131–32, 145
illusion, 32, 39, 43–48, 51–55
imagination, as play, 32–34, 36, 39–41, 95–96, 139, 155–56
imperialism, as play, 16, 22
Isaacs, Susan Sutherland, 106
Iser, Wolfgang, 95–96, 174n14

James, Henry, 152
Jefferies, Robert, 119–20
Jerrold, Douglas, 62, 66; *Black-Ey'd Susan*, 64–65, 67, 70, 72–73, 76–77, 79–81, 83–84; *Mrs. Caudle's Curtain Lectures*, 27; *The Mutiny at the Nore*, 65, 76–77

Johnson, Mark, 32, 177n54
Jordan, Thomas, 106
Joseph, Gerhard, 15
Jowett, Benjamin, 23

Kant, Immanuel, 5, 32, 74, 108, 136–37
Kavanagh, James, 184n7
Kaye, Richard, 157
Kepler, Johannes, 47–48
Kergomard, Pauline, 106
Kingsley, Charles, 23, 149
Kipling, Rudyard, 8, 16, 29, 46
Knox, Robert, 24, 29
Kohn, Alfie, 24, 175n26
Krakauer, John, 120

Lawrence, D.H., 94–95
Lears, Jackson, 36
Leavis, F.R., 92
Leavis, Q.D., 87
leisure, 7, 14, 25–28, 36, 42, 132–33, 149. *See also* recreation
Leo, Alan, 38, 179n86
Levine, George, 24, 175n26
Livingstone, Margaret, 179n109
Locke, John, 103–4, 112
Lombroso, Cesare, 187n75
Lombroso, Paola, 106, 187n75
love, 6, 8, 24, 42, 63, 156, 158–59, 161–65, 168–71
Lyell, Charles, 24

Macaulay, Thomas Babington, 32
MacLiammoir, Michael, 149
Manners, John, 35
Marcus, G.J., 61, 82
Marx, Karl, 74; and Friedrich Engels, 1, 9, 46, 121
Marx, Leo, 140
Maxwell, James Clerk, 47–48
McFarren, George, 52–53
McGann, Jerome, 179n91
melodrama, 4, 8, 41–42, 52–84; domestic melodrama, 61; gothic melodrama, 69; melodramatic mode, 53; nautical

melodrama, 6, 54, 56–58, 60–84, 160; origins, 67–68, 75; and politics, 55–59, 63–64, 71–77, 81, 83
Menikoff, Barry, 124
Meredith, George, 13, 152
Merry England, 1, 35, 57, 71, 84, 180n14. *See also* custom
Miller, J. Hillis, 93
mischief, 15, 18, 28–30, 36, 40, 42, 87, 94, 113, 121, 128, 131, 146
modernity: as illusion, 4, 15, 40, 47–48, 51–52, 171; as ludic, 1–9 *passim*, 13–14, 16, 29–30, 41, 46–48, 53, 57, 88, 99, 119–21, 147; as melodramatic, 53–54; as metahistorical, 2, 19, 40–42 *passim*, 86; and nature, 119–21, 133–34; origins, 3, 42, 46–48; as sensation, 1–3; as sport, 8, 145–46, 149, 171; as unfair, 6, 56, 63, 72
Montcrieff, William Thomas, 64–65, 77–79, 83
Moody, Jane, 51, 67–69, 77
Morris, William, 120
Morrow, Nancy, 16
Morton, Thomas, 62
Muir, John, 4, 7–8, 42, 117–23, 125–35, 137–43, 145, 161, 191n91; "God's First Temples," 127; *The Mountains of California*, 118, 125, 127, 133, 138–41; *My First Summer in the Sierra*, 125–28, 130–33, 137–38, 141–42; *The Story of My Boyhood and Youth*, 129–31, 133–34, 143; *A Thousand-Mile Walk to the Gulf*, 142

Nachmanovitch, Stephen, 43–44, 181n33
Nardo, Anna, 43, 179n92
neuroscience, 47–48
Newman, John Henry, 148
Newton, Isaac, 47–48
Nietzsche, Friedrich, 5, 23, 32, 39, 155
Nunokawa, Jeff, 150

Olmsted, Frederick Law, 134
Ong, Walter, 154–55

Ortega y Gasset, José, 23
Osbourne, Katharine, 122–23, 128
Outram, Leonard, 84

paideia, and play, 30–32, 42, 87, 99, 101, 108, 111, 115, 129. *See also* child play
paradox, 43–44, 153
parody, 28, 61, 73
pastoralism, 6, 120, 132, 140–42
Pater, Walter, 23, 25, 32, 39, 152
Phelan, James, 133
Piaget, Jean, 106, 174n14
Pitt, George Dibdin, 62, 74, 83
Plato, 3, 102, 112, 155
play studies, 5, 19, 88
Plotz, Judith, 31, 107
Pocock, Isaac, 79–80
postmodernism, 3, 146
Pykett, Lyn, 92, 100

race, 24, 28, 29
recreation, 15, 17–19, 26–28, 33, 40, 97, 118–19, 132–34 *passim*, 161. *See also* leisure
Richardson, William, 70
Romanticism, 31–32, 107–8, 113, 118, 134, 140
Rorty, Richard, 5
Rossetti, Dante Gabriel, 39
Ruskin, John, 5, 14, 144–45; *The Stones of Venice*, 35–36; "Traffic," 25
Rybczynski, Witold, 176n31

same-sex desire, 149, 156–58, 161–62, 170
Scarry, Elaine, 59
Schiller, Friedrich, 5, 33, 108
schizophrenia, 44–48, 91
Schreiner, Olive, 29
Scott, Walter, 118, 125
Shakespeare, William, 3–4, 47, 155–56
Shaw, George Bernard, 51, 84
Shelley, Percy Bysshe, 136–37
Sims, George R., 16
Sloterdijk, Peter, 154
Smiles, Samuel, 23

Socrates, 76, 155
Spariosu, Mihai I., 5, 32, 137, 177n54
Spencer, Herbert, 23, 33, 103, 108–9
sports, 7–8, 14–16, 18, 23–25, 28–31 *passim*, 34–35, 37, 40–42, 90, 109–10, 121, 132–33, 144–46, 148–49, 151, 158–62, 165, 167. *See also* competition
Stanley, Arthur, 148–49
Starr, Kevin, 118, 140–41
Stephens, John Russell, 65
Stevenson, Robert Louis, 4, 7–8, 34, 42, 117–32, 134–35, 137, 139–40, 142–43, 145, 161; *The Amateur Emigrant*, 123–24, 127, 137, 142, 189n10; "An Apology for Idlers," 132; "Child's Play," 130; *An Inland Voyage*, 38–39; *Kidnapped*, 124; "San Francisco: A Modern Cosmopolis," 123, 128, 130; *The Silverado Squatters*, 124, 126–32, 135, 139; *Strange Case of Dr. Jekyll and Mr. Hyde*, 27, 128, 134
Stewart, Elizabeth-Anne, 168
Strutt, Joseph, 35
sublime, the, 134–40, 161
Surtees, Robert, 28
Sutton-Smith, Brian, 5, 19–21, 174n14

Taylor, Philip Meadows, 37
Teale, Polly, 89
Tennyson, Alfred, 40–41, 131
Thackeray, William Makepeace, 1–2, 29, 37, 46, 67, 152
theatre, 4, 6, 28, 51–55, 84; actors, 26, 55–56, 78–79, 83–84; audiences, 6, 51–56, 59–62, 71, 77, 81, 84; Covent Garden and Drury Lane, 52, 68–69; minor theatres, 52–56 *passim*, 62, 68–69; theatricality, 15, 26–27. *See also* melodrama

Thompson, E.P., 36, 58, 66
Thoreau, Henry David, 120
tricksters, 28–30, 41–42, 121, 168. *See also* mischief
Trollope, Anthony, 24–25
Tucker, Herbert, 15
Turner, Frederick Jackson, 134
Twain, Mark, 119

Veblen, Thorstein, 27
Vygotsky, L.S., 174n14

Wallace, Alfred Russel, 24
war, as play, 3, 9, 16, 23, 29
Warhol, Robyn, 94, 185n23
Wells, H.G., 106
Weltman, Sharon Aronofsky, 178n72
Wilde, Oscar, 4, 7–9, 42, 144–71, 195n45; *The Ballad of Reading Gaol*, 168–69; "The Critic as Artist," 155; "The Decay of Lying," 152, 155; *De Profundis*, 158–61, 163–67, 169; *The Importance of Being Earnest*, 145, 162; *Lady Windermere's Fan*, 29; *The Picture of Dorian Gray*, 27, 154, 163; *The Portrait of Mr. W.H.*, 155; *Salomé*, 162–63, 165; "The Soul of Man Under Socialism," 149–53, 158–59; *Vera, or the Nihilists*, 162; *A Woman of No Importance*, 145, 148
Williams, William H., 62, 65
Wittgenstein, Ludwig, 20–22
Wollstonecraft, Mary, 104
Wordsworth, William, 31–32, 89, 107–10 *passim*, 112, 119, 137
work, as play, 15–16, 30, 35–36, 132. *See also* paideia
Worster, Donald, 118, 126
Wundt, Wilhelm, 106